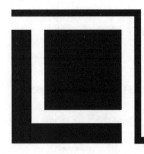

The Business of Ecommerce

Breakthroughs in Application Development Series

David Orchard, Series Editor
Cambridge University Press
New York, New York

and

Solutions Architect
IBM
Burnaby, British Colombia

The Breakthroughs in Application Development series is dedicated to providing hard knowledge in the form of detailed practical guides to leading-edge technologies and business models in modern application development. This series will identify, define, and stimulate emerging trends in the industry, covering such rapidly evolving areas as electronic commerce, e-Business, Inter/intranet development, Web architectures, application integration solutions, and the intersection of business and technology. Each title will focus on a new innovation in the field, presenting new ways of thinking and demonstrating how to put breakthrough technologies into business practice.

1. The Business of Ecommerce: From Corporate Strategy
to Technology • *Paul May*

2. e-Enterprise: Business Models, Architecture,
and Components • *Faisal Hoque*

The Business of Ecommerce

From Corporate Strategy to Technology

PAUL MAY

PUBLISHED BY THE PRESS SYNDICATE OF THE UNIVERSITY OF CAMBRIDGE
The Pitt Building, Trumpington Street, Cambridge, United Kingdom

CAMBRIDGE UNIVERSITY PRESS
The Edinburgh Building, Cambridge CB2 2RU, UK   http://www.cup.cam.ac.uk
40 West 20th Street, New York, NY 10011-4211, USA   http://www.cup.org
10 Stamford Road, Oakleigh, Melbourne 3166, Australia
Ruiz de Alarcón 13, 28014 Madrid, Spain

Published in association with SIGS Books

First published 2000
Reprinted 2000

Design and composition by Susan Ahlquist, Perfect Setting, Wainscott, NY.
Cover Design by Andrea Cammarata

Printed in the United States of America

A catalog record for this book is available from the British Library

Library of Congress Cataloging in Publication data is available

ISBN 0 521 77698 8 paperback

To the memory of my father, Terence Edmund May
23 September 1914 – 8 July 1999

Contents

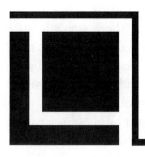

Foreword

The new digital economy and electronic business are evolving so rapidly that it is difficult for anyone to keep abreast. At the end of 1998, 140 million people around the world were connected to the Internet. By May of 1999, when this Department published the *Emerging Digital Economy II,* over 171 million people were connected to the Internet. By September 1999, the number had climbed to over 200 million people. (See www.ecommerce.gov for both *Emerging Digital Economy I* and *II.*) Over the same one year period, the number of Internet hosts rose by 46 percent, the number of Web servers increased by 128 percent, and the number of new Web addresses rose by 137 percent.

The Internet is fundamentally changing the way companies do business. A recent survey of Chief Financial Officers estimated the proportion of U.S. companies that sell their products over the Internet will jump from 24 percent in 1998 to 56 percent by 2000. Using the Internet for selling, however, is only one facet of ecommerce. Businesses increasingly are adopting ecommerce to improve operating processes. One recent study predicted that U.S. companies using Internet technologies to improve core business processes will save over $600 billion on an annual basis by 2002. Firms are seeing efficiency improvements in the area of supply chain management, procurement, marketing, customer service, and order handling and processing.

The Internet and World Wide Web are subversive, creating new models for business and undercutting the old. As Andy Grove,

Chairman of Intel has said, "In five years' time there won't be any Internet companies. All companies will be Internet companies or they will be dead." It may be true that not every business must be a "cyber business" but today every businessperson must understand how his or her business will be affected by the new digital tools.

You have clearly accepted the challenge of learning about electronic commerce. That is the first step in insuring you will be one of the victors and not one of the victims in the new digital economy.

William Daley,
US Secretary of Commerce

Acknowledgments

This book reflects a widespread change in thinking about the relationship between technology and business, and a corresponding shift in the practice of system development. My best mentors in understanding the emergence of ecommerce and its applications have been my consulting clients throughout the years, who have let me share in their opportunities and help realize them. My thanks go to them all, in particular, to Chris Boyce of Chase Manhattan.

I thank my many colleagues in consulting for their advice and support, particularly Simon Powell at Parallax, Simon Bisson and Nigel Fox at ECsoft, and Chris Pring at Bullitt. I also thank Geoff Seel of Financial Object Toolkits for his invaluable help with Chapter 5.

I thank my colleagues at Avenida for their friendship, creativity, and good humor, and, especially, Dave Wilkinson, who helped me to structure and revise Chapter 4.

My thanks also go to my editors at SIGS and Cambridge University Press in New York, who demonstrated patient and supportive care for a first-time author—and who excused most of his Briticisms.

Last (but never least), I thank my wife Helen for the tea, sympathy, and prodding that powered the writing of this book.

Any mistakes in the book are mine.

Introduction

E commerce is a compact word for a wide array of interconnected business concepts, technologies, and cultural phenomena. Technology and business professionals alike need to command this new field of knowledge to ensure they profit from it. At the very least, they need to acquire a level of familiarity and confidence with ecommerce so they can evaluate the opportunities it may afford, to both themselves and their competitors.

This book aims to bring readers up to speed on the topics that matter in ecommerce, from the ease with which a presence can be established on the Web to the challenge of founding an ecommerce channel that delivers continuing, measurable benefits to the business. I offer a number of models that the reader can use to formulate and implement an ecommerce strategy. These models establish frameworks for decision-making, so they can be thought of as tools rather than blueprints. Every model has been derived from repeated real-world experiences in the emerging ecommerce arena.

WHO SHOULD READ THIS BOOK

This book is primarily intended for business managers and IT managers working in commercial, industrial, and nonprofit sectors.

For the business manager, the book is a source of successful electronic commerce business models, a guide to the underlying technologies and application opportunities, and a grounding in the wider organizational, legal, and cultural context of electronic commerce.

IT managers can use the book to broaden and update their command of electronic commerce terminology, technologies, and priorities; to enhance their ability to add value to the business by understanding electronic commerce drivers; and to navigate the electronic commerce space using clear maps of its application areas.

The book should also be useful to consultants seeking an overview of electronic commerce and its relationships to other issues of technological and organizational change.

HOW TO USE THIS BOOK

This book has been written to be read sequentially; however, certain parts can be used in standalone mode if time is short.

Chapter 1 is a twin-tracked introduction to ecommerce exploring the business and technology issues that have created the current ecommerce climate. Technologists interested in the business environment may prefer to concentrate on the business track, while those familiar with concepts such as virtual organizations and globalization may want to familiarize themselves with ecommerce's technology precursors.

Chapter 2 provides a generic model for ecommerce that can be applied in real-world situations. It forms the main analytical apparatus of the book.

Chapter 3 explores six application areas, using examples to develop each theme. Readers may want to concentrate on the three business-to-consumer areas or the three business-to-business areas.

Chapter 4 is a technology primer that draws together the key technologies of ecommerce. Technologists may wish to skim this chapter or to focus on aspects they may not deal with on a daily basis, such as network technologies.

Chapter 5 presents logical, technological, and organizational architectures for ecommerce. This chapter is particularly useful for those readers in established enterprises who are introducing ecommerce to their organizations or looking to re-found their ecommerce activities on more explicit architectural footings.

Chapter 6 gathers together the main legal, technical, and market issues that currently remain open. This chapter is best used as a starting point because any particular application or initiative will run into specific issues that cannot be foreseen in a book.

The book includes a number of sidebars. Some of these sidebars are checklists, while others contain extra material that supports the main text. Some of the sidebars are included as thought-provokers.

I tried to make the book as neutral as possible regarding territory. The concepts, models, and general guidance contained in the book can be actioned by readers regardless of their geographical location, formal organizational status, or industry sector. Despite technology's famous capability to shrink the world, it has not created a common or stable legal framework. Laws relating to the uses of personal information and the conduct of cross-border transactions, among other issues, vary according to jurisdiction and are subject to revision. I cannot guarantee any of the example applications discussed in the text are, or will continue to be, viable in any country.

I have also been neutral regarding gender, using *she* and *he* more or less alternately throughout the text.

Finally, readers may contact me at paul.may@verista.com.

1 Getting Here

Garden Escape is based in Austin, Texas, but its online presence, garden.com, is available to gardeners everywhere, all the time. Founded in September 1995, the site is aimed at controlling a significant share of the $50 billion gardening industry in the U.S. For Christmas 1998, garden.com sold live Christmas trees, boxed and shipped by Federal Express. Customers could also choose decorations for their trees from the site's special tree trimming department.

Meanwhile America Online's members spent $1.2 billion between 26 November and 27 December 1998, with the most popular items being toys and baby items.

Ecommerce has long been awash with statistics. You can now purchase from the Web ready-made Powerpoint slides containing compelling statistics about ecommerce,[1] just in case you need to pep up your own pitch to the board or your investors. Most introductions to the topic have opened with predictions of mouth-watering revenues: billions of dollars generated in sales of goods and services to online consumers, and similar billions predicted for developers and implementors of ecommerce systems. The hard facts and figures that made headlines following 1998's holiday season are now beginning to take over as motivators. There's action in ecommerce, or ebusiness, or e-whatever. Most business people know they need to be part of it. But what *is* it? The e-numbers are palatable; but what's the story?

---

1. The Industry Standard, http://www.thestandard.com

Many definitions of ecommerce exist and all are useful to some extent. For most people, *ecommerce* means selling items over the World Wide Web. Some people include charging for Web content. Others concentrate on the sale of advertising space on Websites and email. Along with these voices are those who argue ecommerce isn't just about transacting with consumers, but it's also crucially concerned with interbusiness trading. If you listen to too many hardware, software, and services vendors, you'll come away with the dizzy sense that just about anything and everything can be ecommerce.

There's no agreement about what ecommerce is or what it might come to be, because ecommerce is the next big thing. In the cynical interpretation of that phrase, ecommerce is a magic marketing word that can be liberally sprinkled on any dish. Whatever ecommerce is, it attracts attention. In the more positive interpretation, ecommerce is a fundamental change in the way business is done. Ecommerce is perceived as the next wave in the evolution of business and it is where we are all migrating.

This book attempts to put some practical shape on ecommerce, its concepts, opportunities, and technologies. It centers around a generic business model for ecommerce. The generic business model is shown in action through an exploration of ecommerce application types. This core definitional material is preceded by some business and technology background, which shows how ecommerce has grown naturally out of prior developments. This book includes a primer on the relevant technologies, designed to give the nontechnical reader an understanding of the core underlying technology issues without requiring him or her to digest a bookstore. The book includes a chapter on architectures for ecommerce, which explores how businesses can exploit ecommerce opportunities in a managed manner. It concludes with a tour of the main outstanding issues in the ecommerce world.

The aim of this book is to equip managers better who want to take advantage of ecommerce. The framework that emerges enables decision-makers to establish boundaries between decisions of different quality and impact. This is as much about determining audiences as it is about distinguishing between technologies. Above all, this is about creating credible applications that generate customer satisfaction and business benefit.

This chapter looks at the prehistory of ecommerce from the twin viewpoints of business and technology. What are the movements within the business and technology spheres that have led up to the emergence of ecommerce as a potent force? In tracing the emergence of business themes, such as relationship marketing and globalization, we can start to see why business evolution demands a technology response that is focused on connectivity, usability, and ubiquity. By considering the divergence and convergence of a group of important technologies in the business and consumer fields, we can appreciate how the technologies of the Internet offer a reliable, consistent, and extensible environment that matches the needs of business evolution.

As the background fills in, we begin to see why ecommerce (or ebusiness or e-verything) can mean a great number of things and why a generic business model, such as the one introduced in Chapter 2, can help those planning ecommerce initiatives—or planning to profit from them—to invest their energies most effectively.

In one sense, this chapter is about the process of "getting here:" identifying the most important business and technology influences that have shaped our present environment. In another sense, we're also concerned with "getting" that environment: recognizing the core characteristics of ecommerce, so we can move on to managing it confidently.

TRACKING BUSINESS CHANGE

Four main types of change pressure business into new and surprising shapes and as they interact, they have the effect of propelling all types of organizations toward an ecommerce way of life. These are the forces of individuation, virtualization, globalization, and intellectualization.

If we are looking for some basic underlying physical laws of business in the twentieth century, we may want to start with the relationship between commercial activity and volume. Modern business is so clearly geared toward volume that we take the relationship for granted. Small businesses are corralled into a notional sector by governmental agencies and by their larger cousins in the banking and legal worlds, marking them as an abnormality. Turnover and headcount are the measures of size and credibility in a system of values that owes more to the legacy of physical plant and market domination than the specific profitability of the concern to its stakeholders.

Much of the business story of ecommerce is about the undoing of this size-ist thinking and the rediscovery of the wealth-creating potential of diversity and niche environments. Specifically, ecommerce is intimately concerned with rediscovering the individuality of customers and their needs, and the creation of frictionless modes of commercial interaction with them.

Before dry goods were first packaged and branded, they were sold loose in stores by the measure. Little differentiation existed among goods that were seen as staples. They were meant to be of averagely acceptable quality and variability. As retail business developed with the spread of transportation and communities in the U.S., so the opportunities for pre-measured and pre-wrapped products increased. Branded goods and services, as we understand them, are part and parcel of the creation of masses: classes of people bound together by common conditions, experiences, and aspirations. Many quintessentially modern everyday brands arose on the back of related mass effects, such as education and entertainment. Breakfast cereals, for example, came to prominence through their association with popular health programs, while Coca Cola was nationally established when Prohibition was exercising its blunt social engineering on a generation of Americans.

Our images of business are dominated by the growth of consumerism in the post-war period, from the building of supermarkets to the management of landfill sites. Retail is a web of buildings, trucks, fuel, and packaging. It deals in standardized products whose benefits are communicated through mass media.

The same trend has been at work in the service sector. The mass scaling of services is evident from the consolidation of banks to the increasing economic significance of telecommunications carriers. As these services grew in volume, they took on more and more character-istics of physical retail business, including branding, customer seg-mentation, and targeting. The banks that literally cornered our growing towns and cities with their heavy statements of security began to dematerialize in a haze of page-promoted offers and a vapor of telephone services.

Looking inside the corporation, it's easy to see the fundamental effect that volume thinking has had on organizations. Traditional organizational structures were based on the organization of armies, the only readily available models of large scale, cooperative, purposive endeavor in the pre-industrial age. Successful organizations strove to build predictable and repeatable structures and processes. The job of management could be tidily described as the articulation of such busi-ness rules and their ceaseless improvement, whether in the recruit-ment of the next platoon of graduate trainees or the swift handling of a customer complaint.

Senior management has been increasingly concerned with applying distance to these rules and to undermining their foundations when necessary. This may involve questioning the practice of hiring new graduates when so many seem to leave the company in their first two years or commissioning the redesign of a service that is attracting a high level of complaints. Of course, in real companies today, these duties tend to be the responsibility of all. The underlying model, however, remains one of a large, complex machine that must be main-tained and steered. It's not for nothing that successful serial CEOs are often also "turnaround" experts.

The undoubted benefits of the mass market approach are pre-dictable quality, repeatable supply, and lower prices through scale economies in design, manufacture, and transportation. The downside is the inevitable homogenization of the customer experience: he is treated as a type, not a person, and he is expected to modify his expec-tations and behavior to fit the design of the product or service. Per-sonal service comes at a premium, whether the tailored item is a business suit or an insurance policy. If the customer insists on devi-ating from the built-in rules of the corporation, then he has to pay for the disruption.

Prophets of a smaller-scale, customer-oriented approach range from visionaries such as Alvin Toffler in *The Third Wave* to guerrillas such as Tom Peters in *In Search Of Excellence*. Most large corporations have made efforts to introduce smaller-scale thinking in their management structures, with much of the 1980s concern for quality and productivity in the automotive industry, for example, often ascribed to the quality benefits of team-centered manufacture. But it's in addressing the customer that the most significant changes are signaled. Increasingly, businesses seek to communicate with customers on a one-to-one basis. Businesses aim to create dialogues that are relevant to the individual customer's condition and concerns. Above all, businesses strive to create relationships, rather than just effecting transactions. In any company, the cost of acquiring a customer is a significant variable and the best business is always repeat business. Designing the business for repeated interactions with retained, quality customers is the stated aim of most leading service companies and the implicit aim of companies engaged in sophisticated, lifestyle product branding.

How can a business foster this level of intimacy with the customer? At first sight, it looks as though we must jettison our segmentation schemes and halt the production lines. If we can no longer simplify the task of adding value to our customers by making some broad assumptions about their wants and needs, then how can we protect the economic efficiency of the corporation? Drawing a chart that shows the ineluctable evolution of a product from mass-produced to individually-demanded is easy, but it's less easy to identify the evolutionary mechanism that takes us all the way. Figure 1-1 shows three stages in a product's development from undifferentiated commodity to individually tailored item.

The final shift, from branded good to personal product, is predicated on gathering and organizing large amounts of real data and acting sensibly on its revealed messages. Companies need an information-based simplification mechanism that replaces (or, at the least, augments) their broad segmentation schemes. Business can only achieve customer intimacy at any meaningful scale through proxies: information systems that delineate the key facts about an individual

FIGURE 1-1. From generic to personal.

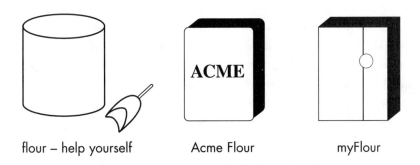

flour – help yourself   Acme Flour   myFlour

customer in a well-defined profile. Once businesses acquire that profile, they need a reliable mechanism for reaching the customer and initiating a stream of transactions with him. As that stream progresses, value accrues to the company through sales. At the same time, each transaction represents an opportunity to learn more about the customer.

The evolution of business from mass marketing to relationship marketing marks a fundamental change in the nature of the enterprise. Any corporation engaged in this shift is essentially learning how to be a learning organization. The corporation is becoming an entity that manages its environment for productivity, rather than simply exploiting it. Simply put, a lot more stuff is suddenly worthy of the enterprise's notice than there used to be. Its communications with its customers have become a valuable ore to be mined.

Consumers commonly believe large corporations know great amounts about them and their habits. This has always been true in theory, but largely impossible to achieve in practice. The systems of banks and retailers, let alone governments, have rarely been well-connected within their respective owning organizations, making it as hard for your bank to summarize you as it is for anyone else. Banks, in fact, made a historical retreat from customer intimacy when they began to consolidate operational decision-making away from their local branches. Our parents may have been assessed for their creditworthiness based on the local manager's knowledge of the street they lived on, the car they parked outside the branch, and the reputation of their business activities, knowledge that is now only dimly shadowed by the data held in its computer centers.

The depth, quality, and connectedness of the customer data they hold is a major barrier for businesses trying to make the shift to relationship marketing. Intellectual solutions have been sought in corporate data modeling, a practice that attempts to apply standardized definitions of customers, products, and transactions so information systems are built from a common blueprint. More brutal, and often more successful, solutions are associated with data warehousing, where massive quantities of operational data are copied into a high-performance database for subsequent analysis.

Both these solutions tend to share a common drawback: they are based on analyzing the data the organization happens to have, rather than on commissioning the information it actually wants. Customers leave shadows on information systems built to track sales, rather than revealing their reasons for purchase. Their lives are sampled as their cards are swiped in terminals, but they are rarely asked what made them choose that card for that purchase. Most companies know too little about the drivers of their customers' behavior.

Retrospective data analysis solutions also share a common disconnect: neither approach, on its own, guarantees the company's behavior will be changed as a result of new knowledge gained.

Gathering new data from customers has always been fraught with difficulty. Even once we have decided what questions to ask, we still need a way to solicit the answers, transcribe them to a system, and analyze them. These activities are always going to represent an interruption to the flow of any transaction and they may even jeopardize its completion. Ideally, we want to acquire customer-specific knowledge as an unnoticed by-product of some core process in which the customer engages. Furthermore, we would like the new knowledge gained to have a guaranteed effect on our next interaction with the customer. The ability to close the loop on the purchase process, so the business can adapt its approach during a dialogue with the customer, is at the heart of the Internet's fascination for marketers.

Imagine a user exploring an online resource, such as a catalog of consumer appliances. If we present a table of products and prices, along with some means whereby our visitor can indicate his selection and make a payment, then we are in business. We don't learn much about the customer, however. We can theorize about why some visitors buy and others don't. We have an automatic, though skimpy, record of who visits our online store, which is at least an improvement on the traditional physical store.

Imagine we now redesign the site so the visitor is presented with alternative paths and with options for accessing different kinds of information. Simply dividing the catalog into kitchen and nonkitchen appliances and requiring the user to click one category will at least tell us how interested in kitchen appliances our visitors are. Perhaps we could highlight one product and advertise a discounted price, and see what happens. We could easily provide pictures of all the items, as well as full-feature descriptions and dimensions. What about adding availability information? What about bundling shipping?

All these improvements provide levels of distinction that enable us to track customer behavior in more detail during a single encounter. When aggregated for a returning visitor over a period of time, we may be able to determine a pattern and act upon it. If, for example, we track a customer who repeatedly visits the site to look at three brands of toaster, we can rule that on his next visit, and for him alone, we will offer him one of the toasters at a 15 percent discount if he buys it today. If we're feeling less pushy, we could invite him to join our Toaster Lover's Club and ask him to tell us more about himself and his toastal orientation, in return for a toast-related screensaver.

This style of relationship, where the customer provides the motive power while the company casts a fluid maze around him, can be carried out with different degrees of subtlety. The more hard information successfully solicited from the customer, the more refined his experience can be. Rather than finding a single benefit to shout about—such as price—we concentrate on crafting compelling messages for receptive eyeballs.

Worth noting in passing is this approach to relationship marketing on the Web challenges the Website construction and management practices of many organizations. We are creating an environment in which the customer designs his own experience. Most corporate Web teams approach the Web presence as a publishing project, managing it through a cycle of design, construction, release, and review. Such sites are customer-driven to the extent that the responsible team takes note of user feedback. They are still motivated by a desire to create a common experience, however, rather than a tailored relationship.

Such microscopic, dynamically generated behavior can, at first, seem antithetical to the predictive arts practiced by marketers. Relationship marketing is often necessarily reduced to the tracking of customer life stages and the making of relevant offers to coincide with transitions from one stage to the next. Birth, graduation, and marriage are all significant milestones that prompt purchase decisions. Moving into a new home, for example, is a signal for a range of businesses to close in on a family. They may need new insurance, furniture, cleaning services, or just therapy. And, while the homeowner is freshly exposed to the unusually large sums of money associated with the purchase of a new home, he may be temporarily better disposed to spending smaller amounts.

Life stage tracking is undoubtedly powerful, but it is a somewhat blunt instrument. The microenvironment of the tracked customer interacting with a responsive Website can seem overly precise in comparison. If every customer's experience becomes truly unique, then we begin to lose sight of any common foundation we can use to structure our offerings. We need *some* landmarks to hold on to or else our engagement with the customer loses purpose and direction. If we are in business to sell toasters, then we have to steer our relationships away from commitments to supply tires, even if the subject crops up in a mutually agreeable conversation between a customer and our perfectly malleable and endlessly suggestible software. (Of course, we could be in the business of supplying unforeseen needs through alliances with other providers, in which case a smooth transition from toasters to car parts would be something of a triumph.)

The middle way between these extremes is to project a series of life events that are less crude than the traditional life stages of marketing, but that can be confidently applied as common infrastructure to encounters with groups of customers. Some of these events can be recruited from the media, which thrives on the creation of streams of "special" events, such as movie and album releases, each a potent occasion for selling things. Other events can be gathered from new product releases, changes in dress fashions, or even the pleasing aspect of a year appearing with three trailing zeroes. Ecommerce, as one dimension of the fashionable Internet, is an ideal environment to experiment with new types of tie-in.

Ultimately, the typical ecommerce relationship will be one that cannot be described in terms other than its collected encounters. Most customer segmentation schemes will be too crude and too perishable for any purpose other than initial conjectures. The customer, trained by games to consume events as a leisure activity, will be creating his own "segment of one" as he interacts with the digital environment. Companies will concentrate on acquiring a share in the individual's attention and spending power. Mindshare, and share of wallet, are the gross measures of this marketing landscape.

Understanding the momentary desires and cumulative behavior of the individual is also increasingly important in interbusiness dealings. The next section explores the topic of cotrading, cooperating businesses, and how temporary and permanent alliances of organizations are coming to define another dimension to ecommerce.

Firefly Finds the Personal Pattern

Firefly (www.firefly.net) was originally a Web-based service that learned about visitors and created groupings of individuals based on their preferences. The visitor told Firefly about her interests in movies or music, and Firefly suggested other items in which she might be interested. Many users reported their surprise at the site's success in pinpointing their interests, with returned suggestions scoring high for relevance. What can be a little sobering is to realize your carefully nurtured eclecticism can be so easily reduced to some kind of recipe.

Firefly is currently owned by Microsoft and its relationship marketing software is productized so others can incorporate it in their applications. The maturity of the market is indicated by the company's highlighting of privacy as an issue and as a strength of their approach. Clearly, drawing conclusions from visitor activity and basing subsequent action upon it is sufficiently well understood that solutions providers must now concentrate on secondary characteristics of their systems. ■

Virtualization: Extended Enterprises and Virtual Organizations

Just as the corporation looking outward to its customers is focusing on the individual, it is also changing internally, moving away from a monolithic, static, and highly engineered structure to a more amorphous nature. An enterprise that decides to build its behavior around the wants and needs of individuals, rather than hypothetical groups, must be able to flex in response to changing information from its environment. An enterprise must be able to reinvent itself on the fly, acquiring capabilities and deploying them as needed. Opportunism becomes its prime strategy for survival and growth.

This organic view of the enterprise is strongly associated with the extended enterprise and the virtual organization. These are both good terms and each has something to tell us about the evolution of business in a period fundamentally impacted by network connectivity. Figure 1-2 shows schematic diagrams of an extended enterprise and a virtual enterprise. Each type of entity is revealed by the microscope as a collection of organizations with the capability to link together in chains.

The *extended enterprise* is a view of the company that takes into account its partner relationships. The effective organization is the sum of the parties it brings to bear on a commercial opportunity, whatever the timeframe of that opportunity. As a traditional business example,

FIGURE 1-2. Extended enterprises and virtual organizations under the microscope.

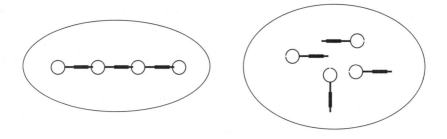

an agent brings capital and talent to serve a short-life opportunity, expecting the team to dissolve when the project is complete. The key model for this type of business is Hollywood. Longer-term opportunities, such as lateral moves into contingent markets or expansions into other territories, are usually served by more permanent relationships, ranging from partnerships to mergers and acquisitions.

The entrepreneurial facet of business has always looked to leverage the value of other players in its environment, but this kind of team-building is commonly seen as the exception rather than the norm. Line management is not usually expected to look outside the company for help in achieving the company's goals and it may attract hostile attention if it does so. Building a force that extends beyond the company you control is fraught with unknowns and makes exceptional demands on personal intervention. This also seems to go against the wisdom that companies should stick to what they know.

Yet most successful companies have taken steps to secure their control over the value chain in which they are implicated. A large retailer, for example, specifies the quality, time, and frequency of delivery of goods from its suppliers, and exerts influence over logistics companies and urban planners. Companies recognize that one way to enhance their profitability is to look along the value chain and address any parts of it which are liable to stick. Reengineering of the extended value chain can be easier to achieve than internal process engineering because the coupling of constituent elements is already looser and the political environment is segmented into identifiable regions. Companies may choose to control or influence other parts of the chain rather than to own them outright, depending on their appetite for risk and their attitude to diversification. Certainly the company's location in a value chain is one key dimension of its strategic thinking—a longitudinal perspective that complements its relationship-marketing perspective on share of customer wallet.

The computer industry is one where extended enterprise relationships are the norm. A manufacturer typically supplies the market through other companies that it may call *channel partners* or Value Added Resellers (VARs). Both terms are significant, the first signaling the manufacturer's view that it can reach its market best through dedicated channels operated by specialists, the second signaling that partners enhance the proposition through the services they wrap around the product.

Companies far outside the high-tech sector have similar views. A long-established extractive industry, for example, works closely with buyers of its raw materials to find new applications for derivative products. This may be simple, forward-thinking, good sense, but it is also a clear sign that successful enterprises recognize the chains they play in and seek to strengthen them wherever possible. Willingness to work with business partners outside of the scope of specific contracts is often the first sign of an extended enterprise's formation and can be the grit around which a valuable organic entity is formed. A branded foods company, for example, diverts a measure of its joint income with a channel partner into a marketing development fund, so both parties cooperate for the long term benefit of both.

An extended enterprise cannot realistically function without constant, operational systems communication among its players. The practicing extended enterprise is a set of system relationships. Those earliest cemented are likely to be inventory enquiry facilities, enabling recognized partners to probe the status of their contributing resources. Shared definitions of business terms, measures, and qualities indicate a longer-term commitment to systems cooperation. Controlled access to operational systems may follow, enabling partners to change the corporate data of other players, as well as to view it.

Not all commentators would recognize such activity as ecommerce, even though the partners are combining electronically in the pursuit of commercial goals. Some companies and consultants use the term *ebusiness* when discussing such relationships because for many, ecommerce has acquired the restricted sense of monetary value transactions. Ecommerce is also often associated exclusively with mass market consumer applications and ebusiness[2] does something to correct that view. The confusion is inevitable because common technologies are involved in all kinds of these applications and because

---

2. *Ebusiness* is a term introduced by IBM in a marketing initiative of 1997, which has subsequently entered the general lexicon.

suppliers and buyers of solutions are rightly more interested in progressing their business goals than describing taxonomies.

The *virtual organization* is usually an extended enterprise that has embraced the notion of permeable organizational boundaries as a core dynamic. Virtual organizations are associated most often with creative service industries where networking for added capability has always been the norm. The media sector is a prime example. Virtual organizations tend also to be unmarked by long and proud histories as monolithic players. The cachet of adaptability and nimbleness is one that sits ill with a lengthy heritage or a portfolio of established brands. It is, however, well suited to Web-based communications and the term *virtual organization* has become almost synonymous with companies trading via the Web.

The Web brings the apparent technical price of creating a company and presenting it to the public within the reach of anyone with a good (or bad) idea. Looking like a million dollars is a serious option for anyone with a grasp of HTML—or of how to grasp someone else's HTML. You don't need to lease an office or a store and all the paraphernalia that goes with it. The low barrier to entry represented by the Web doesn't guarantee the creation of a viable company, however, any more than a free distribution of mild steel to a nation's citizens would result in a revitalized white goods industry. In this aspect, the Web is an enabler, making economically feasible what previously was the preserve only of the well-funded. But it is neither an adjudicator or guarantee of credibility or success, nor, as we shall see, is it inherently capable of doing anything more for a virtual organization than representing its stationery.

A virtual organization is more correctly characterized as one that embodies a varying network of specialists in distinction to a formally constituted enterprise. Such organizations are closer in kind to the earliest commercial enterprises and may be similarly poorly provided for in terms of legal protection and redress. Many virtual organizations may be better labeled as putative corporations because they are often formed to foreshadow a company in its pre-startup, or moonlight-nourished, form. Some districts of the Web are like the iconic Wild West towns of the movies: all storefront, with desert behind.

Whether we choose to label an organization as "virtual" or "extended," if it is determined to assemble the best team to perform a particular project or to satisfy a particular need, then it has to recognize that it is putting the customer in control of its moment-by-moment operational life, as well as its long-term viability. The customer is the lead partner, yanking the value chain and making its component companies dance. As the customer's impulse passes along the chain, it affects each partner's tooling, as well as its momentary behavior. Just as he is increasingly tasked with designing his own engagement experience with the company, the customer is increasingly the designer of the products and services he buys. In the movie industry, we find films being rewritten, reshot, and reedited in the light of the reactions of selected audiences at test-screenings. Ford's family car, Focus, was derided in some parts of the U.K. press for being too blandly the result of using focus groups to design it. Meanwhile, the software industry makes increasing use of so-called beta releases to ensure customers effectively test and respecify its new product generations, recruiting large communities of skilled developers for minimal outlay. With the customer becoming less and less distinguishable from an employee of the companies she patronizes, so the employee is becoming more and more a free agent. Under the pressure of corporate downsizing and sectoral restructuring, workers of all types have been encouraged to let go of any expectation of a "job for life." The positive spin on the casualization of labor finds expression in the "portfolio career"-ists of Charles Handy,[3] or the self-directed, self-productized followers of "Brand You" era Tom Peters and *Fast Company* magazine.[4] It's already clear to companies hiring new graduates in the technology industries that the hiring process is one of mutual inspection and negotiation, and as the life expectancies of companies and managements continue to fall, we will surely see a rise in the number of workers who see themselves as skills for hire, rather than as loyal cogs in an enduring machine.

These blurring boundaries are, on the one hand, discomforting to all of us engaged in business because we keep finding familiar

---

3. See, for example, *The Age of unreason*, Arrow, 1995.
4. *Fast Company*, August-September 1997.

landmarks disappearing into newly defined territories. The control we once had over our proposition—the power to offer our product "in any color so long as it's black"—has passed to the customer. The gratitude we expected from those starting out their careers has melted in the blast of their need to repay the ever-rising costs of a good education. And we are irrevocably aware of our involvement in a value chain we can never shake off.

On the other hand, the freeing up of the business landscape is immensely invigorating. Everywhere the rules of engagement are being simplified and the time scales over which businesses are asked to plan are reducing.

Whether business change is driving IT in the shift toward extended enterprises and virtual organizations or the effect is taking place in reverse is a moot point. At the macro level, the best we can say today is the changes noticeable in both spheres are complementary. Businesses are disintegrating and reformulating in response to customer demand and doing so using electronic means. Organizational boundaries are becoming mobile, permeable, and perishable. Collaborative, short-life encounters and provisional relationships are the key characteristics of the nimble, morphing organizations of today. They must be served by technologies that enable—indeed, promote—promiscuity. Architectures that support both the building of intimate relationships and promiscuous partnering are discussed in Chapter 5.

Globalization: The Shop Window of the World

Borders are disappearing and reappearing around the world as political and trading unions wax and wane. The erosion of trade and communications barriers continues, creating an ever more global economy and making even the most internationalist business appear parochial or alien to some of its new partners and customers. Competition in every sector leaves few businesses with the luxury of concentrating on a home market. To many, this is a cause of insecurity and uncertainty. To others, it is a huge opportunity to change the scope of the business and one that comes at an opportune time for exploiting technological advance.

Traditional concentration on home markets is a result of traditional possibilities. Any physical market owes its existence to a combination of chance elements that creates the right environment for trading. A European city might grow around an easily forded spot on a major river, a place where travelers habitually meet and begin to transact with each other. Intermediaries might settle at the spot knowing they can aggregate the needs of buyers and sellers, matching them to each other far more efficiently than the principals could themselves. They take a fee to cover their expenses and some profit element, and become an integral part of a trading community, where once only an accidental crossing of paths existed. In other cases, markets are attracted to existing centers of production to serve those engaged in the local industries with nonlocal goods. In any case, the physical market is a known place and a phenomenon that is trusted to occur at known times. When only armies and merchants travel, business possibilities are restricted to what can be generated within a relatively static community.

Despite the growth of retail chains and the massive rise in transportation, much of our business thinking is still based around physical locality. However exotic they may be, goods still must be transported to the point of sale. However sophisticated a service may be, it still has to be delivered through human agency. And whoever our customers are, they still must be brought somewhere they can see, touch, and pay for their purchases.

Network technology famously makes nonsense of these restrictions. Most obviously, any consumer can hear about any offer if he is well enough connected. Intangibles can be readily bought and sold, regardless of the transacting parties' locations. We have long accepted that financial instruments are traded in this way and the location of a financial market has much to do with its time zone and regulatory environment, both legal and telecommunications. We are also used to the idea that catalog items can be imported from just about anywhere, as long as a shipping method can be found.

We are less well adjusted to the structural changes that globalization implies. Most people would happily define ecommerce as the selling of goods over the Web and will remark that such goods can come from any country. From the corporate point of view, this channel is usually seen simply as an additional source of customers who are fairly inexpensive to service. Businesses with experience selling to foreign consumers over the Web are now beginning to awaken to a new set of responsibilities and challenges, which goes with the opening up of this new market. As Figure 1-3 suggests, the geographical dispersal of Website users is less important than the features they have in common.

First, and most fundamentally, ecommerce allows businesses to build new aggregate markets from dispersed individuals, which may rival geographical markets in value, loyalty, and cross-marketing opportunity. Web users elect themselves into groups regardless of geography. They recognize commonality of interest in far-flung correspondents and information sources. Perhaps the best example of this attitude is the huge amount of genealogical research activity on the Web, as individuals attempt to trace their family histories across time and space. Businesses engaged in providing family history software, databases of families, and search services host some of the most popular sites. For the first time, an industry that could fairly claim to

FIGURE 1-3. Dispersed markets start to add up.

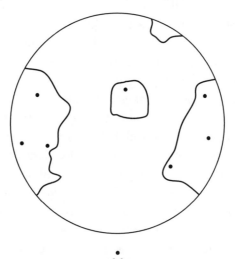

target the entire species as its customers has access to a large proportion of that market. Even more compelling, they have access to customers who have shown an interest in the industry through their use of the Web and who are almost by definition suitably leisured and funded to buy the industry's products and services. Ultimately, we all share some of the same genetic material. The global village is trading happily in information about DNA's travels and liaisons, and the lives it has built along the way.

The chief effect of aggregated markets is businesses now address communities that have formed around elements of a commercial proposition, rather than engineered from a heterogeneous mass. We can compare a community of cheese lovers that has assembled on the Web and attracted the hosting support of cheese manufacturers to the inhabitants of a dairy town who were never supplied with any other form of protein. Business is in the position of supporting and extending existing interests among its users, rather than persuading them to buy a basic proposition. This is, in theory, the dream of marketers, for if marketing is the job of creating customers, then self-creating customers are the equivalent of the engineer's perpetual motion machine.

Most companies simply aren't geared toward markets that create themselves, however. Established companies may have been born of needs demonstrated by a ready market, but they usually sustain their growth by creating demand, rather than hoping for spontaneous growth. The educated, discriminating customer is something of a novelty, certainly when represented in a mass.

Second, globalization makes any business ever-present, as well as omnipresent. Markets wake and transact as the earth spins and any business that puts itself in a global posture needs to operate on a 24-hour basis. The promise of same-day decisions is harder to support when your customer's day is your night, unless that decision can be automated. Furthermore, users of the Internet expect much prompter service than they expect from traditional sources. Email, in particular, is generally cast in a brief, functional form, which would appear impolite if used in a business letter, and is written with the assumption that it should be dealt with as speedily as it was composed. Businesses that ask for customer feedback via email must be ready to deal with it promptly, whenever it arrives, as users who respond to the invitation can react angrily when their effort is ignored.

The third challenge of globalization is often briefly labeled as multilingualism and sometimes is expanded to take into account multiculturalism as well. Clearly, not every potential customer will use English as his first language and the assumption that English is always the language of business is an important hindrance to the growth of ecommerce, excluding as it does huge potential markets. Merely translating text into foreign languages may not always be sufficient because commercial styles vary greatly between cultures. Even in the English-speaking world, business prose falters somewhere in the middle of the Atlantic in a confusion of tones, allusions, and expectations of message structure.

The fourth challenge is that of the enhanced complexity created by the preceding three challenges. Self-selecting markets, timing, and culture interact with the normal processes of the enterprise to undermine its fundamental behavior. Many businesses have surprised themselves with the success of their ecommerce efforts in reaching out to new markets and have turned belatedly to supporting the new channel. Just creating the Website, translating its content into a few major languages, and coping with the oddities of foreign currencies and ZIP codes, turns out not to be enough. These new customers want to engage in dialogue. They want to buy in unusual quantities, at nonstandard terms, and at odd frequencies. They want to access regularly updated content in their own language. They want to know who represents or partners your company in their region. They have questions about tax, quality standards, or environmental compliance that don't apply in your home market. The attractive and apparently lightweight "ubiquitous presence" offered by the Web is a complex and continuing corporate responsibility. Even deciding to withdraw from the new market is difficult, given that you'll apparently be swimming against the tide, while disappointing those in the company who have become used to the enhanced sales.

Globalization also affects business partnerships. Just as companies can now aggregate markets across distributed territories, they are finding that barriers to partnering are also falling. Suggesting that trade has been perfectly liberalized the world over would be wrong and this isn't the place to dilate on the relative merits of free trade and protectionism, and the nature of perfect markets. Businesses the world over are finding opportunities to cooperate across borders, especially where disparities in labor costs are particularly glaring. The Internet enables companies to pass brain-work overseas with little effort. Data input has long been sent offshore and programming has followed suit.

At the strategic level, companies can now forge and maintain relationships with partner companies abroad with greater ease. Locating specialist suppliers using search engines and Web directories has become simple and initial enquiries can be handled efficiently by email. Internet technologies may play no further part in the process after the initial introductions are made, but this is still an important contribution. At the very least, knowing your competitors can roam the world looking for potential partners suggests you may be missing out on potential alliances. Once relationships are in place, email and system-to-system communications can build an extended enterprise on a global basis as easily as they can within one country.

Companies of all sizes are recognizing the world has become their oyster and they don't have the option to send the oyster back. Globalization is not a change companies can elect to ignore. Even those who are protected by local trading laws and cross-border agreements will find their zone of influence shrinking in value relative to the unfettered world outside.

The experience of the telecoms sector paints a useful picture of how other industries may be affected. Built and strengthened by national monopoly protection, telecoms companies worked in concert through international technical standards bodies and tariff agreements to ensure their prosperity. As nations deregulated their telecoms industries and competition was introduced on local, long distance and international routes, the big players' scale economies shrank in comparison to the wider aggregate industry that had been created. New players with new technologies, unburdened by legacy infrastructure and answerable to shareholders ahead of governments, quickly challenged the established players, especially in new markets such as mobile telephony and satellite communications. Companies like Nokia and Ericsson applied their experience of running wireless networks in remote regions to the production of handhelds for urban users, while Hutchison combined its Far East telecoms expertise with Feng Shui marketing sensibilities to create Orange, a leading U.K. digital network.

Telecoms deregulation occurred during the 1980s and 1990s in a domino fashion, showing that interconnected industries cannot insulate themselves from fundamental changes taking place in one or two component organizations. As the world becomes truly wired, we will see the same effects in all industries. Protectionism will likely migrate to those policy regions that are superficially noneconomic, with environmental concerns especially coopted to create subtle discriminators against nonnational products. A nation might make a law to limit emissions or to preserve a cultural value to deflect foreign economic invasion. The evolutionary arms race of international business will continue, its weapons becoming ever more subtle.

The challenges of globalization are such that the opportunities can seem distant and difficult. The global village has been a key part of future-gazers' visions since World War II and especially since the rise of television and air travel. In practice, globalization has not equalized the experiences or expectations of the world community—and certainly not its quality of life. But like every discovery, the wider world cannot be undiscovered. It's up to businesses to map out their own response and to project it faithfully.

Intellectualization: Getting Clever with It

The three effects we have considered—relationship marketing, extended enterprises and globalization—could all be called conceptual shifts in business thinking that demand the intensive use of information technology. The last broad influence we must consider is the purest indicator that we are entering an era where ecommerce is the normal mode of business. The growing intellectualization of business is a symptom that business is migrating to a domain where dialogue and knowledge are the primary content of most commercial activities, rather than a selected few.

By intellectualization, I don't mean business is growing beards, glasses, and polysyllabic critical apparatus. I use the term *intellectualization* to indicate the increase in the variety and value of intangibles, such as branding and after-care service in traditionally based industries, and the growth of information-based products and services in their own right. This is a neat distinction and like all such distinctions it is a little misleading. In fact, detaching the intellectual content from any commercial activity has always been difficult. The smokestack industries of the industrial revolution remain our icon of the simple, heavy approach to generating wealth, which we equate with deskilled labor and poorly differentiated outputs. But the invention of manufacturing processes and machines is hardly a matter of blind luck. Organizing any commercial venture or creating a name that will characterize a product that consumers have never seen before are other examples of intellectual content usually discounted in our rough appreciation of the achievements of the past.

An increased consciousness certainly exists about the intellectual content of products and services and its increasing importance in the proposition, however. Inevitably the basic functional values of any product become worn with use and it becomes necessary to reinvent them. So we find Swatch becoming a successful fashion and collector product when telling the time is no longer a novelty, and no longer the sole preserve of its historic providers.

Stan Davis and Christopher Meyer in their influential book *Blur*[5] major on the inevitability—and the power—of combining product and service elements to create an *offer*, the new class of tradable value. Davis and Meyer point out that the service elements in cars, for example, can represent greater profitability than the product element. Car financing, insurance, and credit protection are all profitable businesses for auto manufacturers, who are ideally placed to sell them alongside the product to which they attach. A vehicle tracker device is a *Blur*red offer with a typical IT content. A tracker is notionally a

5. *Blur: the speed of change in the connected economy,* Stan Davis and Christopher Meyer, Addison-Wesley, 1998.

product because it is a device fitted inside a car. But the customer never sees it because it may be hidden anywhere in the car; and he never uses it. The tracker only activates its promised value if the car is stolen, when it transmits its position to listening satellites. The tracker is, therefore, a combination of notional product and potential service, something that exists only in the plans of fitters and thieves—and possibly therefore the most postmodern item you can buy.

Just as the importance of the service element is redrawing the boundaries of products, so services are increasingly productized. Consulting is one example. Although any reputable management consultancy supplies skilled individuals who will apply their own experiences and insight to a client problem, a client still has the right to expect they will use some sort of established methodology for the project and they will make use of knowledge from elsewhere in their firm. Both expectations drive the consulting service into productization, in that methodologies must be recorded, agreed, taught, priced, and labeled so consultants and clients alike can make use of them, and consultants' knowledge must be recorded and made accessible within the firm's consulting community. Standardization, replication, transference—these are all aspects of productization, even if the end results are never poured into a box.

Many boosters of the digital age predicted its key characteristic would be the emergence of a purely knowledge-based economy. Access to information would automatically create an abstracted economy where the results of brain-work would command value. It had already happened in the entertainment industry, so surely everyone with a story to tell or an idea to sell should be able to make it big in an environment with few barriers to access and a global audience. Yet, it is notoriously difficult to sell "content" on the Web. Web users expect information to be free and have frustrated the attempts of content providers to charge them for it. It's noticeable that the most quoted ecommerce force on the Web is Amazon.com, which sells books, not the information contained in books. Amazon.com's success in selling large quantities of books, CDs, and other products is partly attributable to its insistence on the service elements of its offer, particularly its creation of the largest possible catalogs and its encouragement of customer commentary.

Intellectual property, a quantity that excites legislators and lawyers, is distressingly free on the Web, leading many to despair of making tangible dollars from intangibles in an e-world. But this reaction assumes the creation of intellectual property always rests with enterprises and its consumption with consumers. Experience on the Web proves this to be false, although you have to dig a little to find it. Take, for example, the site of Pfaff.[6]

Pfaff makes knitting machines and has a large, dispersed, and loyal family of users. Its site includes simple discussion forum software that enables Pfaff owners to swap tips, advice, and product information with each other. Pfaff's corporate voice is absent; the company simply provides the forum. Yet this small area of the Web exemplifies the transforming power of the effects we have been discussing in this section. Pfaff's customers are teaching Pfaff about their products, the uses they are put to, and their usability. Their direct comments and their conversations with each other represent fantastically valuable information to marketers. This information is especially valuable because it is contributed through repeated interactions over time and by people who have elected themselves into a self-regulated focus group.

This is the engine of relationship marketing in action, creating an extended enterprise in which the customers potentially dictate the direction of production. Of course, Pfaff's customers can be located anywhere, so they create a community of common interest unrelated to geographical boundaries, a community that would be hard to identify and assemble in any other way. Even if the company could rely on product registration to identify its customers, it could hardly insist they open themselves to regular, detailed probing. Twenty minutes browsing these forums is eloquent testimony that a homespun craft hobby can evolve rapidly into a knowledge-intensive lifestyle offer.

The Web's do-it-yourself ethic is often derided by communications professionals, yet it is arguably the input of individual Web users that has created the most valuable content and inspired professional media concerns to enter the arena. Fan pages for celebrities,

6. http://www.pfaff-talk.com/

sports, and games may even dent the appeal of official merchandising because fans are often motivated by knowledge, rather than souvenirs. Musicians are taking their creations directly to the Web, recognizing that direct contact with their followers provides them with helpful feedback, as well as positioning them as accessible icons. The abstract qualities that combine to generate the winds of fashion are gatherable in cyberspace. The Web isn't the mind of the world, but it is a fair representation of a growing proportion of its thoughts. Those thoughts—whether idle, earnest, or subversive—will be the fuel of new industries.

We began looking at the business background to ecommerce by focusing on the individual customer as the locus of marketing's concerns. We looked at the recruitment of the customer into the extended enterprise and the aggregation of customer communities across geographical and time boundaries. Along the way, we noted how business is flexing and regrouping in harmony with these changes. The intellectualization of business—its transmutation into abstracted forms and its exploitation of content—confirms the defining characteristic of the e-world: an emphasis on person-to-person relationships as the business corollary of ubiquitous systems connectivity.

EXPLOITING TECHNOLOGY CHANGE

Business decision makers can be sure of one thing when it comes to technology: whatever they choose today will be suboptimal for tomorrow. Something better is always on the horizon, but business needs to act in the here and now or it may not see tomorrow. Minimizing the risk inherent in technology decisions is the stuff of later chapters. At this point, we need a basic understanding of the main technology influences on the current shape and capabilities of the ecommerce world.

This section doesn't harp on the build-out of the Internet so much as the strategies, systems, and devices that have converged to delineate the ecommerce space. Ecommerce didn't spring from a vacuum and we look at some unlikely ancestors and relatives for insight into its development. The emphasis is on technologies that point the way toward the ecommerce action: ideas, standards, and systems that show how technology has developed to meet the emerging requirements of the changing business scene.

Consanguinity: Origins and Precursors of Ecommerce

Electronic commerce is culturally a product of the latter half of the 1990s. The Internet migrated to public ownership during 1994, Netscape's IPO was in August 1995, Amazon.com's in May 1997, and IBM launched its "ebusiness" advertising campaign in 1997. Yet the technology of ecommerce was foreshadowed by a number of separate systems, both real and proposed, that helped to create fertile conditions for this seemingly sudden arrival.

Ecommerce has actually been around for 30 years or so, as the long-time users and providers of EDI will irritably tell you. EDI is the acronym for the quaintly named Electronic Data Interchange, a category label for a set of standards and services that has been enabling computer systems to talk to each other since the late 1960s.

An EDI system allows computer systems to exchange standardized documents relating to transactions across dedicated communications networks. Documents representing purchase orders, invoices, and so on are encoded and transmitted between machines belonging to the trading partners, cutting out human handling. Reducing human intervention reduces handling costs in a business process that is generally repetitive and has few exceptions. Automation of the process also guards against inadvertent introduction of errors during transcription at either end of the relationship. EDI is a good example of an automated system that encapsulates highly designed systematic behavior in the workplace, replacing clerical work with the combustible twin characteristics of repetitiveness and accuracy.

EDI has architectural constraints, however, that both hinder its generic applicability to all ecommerce situations and impact its implementation cost. First, EDI standards have proliferated and diverged despite industry attempts to hold the center ground. The ANSI X12 standard predominates in the U.S., where it was introduced to free the proprietary restrictions of the earliest EDI systems.

EDIFACT (Electronic Data Interchange for Administration, Commerce, and Trade) is a United Nations-sponsored standard that is intended to prevail as a worldwide standard. Adopting either standard or an industry-specific subset, requires detailed mapping of data items between those specified by the standard and those used in the business's own systems. Although tools exist to help this process, it is still one that requires insight into the data structures of the target systems.

Second, EDI systems are designed to run on specialized network infrastructure or Value Added Networks (VANs). Such VANs have pricing models that predate ISPs and that are not comparable. This is hardly surprising considering the Internet was built largely with public money, while VANs are the core plant of private concerns. Even if telecommunications costs were not an issue, EDI would suffer in comparison to Internet-mediated ecommerce systems because no VAN has the reach of the Internet. EDI certainly has no toehold in the consumer market.

Third, the costs of EDI tend to make sense only in large volume applications. Specialized EDI software and hardware, together with subscription and maintenance charges, make the up-front investment palatable only for companies expecting to channel a large part of their business through the system. A manual purchase order may cost a large company between $50 and $100 to process, compared to less than $1 for an EDI purchase order.

These facts restrict the applicability of EDI to users who can agree on a message standard and a potentially limited set of correspondent business partners, and who can afford the software systems and network fees associated with its implementation. Consequently, EDI has had its biggest impact in industries where a relatively small number of players influence a relatively large volume of business, such as automotive component supply. In this case the industry can also readily standardize its messaging model around the predominant product sets.

EDI is evidently a mature technology, though it seems constrained to act as a solution for large players only. As we shall see, EDI has been refitted for the Internet age, giving it a new lease on life and bringing it within the reach of smaller companies. Most important, EDI is a system-to-system strategy and, therefore, has little apparently in common with the face of ecommerce as it is perceived today: an inter-active medium targeted at human users. The pre-Internet world had a colorful commercial information service aimed at the ordinary cus-tomer in the shape of broadcast teletext and its more responsive cousin, viewdata.

Teletext uses spare lines in a broadcast TV picture to encode pages of information, which can then be called up on the screen by the user. News, sport, entertainment listings, and travel information are partic-ularly popular teletext services, which pre-date Web analogues by 20 years. Formally launched in the U.K. in 1977 after three years of trials, teletext steadily established itself as an information source in the home setting.

Viewdata marries teletext-style page rendering with online data delivery and has been particularly successful in the travel industry. The French Minitel system, a viewdata terminal supplied to telephone sub-scribers in place of the phone book, created a successful national online information and services industry within France during the 1980s.

Such technologies failed to change the world to the extent promised (or hyped) today by ecommerce. We could cite many reasons for their failure, from the multiplicity of technical standards and dedicated devices needed to deliver them, to simple misjudgment of consumer readiness for a digital age. No shortage of predictions of a wired-up world have occurred, from the "paperless trading" promised by EDI to the defining fictions of William Gibson.[7] Yet experience over the last 30 years of the century has tended to demonstrate that while niches of ecommerce or ecommerce-like behavior have flourished, the general rev-olution has remained stubbornly on the drawing board.

The technology products that businesses have tended to buy have worked against realizing such visions. Businesses do not invest in world-changing technologies, but in solutions to pressing problems. The IT industry's cherished early adopters are few and far between. If we were directing business evolution from a secure position in the clouds then, doubtless, we would have decreed an earlier spread of email rather than the explosion in fax use that occurred in the

7. Gibson's novel *Neuromancer* (1994 reissue, Ace Books) brought *cyberspace* into the
   language in 1984.

mid-1980s. The technology purist looks at the aggregate ingenuity and investment devoted to generating a document image from computer-readable code, printing it onto paper, scanning the image into another set of 0's and 1's, squirting that down a telephone line to a receiver where it is printed out, scanned again, and processed by character recognition software into computer-readable text—and weeps. Yet paper, and its human handling, has been the constant factor in the spread of technology throughout business. Paper has proved the most reliable and flexible common currency for integrating systems. The input and output of human-readable text continues to dominate our thinking about where devices begin and end.

Consumers also tend to buy solutions, not technologies. Most electronic devices we buy contain clock displays, leading to a huge degree of technological redundancy—and a twice-yearly chore around daylight-saving. We buy separate audio players for the living room, kitchen, and car. Few homeowners wire their houses for audio or video integration, let alone install full computer networks.

EDI was born as a strategy for electronic trading between businesses, while teletext systems were intended to display information to consumers. If the two tracks had crossed, then we would have something like today's Web. What the tracks share is a myopia about individual empowerment. EDI is geared toward creating diplomatic relations between hefty trading partners, while teletext systems are user-selectable publishing media.

More obviously, the two tracks have no common technology base. No reason exists why they should, yet with perfect hindsight we can see how the common technologies of the Internet create a new class of opportunities for ecommerce and publishing alike—and allow each to borrow characteristics of the other. With a common technology base taking care of systems connectivity, we no longer have to take a set of basic decisions when we build a distributed system. We needn't consider the basic mechanisms of data transmission, presentation, or user interaction. Internet technologies provide a level of plumbing that enables us to concentrate on the novel features of the application we seek to build. When EDI was conceived, systems integrators could not even assume the systems they were attempting to engage in dialogue coded text according to the same scheme. Teletext borrowed spare transmission capacity to relay information in a more efficient manner than that used by analogue television pictures and it targeted a dumb device.

Many other candidate technologies could be labeled precursors of contemporary ecommerce, but EDI and teletext seem the most relevant from the point-of-view of later developments. Arguably, automated teller machines and home shopping channels have been just as influential in preparing the ground for mass market ecommerce. But neither of these developments required a radical reassessment of the role of an existing technology, as do EDI and teletext. ATMs are essentially safes with computerized doors, while home shopping channels require the viewer to act as the bridge between broadcast and telecoms systems. EDI has the potential to flip the sense of a system's role in its host company, from being a faithful processor of essentially private matters to a gateway for intercompany cooperation. Teletext makes the TV act as a device for delivering structured data. The ecommerce technology landscape of the late 1990s owes much to the repositioning of familiar landmarks and the revelation of the potential they hold beyond their original purposes.

Affinity: The Rise of the Web

Vannevar Bush envisaged a vast web of interrelated documents in his article "As we may think," published in the *Atlantic Monthly* of July 1945. Introduced by the editor as "an incentive for scientists when the fighting has ceased," Bush's article pulls together a range of technologies we would now call embryonic IT systems and projects their future development in the service of knowledge.

As remarkable as his vision of the *memex*, an imagined workstation that associates all kinds of documents with each other depending on links specified by the user, is Bush's argument for the integration of a mass of technologies rarely related at the time he was writing. Photocells, thermionic tubes, and relay circuits appear alongside speech input devices and devices that sound suspiciously like magnetic disks. While acknowledging that such machines will first serve the basic needs of scientists, Bush discusses their impact in business specifically by imagining automated retail scenarios, before developing his image of the "intimate supplement" to memory realized by the memex.

Bush's memex user drives an entire world of information from his special desk, just as knowledge-workers do today with the Web. The most striking difference between the memex and the Web is that Bush's memex user also supplies associations among information resources. He may import collections of associated items, but he also builds his own "trails."

Ted Nelson extended Bush's ideas with his invention of the term *hypertext* and subsequent pursuit of his Xanadu project. But the realization of an interconnected complex of documents, widely accessible and open to growth, had to wait for the emergence of the World Wide Web.

The origin of the World Wide Web in the project work of the scientific community at CERN in Geneva has passed into the folklore of the digital age. Many people know Tim Berners-Lee conceived the Web and the HTTP protocol at its heart as a means of tying together citations in research papers. Underlying Internet protocols enabled Berners-Lee to concentrate at a business level of abstraction without having to build data transport or persistence mechanisms. What is less well known is that Berners-Lee envisaged the Web as a writeable system, not just a readable system. Users of documents would be able to add their own links to them. The Web we know today is a somewhat passive version of the collaborative tool its inventor originally described. We "surf" the Web using a "browser" and, although we can make "bookmarks," we can't create a new trail within the Web or annotate our explorations for those who follow. And, although the Web's founders quickly realized its potential for commercial applications, they had no requirement themselves to incorporate facilities for making transactions or ensuring security.

Numerous elements have been added to the basic Web model to improve its interactivity, with further fundamental changes on the horizon. In the meantime, the Web as experienced by most consumers and corporate users is primarily a medium for the exchange of information rather than value. In its unadorned form, the Web is an environment positively hostile to commerce.

First, the Web is inherently stateless. This means when a client (such as a browser) requests a resource (such as an HTML file) from a server, the server simply throws the resource back at the client. The client and server don't establish a session with each other. In other words, no state information is maintained for the client/server relationship. The server regards each request as arriving out of the blue. The industry has developed many ways around the problem of short-term state, starting with scripts invoked through Common Gateway Interface (CGI), right up to embedded server scripts such as Microsoft's Active Server Pages (ASP) and server-side components such as Java servlets.

This flurry of new-minted jargon gives a hint of the complexity that can accompany the extension of a basic technology. Recognizing that a nontrivial application is likely to require the preservation of state is not enough. We then have to navigate a range of candidate solution types, determining along the way a new set of selection criteria.

If short-term state relates to a server's capability to remember to whom it is talking for the duration of an encounter, then long-term state is the capability to recognize clients between encounters. Implementing long-term state in a Web-based system can be done in two basic ways. One requires the server to make a private note on the client system, which it can look at the next time they connect. This is called a *cookie*. The second method is to require the user to register some basic details, which are then recorded by the server in its database. Many users object to cookies on privacy grounds. The idea that a distant site is writing and reading benign information to their hard disk is also simply unpalatable to some users. Users who are unfamiliar with the cookie concept and who have installed or inherited browsers configured to accept all proffered cookies may accidentally delete the cookie files from their machine and then find themselves denied access to their familiar online destinations.

Using a server-side database to register users is a relatively simple procedure, where we extend the use of our chosen short-term state strategy to include a backend database. Asking users to fill in registration forms is another matter. Some users object to giving away any personal or identifying information, even if the site promises to use it only to recognize returning visitors. Others may have no moral objection, but may simply not want to spend the time filling in the same basic information in different formats on different sites. Sites that ask users to give themselves user names and passwords also pass an added burden to users, whose list of names and passwords grow with every relationship into which they enter. If users keep the same name-password pairs for every site with which they register, then they are compromising their global security. Because many users keep the same name-password pair for all systems they use, including business systems not in any way attached to the outside world, potentially they are also compromising the security of those private systems. Microsoft's Internet Explorer browser offers to remember name-password pairs on the users' behalf. However, I suspect few users could list the places they are registered and, if an employer required them to change the passwords they used on the Web, few would be able to do so with complete confidence.

The Web is inherently insecure and this is the second fundamental drawback to its use in a commercial setting. Neither the Web's protocols nor the underlying mechanisms of the Internet ensure the integrity of any data sent using them. Secure Sockets Layer (SSL) and certificates can be used to improve the security of message contents and to guarantee the identity of their senders, as discussed further in Chapter 4. But, again, these are relatively complex adornments to the simple elegance of the Web in its native form.

The third basic characteristic of the Web that makes it unfriendly to commerce is its lack of an integral payment mechanism. This is not a criticism of the Web because it was not conceived as a medium of value transmission but, nevertheless, this is a substantial barrier to commerce. The Web lends itself well to the exchange of information and the initial commercialization of the Web naturally concentrated on providing product information and corporate positioning statements, functions the Web performs with grace and efficiency. Taking payment dislocates the mechanism; we find ourselves in an unfamiliar hinterland of competing payment solutions, based on different trading and technology models and offered by a bewildering range of suppliers.

Taken together, these characteristics of the Web in its native form ensure that while it enables business encounters, it inhibits business transactions and relationships. The remedial measures we have noted along the way trail their own acronyms and dizzying descents into computer science-speak. It is unlikely that the Web will be swept away and replaced by a transparent commerce infrastructure. The Web has embarked on a process of evolution, and it will develop new capabilities in a complex response to market conditions. If we were setting out to design a commerce system from scratch, then doubtless we would do it another way. We might more logically take the payment mechanism as our point of departure, rather than attempting to co-opt a research-oriented system.

Mondex is one organization that started from this alternative entry-point. Born as a blue skies project within a British bank, Mondex proposed a form of secure, digital cash that would be implemented using smart-card technology. The drivers for the initiative included the great costs to industry of handling cash. Mondex emerged during 1994, at the same time the Internet was transferring to the public realm. At that time, the idea of storing value in a range of currencies on a card and using the card to effect transactions in a series of modified, yet essentially recognizable commercial situations, was a more compelling vision of mass market change than the immature Web. Cards are portable, cheap to manufacture, and understood by millions of users. Computer systems, on the other hand, are frightening collections of boxes that frequently break down and remind everyone unpleasantly of work. Mondex demonstrated transactions using kiosks and modified telephones, and quickly moved to community-wide tests.

Digital cash of all kinds has made little headway to date, despite its obvious theoretical appeal. Digital cash is the consumer analogue of EDI: a standardized means of trading electronically, whose complexity is hidden from the end user. Yet, mass market ecommerce is still stubbornly yoked to the fortunes of the Web and the chief means of payment via the Web is the credit card transaction. History is strewn with failed technologies that were unquestionably superior to those that prevailed or simply failed to ignite the markets they were designed to launch. Pen-based computing burned up a mountain of

Silicon Valley investment before the Palm series triumphed on the scorched ground left by its industry forerunners. Success with technology can't just be a matter of technology. Sometimes, as with the Web, a vision is co-opted to serve purposes that weren't of primary concern to its begetters, while the best laid plans of experts gather dust. This pattern threatens to emerge again in the context of another apparently no-brainer technology poised to grab the ecommerce center stage: interactive television.

Interactivity: The Protracted Dawn of Interactive TV

While the Web has been growing relentlessly as an information and entertainment medium, complete with predictions about its future dominance over other delivery mechanisms, television has been developing in the direction of an interactive, computing-driven environment.

The convergence of television and computing has long seemed natural to those who see an inevitability in shared technology components. But apart from the fact that computers and televisions both use screens as output devices, little natural common ground exists between the two classes of machine, at least from the neutral point of the view of the user. To the extent that the screen of a computer and a modern TV set are both commonly accompanied by input devices, such as keyboards, mice, and "zappers," then each machine at least has the potential for interactivity. Untold millions of computers are daily reduced to emulating magic lantern shows, as they grind through presentations or animate a screen saver.

The technology to make television interactive is not hard to find, though no widely accepted standard exists. Digital cable systems can accept user input directly through the delivery cable, whereas satellite broadcasters rely on telephone links for receiving data from users.

The real issues in interactive TV are not about technology standards, but about applications and context of use. These issues belong under the technology topic because they directly address technology's role in enabling some kind of commercial behavior. Interactive TV does not appear to arise from any well-understood demand or shift in habits on the part of consumers. Interactive TV is primarily a technological potential that is seeking a commercial rationale, though it's an item of faith for many that video-on-demand and pay-per-view sport will prove the commercial viability of the medium.

To consider applications first, what interactivity brings to TV beyond a handful of simple features is unclear. An electronic program guide, which allows the user to browse the various content channels on offer and make his selection, is an obvious necessity when the number of channels grows beyond the scope of a printed publication. The capability to choose camera angles for sporting events may have its fans, though it is also possible few sports fans will value the opportunity of doing a professional director's work for him. Real-time voting on everything from talent shows to political propositions becomes possible, although these are already carried out successfully via phone systems. Multiuser games with high-quality graphics and sound may provide more consumer appeal, though, again, these are well established in non-TV settings.

Interactive TV is currently emerging from its trial stages. Open.... is the name of the interactive digital TV service being rolled out by British Interactive Broadcasting during 1999. Open.... has attracted many leading retailers and brands to its platform, including a number combined in "Britain's first electronic high street," called Shop! Whether such services will change our lives or just be remembered for their creative punctuation remains to be seen.

Each of the potential applications for interactive TV poses a distinct problem of use context, which is the second problem with interactive TV. Television is consumed largely by groups, usually families. TV is absorbed fairly passively and often provides a background to home life rather than a focus of attention. People sit at a distance from the television and interact with it by squeezing a zapper. They don't get up close to the TV and consume it as individuals.

The model of use is, in fact, completely the reverse of that for the PC. PC users sit a foot or so from the screen, which performs for them alone. They are used to controlling its behavior at a detailed level, choosing from options that change between applications and interpreting the navigation design of Websites and software packages.

These two types of behavior have been labeled "lean back" and "lean in," respectively. Entertainment, mass communications, and low levels of complexity are deemed to go with lean back contexts. Decision-making, self-direction, and inquiry are associated with the lean in mode.

Where does this leave ecommerce? We want to reach large numbers of consumers through a ubiquitous, familiar, easy-to-operate medium, which has also traditionally defined the production and narrative standards for the sales process—it must be TV. Yet we also want the individual who controls the purchase decision to complete that decision and to make a valid transaction with us. There's a collision between TV-type behavior and PC-type behavior, which is not easy to reconcile. Who, in a family group, has ownership of the decision to buy? Many members may influence that decision, but an individual must make the transaction. If you are a marketer, seeking to track the viewing and purchasing behavior of a group of consumers, how do you establish which individual in a household is determining which outcomes?

If TV falls down as an ecommerce mechanism at the moment of commercial truth, perhaps business should concentrate on upscaling the role of the Web. If this were done, the Web could become more and more of a TV-like delivery channel, allowing companies to sell products and services using the strategies of broadcast media combined with refined knowledge about niche groups. Indeed, much of the investment poured into the Web over the last five years or so has been aimed at creating that transition. The excitement about "push" technologies in 1997—methods for streaming tailored content to users, rather than requiring them to seek it out on Websites—was intimately connected with this hope. The main problem with this vision is PC users do not tend to use their machines in a TV-like way. They may have a news headline service streamed to a window on their desktop at work, but they are unlikely to order up the same kind of service at home. Streaming news seems to have found a role as a distraction in the work environment, but it hasn't yet proved itself an integral part of anyone's private life. WebTV, now part of Microsoft, aims to bring the Web model directly to the TV.

Of course, the lack of evidence for an effective user response to the convergence of television and Web formats may simply be due to cultural lag. People may change their attitudes toward television consumption, especially as their use of other types of screen-based systems in other areas of their lives continues to grow. The potential for interactive TV to become the main means of home shopping is clearly huge and suggests the problem of identifying and activating the purchasing decision-maker in the home is one worth investing effort in cracking.

With this in mind, many businesses could regard selling via the Web as a trial-run for mass market ecommerce, rather than as a channel in its own right. Taking your business on to the Web exercises a number of corporate muscles and may lead you to discover you need additional powers to compete in an environment where the customer can be taken from passing interest to committed purchaser in an apparently seamless process. In the long run, the basic technologies that deliver customer interactivity to the home may coalesce around a handful of standards or diversify among a number of competing approaches. Businesses looking to exploit the generic opportunity need to insulate themselves from the basic technologies and be confident they can take advantage of whatever infrastructures perform reliably and reach the individuals in whom they are interested.

So what should organizations try to learn as they use the Web for ecommerce? First, they need to acquire the skills and habits of communicating effectively in words and pictures with individual consumers. Companies geared to producing annual reports or billboard advertising may find their capability to sustain a service with many of the characteristics of news and entertainment media is limited. Most companies do not provide running commentaries on their activities or explain their decisions, and when they do, it is for shareholders or regulators. The mysteries of narrative, of addressing audiences of diverse ages and backgrounds, and of subtly discouraging visitors they do not want, are all likely to be missing within the company or locked away within team members far from the corporate communications headquarters. Next, from the point of view of the customer, is the company's capability to engage in dialogue with her. Most corporate

Websites solicit communication from visitors, but many companies aren't equipped to deal with the communication when it arrives. Web users respond faithfully to communications couched in direct, personal terms, and feel let down when they realize their friendly, solicited inquiry disappears into a bureaucratic black hole or—worse—results in a shower of junk mail. No company can judge ahead of time what effect their Web presence will have on their customer services department or how the site's design and promotion will affect the level of inquiries derived from it. Companies need to be aware that it's not just machines that require scalability—teams do, too.

Even more fundamentally, businesses can learn some important—and frightening—facts about their fulfillment capability. The delivery commitment they make in their traditional business cannot be carried over to the Web channel without providing for that channel's effect on fulfillment systems. Many ecommerce Websites have been set up to take orders, which are then printed out by the Webmaster and routed to the sales department via the internal mail. Information is rekeyed and the process is delayed. More important, the Web channel introduces a measure of unpredictable demand. Orders from the Web may be influenced by changes to content, design, or even pricing policy made without reference to the normal decision-making channels. The connection between the site's role in demand stimulation and customer behavior is clouded by a number of unknowables. For example, the site may be suddenly linked to by a popular site, drawing in a sudden rush of new customers, which later dries up when the referring site drops the link.

As well as experiencing the strange new commercial weather of the Web, businesses do well to learn about topics ranging from brand positioning and inflection to aligning sales and pricing systems across the organization. These are all topics we return to in Chapter 5.

However technology convergence plays out, it's certain any successful mass market ecommerce strategy entails reorganization within the enterprise. When your ecommerce team talks about communications, is it thinking about customer propositions and input or about the wiring of its LAN?

Connectivity: The Intelligent Environment

The TV set has been fingered as a potential universal ecommerce device by many observers. But, as we have seen, its role in our lives does not make it the natural choice for effective ecommerce. If the mere presence of a screen is not enough to ensure a mass market ecommerce environment, then perhaps we should look in another direction for an embryonic ecommerce device. And, if we're looking for a well-connected device that we can firmly identify with an individual user, then the mobile phone is the leading contender.

Mobile phones have certainly not suffered from any cultural lag in their uptake. Their daily use is widespread among all types of users and competition between network and device suppliers is fierce. The principle that everyone is always reachable has permeated business culture and those who have reorganized (or disorganized) their habits around its use begin to relate to the world as a responsive, always-on environment. What seems natural is the personal buying behavior of individuals will migrate to such devices. The term *mobile commerce* has been used to refer to standards efforts in this area, but the salient value to the potential user is not so much mobility as its corollary: freedom from physical network attachment. The growth in use of mobile phones, laptops, and Personal Digital Assistants (PDAs) also parallels a general shift in working habits away from permanent, deskbound security to a more peripatetic combination work- and lifestyle.

Many technology players have extrapolated from this situation and are gearing themselves to a world where the environment is "intelligent," either by trying to build that future or to design products and services for it. One way of describing the technology character of this future in broad terms is to build on the model of thin-client computing. The following is a gross simplification of some core architectural concerns that are explored in more detail in Chapter 5.

Systems that are, to any extent, distributed exhibit some kind of client-server architecture. This means some components of the system take the role of servers or suppliers of data and functionality, and others take the role of clients or users of data and functionality. The respective responsibilities of the components in a system are designed so they work together to create the overall behavior of the required system. The extent to which a component is active or passive is, therefore, also a matter of design.

In a two-tier client-server system, one client component collaborates with one server component. The server generally resides on a hefty machine, specified to serve high volumes of requests from clients. The client, traditionally developed to run on a PC, may do a lot of work or a little. This kind of architecture was particularly well suited to early GUI applications. The client would handle the rendering of the GUI and interpret inputs and outputs to it. The client would then converse on a need-to-know basis with the server. So, rather than the client telling the server about every move of the mouse, it would deal with user interaction until an event—such as the clicking of a button—had been completed and only then turn to the server.

This style of architecture has come to be known as *fat client* computing. The desktop power of the average PC and its storage capabilities led designers to locate more and more functionality at the client side. Servers were often reduced to the role of data faucets, pouring corporate data to a multitude of clients, which processed it in their own ways.

Fat client computing has been successful in delivering desktop applications and has been particularly effective in asserting departmental control over systems in organizations with powerful central IT functions. But, as the working environment becomes more dispersed, changeable, and fast-moving, this style of development creates a brake on progress. First, fat clients demand relatively large machine sizes to function well. Porting the average fat client to a handheld device isn't possible. The device will be restrained by how much memory it contains and the speed of its processor. Accessing data held on a disk brings engineering problems because any component with moving parts multiplies the build complexity of the product while reducing its reliability. Moving parts require power, which is at a premium in a mobile device. And the scale and form factor of any truly portable device is likely to preclude the kind of detailed user interface designed for the desktop.

Second, client software must be loaded on each machine that will use the system. This is fine for the first version of any system, but it becomes problematic when new releases are issued, when new users are added to the system, or when the client hardware or software environment changes. It quickly becomes hard to track which machines are using which version of the client software. If the user population is split by version, then the server component has to be changed to deal with different types of interaction. Other software loaded on the client machine may be incompatible with the existing client component and cause the system to behave in unforeseen ways. The long-term complexity created by fat client computing is a significant management overhead and a potential cause of business process failure, which, by its nature, can be hard to quantify. These pressures are at the heart of corporate moves toward intranet systems and interest in network computers. Organizations naturally come to different conclusions about the total cost of ownership of systems built to a fat client architecture and may be able to justify their development on the basis of short-term gain. The trend in corporate systems development is far away from fat client computing, however.

Third, attitudes to network and network traffic have changed considerably over the years. Fat clients require thin pipes; client and server agree not to bother each other unless they have something important to say. Where network access was at a premium and, particularly, when communications outside buildings were required, such a strategy made economic sense. But communications costs have fallen as technologies have improved and diversified. The speed of data transfer increases as new encoding and transmission schemes are invented, while new methods of physically transferring data create competitiveness in network capacity supply. At the same time, network users notionally benefit from the infrastructural economics of networks. Once installed, a communications network is a resource to be maximized and suboptimal use represents a poor use of the investment. Just as systems designed to make good use of scarce storage capacity famously gave us the Year 2000 (Y2K) problem at a time when storage had become cheap, so systems designed to make little use of intermachine communications have given us a legacy of monolithic systems that are tied to heavy machines and permanent connections.

Thin client systems, by comparison, place few software burdens on the client device and make minimal assumptions about its capabilities. They assume an efficient, high-capacity data pipe is available. Most of the work is done at the server side. When it comes to systems management, the thin client model is closer in kind to the dumb terminal systems of the past, where most of the intelligence was centered in the mainframe.

The thin client model also has characteristics in common with voice telephone system development, where a relatively simple device with a restricted user interface has long been used to access all kinds of services. Telephones were designed to be intuitive to use and were regarded as functioning tentacles of the network itself—terminal devices. Picking up the receiver and hearing the dial tone is all a user needs to do to actuate the system and ensure service is available. Scott McNealy, CEO of Sun Microsystems, the computer industry's leading booster of the thin client model, coined the word Webtone to refer to ever-present, ubiquitous, easily accessible, and utterly reliable network connectivity.

If mobile computing devices can rely on such a service, then we can build an unrestrained computing environment that will be perfect for mass market, personalized ecommerce. The locus for customer interaction will not be the home *or* the office, but everywhere. The intelligent house and intelligent office will be cooperating members of a more pervasive computing environment (see the following sidebar).

Sun Microsystems is striving to make this vision reality in its Jini initiative. *Jini,* which is based on Sun's Java technology, enables system components to query and negotiate with each other using common standards. Resources that become available to the network announce themselves and their capabilities, so a distributed system essentially configures itself. Jini effectively erases the boundaries between heterogeneous systems in a real-time, exploratory fashion. It heralds a shift away from tailored systems integration solutions

Services to Your Shirt Pocket

If you could carry the ultimate thin client device, attuned to a persistent Webtone pervading the environment, what would you want to do with it? Just because we can imagine such a device, we can't necessarily list the applications that would follow (or generate) its uptake. But ecommerce has developed through individual visions and speculations, so it can't do any harm to guess at the services people might want in an intelligent environment.

Let's start with the intelligent toaster. This device has become part of the mythology of the high-tech world. If your toaster could talk to other machines, what would it talk about? It could catch up on new types of baked products and anticipate their characteristics by adjusting its cooking times and slice handling mechanism. Your toaster could even place a trial order for you. Perhaps it could follow fashions in brownness, ensuring your breakfast toast matches that being eaten by the *digeratti*.

So far, so useless. I'm not so sure my kitchen is going to break out in a riot of conversation and, even if it does, I don't think I have the personal bandwidth to deal with it.

But if I can carry around a device that can happily deal in my investments for me, perhaps alerting me when it's about to make a trade on the edge of my comfort zone, then maybe I'll give it pocket room. Perhaps it tunes into traffic and travel services as I move around, suggesting new routes to me as it learns of congestion up ahead. Such services are already available in cars, but a personal service that ranged across all forms of transport would transform the lives of those in busy urban areas. Possibly it remembers all the things I'm most

to generic, collaborative support environments for interacting systems. Several other companies are pursuing strategies for enabling dynamic collaborative systems, but Sun has provided the highest-profile articulation of a truly sociable systems environment.

Continuity: The Technology Expectation

EDI, the Web, interactive TV, universal ecommerce devices—ecommerce technology options seem diverse and diffuse. As we have hinted, however, the technology standards of the Internet are helping them to converge. This secondary effect of the Internet—the influence of its standards on the development of subsequent systems—permeates all areas of ecommerce endeavor.

The first beneficiary is EDI. Web front-ends enable users to input data to EDI systems by filling in HTML forms, allowing rapid development of low-use systems. This is an effective way of enabling smaller companies to participate in EDI associations because the Web, together with a certain amount of data rekeying, replaces the need for sophisticated systems connectivity. Gateways now connect EDI systems with Web-based systems at a lower level, porting messages to and from systems that emulate EDI behaviors.

While the Web brings some further reach to EDI, EDI has something to teach Web-based systems. As a strategy for representing and shipping structured business information, EDI is a more highly

interested in and probes likely sources of satisfaction on my behalf, only bothering me when it's negotiated something it knows I'll value. It could be tracking, sifting, and querying offers to supply me with food, power, and entertainment while it assesses which charities I should be supporting.

Some people say that progress allows ordinary people to live the lives formerly restricted to kings. Today, we consume the kind of food, entertainment, and travel that once only the most powerful could command. Perhaps ecommerce in an intelligent environment will also equip us with wise councils, obedient departments of state, and endlessly discrete spy networks, all toiling to ensure our comfort and prestige. 🔲

organized structure than the pure HTML page. By combining EDI message structures with XML, a data-aware successor to HTML we consider later, the Web can rapidly become a vehicle for system-to-system interactions at the business-to-business level. With EDI/XML, Web system developers can code in terms of business documents rather than notional data structures implied by HTML text heading tags or the positioning of text within an HTML table.

On a broader front, the phenomenal success of the Web and its navigational metaphor are the chief influences on current system design. Just as the early to mid-1990s saw the systems community move en masse to Windows-based systems, so the latter half of the decade has seen the "Web front end" become the user interface of choice for most business systems. This is partly because running a system in a browser environment takes care of user platform differences because a correctly designed Web-fronted system will run on any platform that can run a Web browser. Although this is the economic argument most often cited for the move to the Web, a more defensible argument for many companies is that systems presented via a Web interface bring with them an expectation of transparent usability. For most of us, Websites appeared in the public domain first, before we were ever exposed to a corporate intranet site. We approached the Web as ordinary users, who were not going to be invited anywhere for a one-day course in reading the designer's mind. We were trained, through exploration, to click and go; we each evolved our own opinions about what constitutes good and bad visual design. A generation limited to using the systems provided by its employers were suddenly exposed to an ever-growing range of alternative approaches and became adepts as well as informed critics.

The Web is a systems delivery mechanism that requires "zero installation" and no training, and that helps to obscure the boundary between systems that are work and those that are leisure. Business systems become increasingly user-friendly because ease of use leads to enhanced productivity. Consumer Websites become more intelligent as consumer lifestyles become more complex and information-hungry. Little process difference exists between organizing a family holiday, with its intermeshing requirements for timing, diversions, comforts and cost, and organizing a due-diligence assessment of a target company. Indeed, the air miles from one might be used to subsidize the other.

Few Web-based systems have been built entirely from scratch. Most are veneers applied to existing systems. The partitioning of systems into layers and the organization of interlayer communication has been a key issue in systems design since the general introduction of the GUI. The Web adds to the partitioning challenge by replacing a generation of GUI tools. It also undermines much of the learning associated with Windows-style GUIs because many Web-based systems forego nonmodality for form-style interaction. (Nonmodality enables users to click a range of legal options at any one time, whereas modal interaction forces the user to complete tasks in a pre-set order.) Architecting for the Web and dealing with its impact at all layers of the design model, is explored further in Chapter 5.

A basic, shared level of expectation of systems capability has emerged during the last few years. Rarely is it articulated as such a consensus, yet when it is acknowledged and paired with the business change drivers we have looked at, it becomes a powerful basis for action. Putting aside for the moment the specific challenges of building any one solution, we can see ecommerce overlays a technology environment that is highly connected, intuitively usable, and universally accessible. These are the minimum technical requirements for any ecommerce initiative: they interlock with business's shift to individuated, connected, aggregated opportunities.

2 A Generic Business Model for Ecommerce

In Chapter 1, we considered the business and technology influences that have shaped the current ecommerce environment. This chapter shifts the focus to the individual organization and describes a generic business model that managements can use to found their ecommerce strategies.

This model is not a financial or organizational blueprint for creating a successful ecommerce line of business. Instead, this is a model in the sense that it provides a set of related concepts, which can be used to orient management thinking. The aim of the model is to establish a baseline vocabulary management can use to generate specific projects.

The model is a little like a game board. The playing surface for ecommerce is suggested in the section "A New Map," where a map of the ecommerce space is outlined, subdividing it into characteristic zones. The playing pieces and the rules whereby they move, are explored in the section "Role Types," which concentrates on the types of roles players can adopt. The opening section considers the local business drivers that bring decision makers to the table.

LOCAL BUSINESS DRIVERS

Sweeping changes in the business and technology domains create the broader weather patterns of our age, but the individual organization feels the effects of these forces in a more visceral way. In this section, the broader forces are dissolved into their local manifestation in the immediate business environment. The principal focus is, therefore, on existing businesses. The process yields four local business drivers that are commonly felt as urgent stimuli.

The first of these four drivers is the compulsion to catch up with competitors—or to steal a march on them. We take for granted that competitive edge is a leading concern for all businesses; its role as a survival component in the business's strategy makes it a stand-out issue, especially where novel channels are at stake.

The second driver is the requirement to develop a credible ecommerce channel from whatever online assets the business already has—assuming it has a presence of some kind established.

The third driver, cost reduction, can be a creative force when accepted as an essential part of an ecommerce project.

Finally, we consider how the drive to improve partner inclusion can shape an ecommerce strategy in a direction that improves the business's infrastructural capability to play as an extended enterprise.

Each of these drivers can be harnessed as a propulsive force for the business, rather than a deflective or immobilizing one. The emphasis here is on capturing the free energy that crackles around the ecommerce decision space and connecting it to the innovation and development processes.

Catching Up and Being Caught

Everyone has his or her favorite ecommerce success story and that story is Amazon.com. "Earth's biggest bookstore" brought the main message of ecommerce to a wide business public with its rapid dominance of online book retailing and its effect on traditional booksellers. The first lesson of Amazon.com, to most onlookers is it can offer a range and quantity of products that would defeat a physically tethered store. The second lesson is generally held to be that an online force can achieve market ubiquity without acquiring retail real estate. The third lesson is that ecommerce directly challenges established players and upstarts can rapidly establish themselves as leaders; barriers to market entry are on the floor.

These lessons have been rehearsed so often it's not uncommon for people to dismiss Amazon itself as a rather obvious and somehow trivial phenomenon—a mere trigger for the business world's rush online. Yet Amazon's success was less predictable than is sometimes now charged and its lessons are more complex than the general summary would suggest.

Jeff Bezos famously lit upon books as an ideal product for selling over the Web because the potentially complete stockholding of every published book would be impossible for a traditional store to carry. His analysis told him quantity and diversity within a catalog would be the key differentiator between purchasing online and purchasing through a physical channel. In other words, it's not books as such that drove Amazon, but that lots and lots of different books are available. The book trade has always been "virtual," in the sense that any customer can order any book in print from any regular bookstore. Amazon brought a new level of efficiency to this service and improved its availability. The winning insight was that an under-resourced sales channel could be enhanced by technology, not that people would want to buy books over the Web.

Amazon's expansion into music CDs illustrates a similar point. The music market, with its complex makeup of genres and eras, is hard for customers to navigate. Physical stores have to bet on big-selling artists, giving them prominence and promotion. Yet the aggregated potential revenue from niche tastes and obscurities would give even the greatest acts a run for their money. An online retailer can offer all this product as easily as it can offer the top ten. It can even offer an attractive route to market for small labels, by carrying their catalog details and stocking small quantities on a sale or return basis. The Web isn't the most obvious channel for selling music: audio clips require plug-in streaming technology and can be hungry for bandwidth. But it's an ideal channel for selling standard-format items that come in a bewildering range of variants.

Amazon's first lesson is not, therefore, so much that vaporizing the physical store inevitably leads to market dominance, but that picking a product of inherent and proven diversity leverages the behavior of the Web. What about the tantalizing notion that physical storefronts can be jettisoned in favor of cheaper, virtual ones built from pixels? It may be cheaper to write a page of HTML than it is to fit out a store, but there's more to the virtual store than the code of its home page. We have more to say on this theme later.

Amazon.com is the quintessential ecommerce player: a brand born for the Web and wedded to its .com suffix. Fidelity Investments has proved that established players can also triumph on the Web. From the launch of its first trading and retirement planning sites in 1995, Fidelity tracked impressive growth across the first three years online. By March 1998, the company could announce that Fidelity's total assets held by registered online customers had reached $73 billion. The NetBenefits service for 401(k) and 403(b) retirement savers enables users to model and modify their portfolios online, further extending the company's service capability.

While Fidelity is a fine example of an organization that has embraced the Web as a means of doing business, its success is no guarantee that any other existing business can become an ecommerce force with such apparent ease. And while Fidelity's brand and loyal customer base have played a part in the establishment and growth of its ecommerce lines, the *applications* have created that success. The ability to administer her own portfolio at any time, without having to interact with a customer services representative, is a clear benefit to the customer. At the same time, the company is saving on staff time by enabling the customer to drive her own portfolio. Trading and asset management fit the characteristics of the Web channel, just as books and CDs do. A stock trade is apparently complex because of the huge number of potential stocks that could be traded and the variability of prices. But once the values of these variables are fixed, it is a standard product. Big catalogs and changing prices—these are better indicators of a market's early suitability for ecommerce than the prestige of a company's brand.

Amazon and Fidelity are just two of the highest profile leaders in mass-market ecommerce, but they represent a group of players that exerts extraordinary pressure on business decision-makers. A wave of "me-too" activity began to swell during 1998, with apparently every business dot-com'ing itself and looking to position itself as an ecommerce-enabled enterprise—whatever that might mean. The anxiety contains a paradox: the feeling the pioneers have grabbed all the easy pickings, mixed with a belief that anyone can replicate their formula.

Catching up and avoiding being caught have become the prime business drivers behind ecommerce. Value can, in fact, be gained from imitation, but it must be done consciously and with a positive goal in mind. Blindly mimicking the competition can be harmful, for while the copycat spends his way into the shadow of a competitor without grasping his substance, he hollows out the unique values of his own enterprise. Nothing ignites the cynicism of an organization's people faster than a scramble to wear the clothing of a competitor. Amazon.com could possibly lose its place to another player, but we suspect it would be to another *kind* of player, not a competitor using the same formula.

Positive imitation allows companies to develop online presences that leverage the experience of earlier entrants. The best way to learn visual design standards is to construct your own critique of the sites you visit. Buying as many different kinds of products and services as you can over the Web, and noting how easy it is to buy, to revise your selection, and to find your way around the site, is a vital educational process that is dangerous to omit. How few ecommerce managers buy on the Web is surprising, yet showing disdain for hands-on experience is as dangerous here as in any other area of the business. Immersion leads to informed action.

As well as profiting from the public experience of its peers and competitors, a company may use imitation to learn how to inflect its brand in the new channel. We use the term *inflect* to suggest existing brands usually require a subtle set of changes to make them suitable for online use. This may simply mean corporate logos are abandoned because they do not reproduce well on screen or because they are too strongly suggestive of printed matter. More fundamentally, the brand may need to be enhanced to make it mesh with other visual design elements, such as animations and pop-ups. The Web abounds with good and bad examples of brand inflection, but the corporate identity industry has yet to write the book on this important subject.

Of course, the outward form of a competitor's ecommerce activities may not be the only driver to imitation. Some companies are attracted to the ecommerce bandwagon less by the commercial performance of leading players than the stock market performance of Internet stocks. Stocks associated with the Internet have reached valuations far in excess of their commercial performance. While most commentators agree the market as a whole has been overvalued, a general consensus exists that ecommerce will somehow save the basic rationale for high valuations of companies that have yet to deliver profits. The argument goes that, if ecommerce generates transactions to any interesting fraction of the predictions on offer, then companies at the core of the movement stand to gain. It's as if any firm with a hole or a shovel is worth backing if it's somewhere near the gold rush. Investor hype backwashes onto management when the company sees its stock market performance in relative decline, compared to upstarts with Internet cachet. Established retailers in particular are prey to an understandable rage that new entrants with untried formulae, unknown brands, and poorly defined business plans soak up the ecommerce investment action, while their own proven expertise, brand equity, and relationships seem to count for little. In some cases, the established company's second thoughts about the Web—it's another channel—may be mature and actionable, but fail to help the company's valuation. The dot-com'ing of the company, on the other hand, can send a signal to the stock market that it should acquire the luster of an ecommerce

---

A Checklist for Imitation

1. How have our traditional competitors approached doing business on the Web?

2. Who are our nontraditional competitors on the Web?

3. Who is doing business unlike ours that we admire?

4. Who seems to be imitating us? Have they improved on our job?

5. Do we have a set of parallel agendas for our Web projects? If so, which are public and which are private? Do we have any protected agendas—ones we can share with our business partners? ■

upstart and be re-evaluated accordingly. To suggest we can wish this sort of action away would be naïve, but for management to know if it is managing for real ecommerce success or just for public positioning is crucially important.

By the same token, what is quite possible is, by the time you read this, every Internet stock may have crashed magnificently in a general wipe out, triggered by the failure of some prominent leaders. If so, you could be looking at the ideal time to mount your ecommerce initiative.

Some of the motivations we have touched on here may seem cynical. Imitation is, however, the most common driver for established businesses moving into ecommerce and, when handled with sensitivity, it can be a positive influence. Even undirected imitation or a stock market maneuver can spark committed and creative ecommerce revenue streams. Not being changed by the e-world once you become a player in it is difficult.

Catching up is always easier to accomplish if you capture some of the leaders for your own team. So, should businesses ease their migration by hiring in pre-formed Internet teams or even acquiring existing Web-based or ecommerce-led businesses? After all, if we are all moving to this new place, it may not hurt to have a few of the pathfinders on board. A common fear for managers contemplating ecommerce is that resources spent to date on a static Web presence have been wrongly allocated and an expansion of the site's capabilities will only lead to more losses and to the starvation of other projects within the business. In this case, prior experience with an ecommerce site—including failure—can save the acquiring company a great deal of pain.

This approach can work well for technical staff hires, especially if a real effort is made to make the new team a focus for growth in skills within the company as a whole. Acquiring an ecommerce business is currently still a low-volume and high-risk activity carried out mostly among the ecommerce players themselves. As the industry develops, we will probably see more capability-driven acquisition moves. At present, the number of analysts qualified to advise on such activities is probably too low to sustain a viable market. The following sidebar

Turning Zapata into zap.com

One of 1998's most entertaining running stories was the engagement of the Zapata Corporation and the Web. The twists and turns of the story provoked a lot of comment in the online industries and provided much continuing food for thought.

Zapata is best known as a fish-oil concern, though the family that owns it has diversified interests, which have changed greatly over the years. In the spring of 1998, Zapata ran advertisements in U.S. newspapers offering to buy Web zines, in a bid to create an entertainment portal named zap.com. Later in the year, the company attempted to buy Excite, but was rebuffed. In October, Zapata announced it was pulling out of the Internet game altogether and reversed its acquisition and investment deals with about 30 online companies. By January 1999, the portal strategy seemed back in play, as Internet stock prices returned from temporary doldrums.   ◼

on Zapata provides some thoughts on whether a company can easily buy Web credibility and why it may wish to do so.

Whatever the ostensible motivations for adopting an ecommerce position, management needs to move to a securely founded strategy. If imitation is one pillar of this strategy, then the other three are channel development, cost reduction, and partner inclusion, which are the topics of the next three sections.

Channel Development

It used to be enough to have a site; then you needed to claim you had a presence. Ecommerce demands that businesses go beyond both of these essentially static concepts and develop channels. The word *channel* is being used in two senses. Ecommerce is helping to blend these two meanings into each other.

In the media world, a *channel* is a branded carrier of entertainment or information to an audience. The physical manifestation of the channel—a segment of bandwidth, or an address, or a collection of printed pages—is intimately bound with the content it carries to create a strongly identified personality. Certain types of message and presentation have become fitted over time with particular channel types, creating a set of traditional media models with their own dynamics. Sports coverage, for example, is different across radio, television, newspaper and online channels. Radio may offer a ball-by-ball commentary on a game and plenty of expert opinion, while a newspaper may offer a more lyrical and weighty appraisal of the game and its highlights. Each channel is performing a different role with respect to the same input. Each may ultimately be addressing overlapping audiences yet, in each case, the channel's users choose it for its distinctive qualities. These criteria include convenience, access to technology, and habit, as well as the more overtly content-oriented criteria, such as loyalty to a star commentator.

As media channels have developed, they have multiplied and specialized. Formerly organized largely on geographical lines, news and entertainment channels now form around types of content or audience interests. Television channels such as MTV come to define generations of consumers. Strongly branded channels create a new geography of affiliation.

The other use of the term *channel* is that of the marketer. In this meaning, a *channel* is any permanent route to a group of customers. Channels are conduits for a company's products and services, with consuming populations fitted at their outlets. An organization may have direct channels, such as a sales force that is part of its payroll. It may also have indirect channels, via its business partners.

Both uses of the word *channel* incorporate the concept of a fixed, identifiable route along which messages may be passed to consumers. But in the traditional media world, a distinction exists between those who provide primary content for the channel and those who use it to send commercial messages. Authors and producers tend to regard advertising as a layer superimposed on the chief purpose of the channel, a necessary evil to be clearly demarcated in style and format from its main body. For marketers, content generates audiences for commercial messages and can help to deliver suitable demographics. Marketers also deal with a wide variety of channels that are untainted by any of the news or entertainment values associated with the media. Mail order catalogs, for example, should be good-looking and easy to use, but they don't require too much editorial agonizing. Where a catalog includes magazine-style copy, it can legitimately be biased toward sales. Marketing channels made up of teams or partner companies are even further removed from media practice. While a company's marketing department would certainly communicate with, for example, the sales representatives of a major retailer carrying its goods, that communication may be combined with product training, motivational exercises, and award evenings—a level of active engagement that seems far removed from the editorial practices we associate with media channels.

The arrival of ecommerce has propelled the channel concept to the top of corporate concerns. Clearly, the success of mass-market ecommerce pioneers such as Amazon and Fidelity proves the Web must at least be regarded as a route to a market: a persistent, brandable channel to an audience. At the same time, the Web is an information and entertainment medium, and, as such, it isn't a cost-free pipe. The Web isn't a place where goods are piled up and customers arrive to take them away, but a place where stories are told, dialogues are initiated, and facts are discovered. Above all, the Web remains a stubbornly *literate* medium. To the despair of those oriented to richly visual modes of communication, the Web continues to be a place where users are readers—and usually writers, too. Web users expect to access useful information, in large quantities, of high quality, and at no cost.

To make the transition to doing business on the Web, companies need to develop a sense of the Web as a channel. A traditional, static Web presence isn't an ecommerce channel. How can we go about developing a presence into an ecommerce channel?

Despite the currency of ecommerce and its variants, a surprising number of companies remain stuck at the presence point, apparently unable to develop their virtual real estate for any purpose beyond advertising their arrival. The basic commercial Website pattern has established itself and can be summed up by the typical navigation bar: **home | products | services | jobs | about | contact**. Some organizations strive to add further interest with manifestos, contests, or downloadable goodies. In general, however, the majority of commercial Websites are highly static.

The pure presence site performs a number of useful roles. It enables the company to learn some of the technology and media disciplines of the online world, even if those lessons are sometimes restricted to an imitative catching up with the industry average. The pure presence site also enables the company to gather some visitor traffic data, although because the visits are geared to general messages, it is doubtful how useful their analysis is. After the gee-whiz effect of charting the geographical distribution of domains hitting their site has worn off, corporates realize they can take little immediate action on the basis of raw traffic to a simple presence.

Does this mean ecommerce initiatives should abandon the *de facto* standard commercial Website pattern and try to create something more purely transactional? Some players have taken this attitude in developing the portal strategy. While a standard commercial presence may be a destination site for someone seeking information about a specific product or topic, a portal acts as a jumping-off point to other resources. A portal's perceived value to a user is its coverage and convenience. As a gateway to services, it may not seek direct revenues from users; instead, a portal is likely to support itself by selling advertising space or by taking a fee from services to which it links. Both these revenue streams are predicated on provable traffic levels, making the portal game a battle of giants. The portal strategy derives from the Internet industry's discovery that Netscape generated significant revenues from its home page because many users left their Netscape Navigator browsers set to that address as their default home page. Netscape used this default traffic to establish, along with other players, the market value of advertising space on high-traffic sites. The company developed NetCenter as a value-added portal, adding services such as free email to create a site that offers customer benefits rather than a simple default starting point. Portals are evolving their own style: often low in frills, they are characterized by an Amazonian bigness and an action-oriented interface. The portal-keeper has a somewhat paradoxical aim: to send you on your way, but to inspire you to return again and again. Services such as free email and calendars are weapons in this fight—mass market applications requiring hefty investment.

The portal is a logical development for online directory services such as Yahoo and Excite, but not so obviously a way forward for any other kind of business. Most businesses regard themselves as destinations and even intermediary businesses promote themselves as general partners of choice. Few companies as yet have made the transition to the new thinking about intermediary roles that we explore in the section "Role Types," though vertical portals (or *vortals*) are starting to address the directory needs of specific industries and interest groups. In general, companies succeeding with mass market ecommerce on the Web have shown that extending beyond mere presence into community is the key.

Designing your Website as a community involves concentrating on its main destination value for users and building content and interaction around that theme. The model here again is Amazon. Although the ostensible core customer value of Amazon's proposition is its gigantic catalog, the feature of the site that creates customer interest and loyalty is the reviewing of books and CDs. The ability to read what other buyers think of a product—often including its author—creates an unusual atmosphere of shared purpose. It's a little like a collision between a bookstore and a reading club. A real bookstore that encouraged this level of discussion would be a noisy and anarchic place, and a reading circle that jumped from topic to topic would be equally irritating. The virtual store, therefore, manages to apply a layer of experience that would defeat a traditional delivery mechanism. It represents a place that is always open for you to drop into, where some opinion can be found, and where your opinions count, as well. Better sociological and political definitions of community exist, but this seems a good pragmatic one to go on with as any.

The input of other community members forms a large part of the appeal for this type of site. It's noteworthy that users of this kind of site don't demand author fees. They don't see the offer of an album review as a commercial transaction, but as a contribution to the community: the chance to share their enthusiasm with others or to place their criticism before people who may be interested. Alongside this do-it-yourself ethic, good community sites add an authorial voice, to ensure a sense of personality exists on the site. Responding to visitor queries is a vital part of this stance. A community site team may spend as much time responding to customers as it does creating original content.

Raising the game from presence to community requires a shift in our thinking about the media content of the ecommerce activity. We need to generate new content on a continuous basis. We need to find a voice we can use to ensure consistency of tone across the site and to train writers in its use. Above all, we need to accept inbound customer communications and respond to them thoughtfully and rapidly. Taking the orders begins to look trivial in comparison: we can have a system do that.

The decision to develop an existing presence into a community or a portal often rests on an assessment of the presences's main customer benefits. Does it have credibility as a directory of resources or services elsewhere on the Web? In that case, it may be an embryonic portal. If, on the other hand, visitor feedback suggests that specialized content is a key attraction, then the presence may be better suited to development along the community path. The two paths are represented in Figure 2-1.

For most businesses, the time for experimenting with Web presence is over. Management must be ready to manage the phase that follows. With a community-oriented ecommerce presence, the team moves away from mirroring the company's brochures and press

FIGURE 2-1. First steps in developing beyond presence.

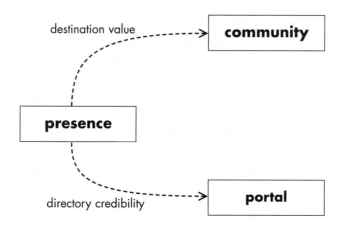

releases, and embarks on a heightened customer relations program crossed with a professional media channel. This is new stuff, but it's not what most people think of when they talk about business and the Web. Furthermore, the phase we are moving into should be seen as part of the business, not a weird add-on. The symbolic act of stripping the term *Webmaster* from the organization chart can help to emphasize the company's activities on the Web are mainstream business processes, rather than mysteries performed by the strangely gifted. We need to ensure a sustainable, resourced, scalable, and, above all, goal-directed business process. This calls for all the traditional planning and execution skills of management.

At root, management needs to set explicit goals for ecommerce channel development. Measures are the easiest attributes to identify in the goal-setting exercise: numbers of visits, visitors, inquiries, and sales are the obvious candidates. Less easy to establish is the realism of the goals set. Should every company swallow the sales figures of the pioneers and choose a percentage of the nearest analogue? Many retail organizations treat their ecommerce channel as a retail outlet and target it accordingly, using traffic estimates as analogues for local populations.

We suggest the early goals in a managed ecommerce channel don't focus too much on general sales volumes. Setting them may seem macho, but you will find little evidence to support your choice of number. You can achieve greater realism by fixing on a pair of early goals: a dull one and an interesting one.

The less glamorous goal is to repay the return on investment (ROI) for the ecommerce channel. Focusing on achieving payback within a challenging timeframe can help to solidify the feature scope of the project, as well as emphasize the seriousness of the undertaking. "We only need to sell ten a month to make a profit" is a fine mantra for any initiative and it demonstrates that the ecommerce stream is a revenue engine like any other in the business.

The more interesting goal position is to choose a specific product or service and target ecommerce sales for it. At this point, some companies realize they need to develop a radically new offer for the Web, rather than simply pushing existing lines through a new channel. This can be a breakthrough point: a moment when the team's perspective changes and we can start to see new business emerging from a cocoon of new media. We have more to say about the birthing process when we consider Pathfinder Applications in Chapter 3. Meanwhile, an early goal for the ecommerce channel may be to isolate a set of underperforming products with some characteristics that can be turned to a positive effect on the Web. Recalling the business changes we explored in Chapter 1, we should look for anything we have that could benefit from those movements. Do we have something that can be individualized, virtualized, globalized, or intellectualized?

For example, imagine we have a warehouse full of stock manufactured in 1970s styling: perhaps the company once created a *Saturday Night Fever* lawnmower that never caught on. We could sell them to an intermediary for disposal, but we're nervous about goods with our brand name reaching the market in this way. At the same time, little interest exists in embarking on the problem of finding a suitable business partner. Scrapping them would cost us more than storing them because we fitted them with a special high-pitch motor that can only be removed by experts.

Our Web presence gives us an ideal way to place the stock with buyers. We can summon the lurid appeal of the disco era with some good (?) visual design and connect with its current adherents by linking to disco-related sites. Pictures and technical data will clinch some sales and all can be achieved at low cost. We must be careful not to undermine our own brand, but Web users expect sites to show a little humor. We may even get some good publicity. We've intellectualized the offer by linking it to fashion and exploited the global dispersal of a market of enthusiasts.

Is this a flippant notion? It's a flippant example, but a serious effect is at play here. This is the idea that the wider possibilities of ecommerce can redefine our corporate attitudes to applicability. Our theories about what sells and what doesn't are based on our experiences with masses in segments, not masses of individuals. The Web enables us to tap straight into the interests of individual customers. In that respect, no offer is off-limits. By rethinking the outlets for what we have, we are also performing the analysis function that every business manager holds nearest to his or her heart: the maximizing of assets.

This suggested early path gives broad direction to those who want to develop a Web presence into an ecommerce channel. Its main value is in helping to remove the perceptual roadblocks that often frustrate managers surveying their existing Web investments. But the path is not a long-term strategy. It points the way toward a clutch of fundamental internal and external factors that must inform any complete strategy—namely, the attitudes, skills, and outcomes we need to engineer into our internal processes and the evolving environment our channel will play against.

Cost Reduction

Every business shares some common points of pain that can be alleviated by ecommerce. As well as providing an expansionary dimension to the business, ecommerce can have salutary effects on cost efficiencies in several areas.

The most radical contribution to cost reduction is the dematerialization of finished goods that technology enables. All built inventory represents a drain on resources. Unsold, finished goods take up space and financing. They are also the least liquid of assets. An assembled and painted automobile cannot simply be reversed into its constituent parts, spitting back the energy expended in its manufacture. The capability to illustrate, configure, and compare products that haven't been built is the prime value of virtuality at the engagement level of ecommerce. Showrooms of sophisticated products with complex optional features can be stocked, rendered, and opened to a multitude of visitors, without a single real-world tool swinging into action. Customers can choose their own products through the ecommerce channel and their confirmation issues a build signal to the back-end construction facility. The dream of mass customization is possible, given sufficient systems intimacy within the organization. For businesses offering simpler products, virtuality enables them to reduce their stockholdings, sourcing only when they need to ship.

Reducing costs associated with finished stock is a constant management concern that ecommerce supports. Ecommerce is also an ally in the struggle to reduce process costs, particularly those associated with unnecessary or duplicated labor.

One of the first cost advantages of ecommerce is the saving of labor in information publication afforded by the Web medium. With templated Websites and good authoring tools, information can be added to a site and delivered to the customer without further intervention from a media agency, assuming the site has been well designed and branded from its inception. Although the limitations of the Web in terms of true color rendition, exact positioning, and loss of texture constitute frustrations for visual

Revenue Categories for Mass Market Ecommerce

Additive channel	sell more of our traditional lines to new markets
New offer channel	invent a new product or service for the ecommerce channel
Subscription	charge for access to content
Advertising	sell ad space on the site
Sponsorship	apply a brand to a content offering
Licensing	restrict your channel to paying carriers
Portaling	charge destinations for sending users there (also seen in "click-through" advertising)
Commission	take a percentage on transactions effected through the channel
Tolling	take a percentage on transactions effected through your mechanism

designers, these constraints all serve to simplify the production of product catalogs and customer communications. Distributing your catalog, with its costs in mailing list maintenance, packaging, and posting becomes easier, if less exact. If you currently distribute a catalog through a retail network, then you can effectively reduce your retail stock by one item. You may not always know who is accessing your catalog if you aren't enforcing a registration scheme in your ecommerce channel, but then you can never be sure how your printed catalog is used. Most importantly, using the Web as a distribution mechanism for your product and price information means you can ensure the complete withdrawal of outdated versions by making a once-only change at the Website. You no longer have to honor outdated prices or advertise a price applicability period. You can withdraw product listings when you withdraw the product from sale, thus synchronizing business decisions with their market effect. You can also increase the frequency of your updates with no incremental effect on printing and distribution costs.

Process costs can also be improved through more effective use of freed sales staff. Customers buying in the ecommerce channel need less one-on-one guidance around the company's basic offerings and generally expect to explore high-level features and benefits on their own. Customer-facing staff can then be reassigned to more valuable tasks that assist with sales, making specific interventions when required, in particular the more complex queries that arise once an online user has exhausted the channel's more simplistic content. Some ecommerce Websites enable the user to initiate a voice callback from the company by clicking a suitable help button. Most likely, ecommerce channels delivered by interactive television will continue to make use of optional voice communications, as well, because the offer of a free 800 number is such an established part of television's call to action. Retail staff can be upskilled into more consultative roles in this way. They may be encouraged to add to the site's sense of community by making their own product recommendations or by answering incoming email.

Implicit in this model is the shifting of labor from the business to the customer. By navigating the search space himself, specifying products exactly for his shopping basket, and entering his own payment and delivery details, the customer acts as an unpaid clerk for the company. By selecting a displayed product, the customer ensures the correct product code is transmitted to the underlying order and fulfillment systems, eliminating an area of common transcription error and attendant product returns.

The signs are that most customers to date see their clerical role as a benefit. They want to drive the purchase transaction themselves and they often feel more secure about the recorded accuracy of their details if they have keyed them personally, rather than written them on a form or spelled them out to a customer services representative. Sometimes called *downstreaming* or *customer self-administration*, this shift in clerical responsibility is a key benefit of ecommerce and one that brings advantages to both parties.

The final noteworthy opportunity for process cost reduction in the ecommerce channel is in the area of payments processing. Not only do we ask the customer to input her payment details, but we pass those on directly to our payments system with no human intervention or workflow delay. Businesses may even choose to outsource their payments handling entirely to a third-party agency that verifies the payment and posts it directly to the merchant's bank account. In effect, the ecommerce channel turns every networked device into a potential credit card swipe or EFTPOS terminal. The point of sale (POS) in EFTPOS is significant. The point of sale has shattered into an infinity of points, each virtualized in the design of an ecommerce site.

Back in the assets section of the balance sheet, what other costs can we attack other than reductions in finished goods? As we noted before, pixels generally come in cheaper than bricks, so we may expect some savings in provisioning for retail space. This area needs careful analysis on a case by case basis, however, because a commitment to channel development will provide a serious counter-balance to any savings. A common mistake is to budget only for visual design and site hosting costs, while forgetting the costs of ongoing maintenance and backend systems integration. Some organizations even fail to budget for the technical running costs of the site, having failed to consider that their

ISP will be unable to host the functionality they require, let alone the backend integration.

Savings should still be able to be achieved in physical accommodation costs away from the retail arena. Customer support services can be located in less expensive real estate areas and even in other countries. Some organizations now site their customer-support capabilities abroad to obtain a combination of cheaper labor costs, cheaper accommodation costs, and longer coverage of the working—or rather transacting—day.

The organization that faces its markets through an ecommerce channel is also well equipped—both technically and culturally—to consider moving more of its people to a work-at-home basis. The economics of working at home are outside the scope of this book, but it is worth considering that the mass of consumers we envision using ecommerce in a naturalistic, workaday setting also play employee roles. The changes in habits and aspirations leading more and more people to transact online are the same forces leading them to choose more flexible working arrangements.

Further cost efficiencies on the assets side come from leveraging the power of systems the business relies upon and already owns. Ecommerce has one claim to novelty when compared to some of the waves of hot technology, which we have seen in the past: ecommerce systems vendors and technology practitioners rarely state that an organization must abandon its existing systems investment and start anew. Ecommerce may be revolutionary in business terms but, from the point of view of the business systems architect, its effects are additive. A Web interface can bring a new lease on life to a company's sales systems, extending their utility by many years. In particular, ordering systems that have been written—or, more commonly, rewritten from earlier incarnations—to be easier to use by the organization's staff are prime candidates for exposure to the customer. Every software vendor and services company offers "Web-enabled" as a feature and it is rare that a sound legacy system of this kind cannot be Web-ized and turned over to the customer as user. Of course, better and worse ways exist of achieving this goal, and we examine them in Chapter 5. Once the costs of amendment have been determined, they can be set in the context of estimates for virgin development, testing, and implementation. The value of the existing base legacy system may also usefully be reassessed, if only for internal accounting practices.

The remaining cost efficiencies associated with a move to ecommerce are less direct than those we have so far considered. These are more correctly influences on the cost and quality climate than measurable savings in their own right.

The first of these beneficial influences is the Internet's culture of low-cost systems, which has a pleasant effect on expectations of IT across the board. Complicated manuals and long training sessions have disappeared with the high-usability standards of the best Web interfaces. Long development phases, with technicians cordoned off from users except during walkthrough sessions, have given away to rapid prototyping and design-by-example. Third-party development costs for Web-based systems are well below those associated with traditional business systems. Software developers correctly argue that ecommerce systems require levels of robustness, processing complexity, integration, and scalability associated with mainstream business systems. An ecommerce system is a computing problem, whereas a static Website is a publishing problem. Despite this reasoning, Internet technologies have increased competition in a way that drives down development costs for all types of systems. Internet technologies are open technologies so, although developers may differ in their designs and tools, none can create a fundamental lock-out for their client. Another supplier can always replicate their work using other methods.

The second indirect influence is concerned with time. Because the technical infrastructure for the user interface is well known and because a variety of mature development tools exists, building ecommerce systems for Internet standard networks can be rapid. The Internet's culture is one of rapid change and lightning readiness for market, characteristics embodied by the vendors who supply the principal tools of ecommerce development and the chief examples of ecommerce success. Internet technologies, Web interfaces, and ecommerce expectations combine to provide a greater emphasis on successful, timely delivery than the IT industry has enjoyed in the past. Add to this mix that ecommerce is a customer-facing phenomenon and the pressure to deliver competitive solutions becomes a principal driver of rapid value.

Partner Inclusion

So far in this chapter, we have concentrated on the enterprise and its communications and transactions with customers. But as we discussed in Chapter 1, organizations themselves are changing and the development of extended enterprises and virtual organizations provides another shaping influence on the generic business model of ecommerce. *Partner inclusion* is the practical outcome of an organization's involvement in collaborative efforts. It is the systems embodiment of the social impulse to cooperate.

The first step to partner inclusion is data lookup. Most routine communications between business partners entail one person looking up an isolated fact on one system and relaying it to a person at a partner company, who often, in turn, submits it to another system. These data items are frequently prices and dates, particularly commodity and component prices and delivery dates. Routine lookups may also include details of specifications, tolerances, variations, applicability date ranges, alternatives, and addresses.

If these items sound specifically related to relationships between manufacturers and their suppliers, consider the routine interactions between a marketing department and its media agencies. Here the data items being queried may include ad rates in various titles, delivery dates for copy, and agency fee rates for different types of service.

Providing an automatic lookup facility for a trusted external party has clear operational benefits. The need to raise the blinds on the organization in this limited way gave rise to the concept of the *extranet*, a controlled extension to the company's intranet. As a way of signaling that a company's information can be extended to its business partners using existing technology, extranet is a useful term. In many companies, however, the intranet is largely perceived and managed as a static publishing mechanism—the in-house analogue of the static Internet Web presence. By implication, extranet sites are rarely conceived as dynamic applications. Together with the inescapably technical sound of the word itself, the association with static information publication makes extranet a less than useful word in the ecommerce context. We prefer to use business-to-business (b2b) to denote dynamic systems relationships between business partners.

Business partner access to routine lookup data is often provided by a dial-in facility. Here the user may not be exposed to a Web interface. The partner may simply be given the same style of systems access as a regular employee, albeit with more greatly restricted access controlled by his logon. Web-based access mechanisms enable the partner to specify a URL to access lookup resources, giving a name and password for access. This is simple to implement using any leading Web server software.

Lookup facilities like these imply partner access to data is an as-and-when activity, triggered by unpredictable events in the partner business. This is often incorrect and results from a superficial analysis of existing practices. Staff at the partner company may call with queries throughout the day or bulk their queries for regular calls. Both practices may conceal that substantially the same information is requested on a repeated basis. The requesting party may simply be serving the update needs of its own internal system and may have organized the work in such a way as to spread the load on its human resources. If the company carries information from several different partners, management may have allocated the task of gathering updates to those knowledgeable in the affected products or those who have good personal relationships with staff at the supplier side.

System-to-system links could remove this level of organization entirely. Where regular lookup can be rationalized as a data exchange relationship, an upload/download regime can be formalized with relatively low-tech software tools. For example, one partner can specify the information it needs on a regular basis and the supplier can copy it to a file for FTP[1] to the partner every day. Simple scripts at both sides of the partnership can ensure files are transmitted and received

---

1. FTP: File Transfer Protocol. The standard means of moving files between machines connected by Internet standards.

without operator intervention. Some programming effort will be involved in creating the extract and update routines at either end, but these needn't be mammoth tasks. Concentrating on those data items that are truly regular for the automated update mechanism and excluding exceptional items or groups of interrelated items, makes for a simple relationship that removes 80 percent of the update labor, leaving the staff to deal personally with the more complex items. This is a pragmatic approach that we could think of as minimally invasive co-surgery: we make the smallest possible interventions that enable two bodies to act as one over a strictly limited range of behaviors.

The business issue here is one of synchronization between the partners in a chain. It generates a systems issue because systems embody the routine processes that run our organizations. Some companies are concerned about revealing even routinely shared information to their partners using a systems solution, however. Why should this be? Worries about security are refutable. No reason exists why enabling lookup or file exchange should expose your entire organization to data theft or corruption. It could be the sense of unease derives from the symbolic weight of systems connection with another party. This is one reason minimally invasive surgery is a good pragmatic step for organizations: systems level cooperation doesn't have to feel like a drastic declaration of blood brotherhood.

Do organizations venerate their boundaries more deeply than the move to extended enterprises and virtual organizations suggests? Our guess is, while we tend to accept the intellectual value of more collaborative relationships with other parties, we retain an emotional attachment to the integrity of our own home organization and, perhaps, a degree of fear about exposing its innermost workings to outsiders. It's not uncommon for someone to suggest "we don't want them knowing how easy it is"—usually a sign of over-familiarity with the company's processes, rather than a fair appraisal of its activities.

One of the best-known examples of a Web-based lookup facility provides a resounding counterblast to the idea that revelation equates to weakness. Federal Express (FedEx) introduced a facility on its Website where customers can enter the identifier of a package and get an instant update on its status. Far from suggesting that what FedEx does is easy, the facility makes a strong statement that confidently knowing the whereabouts of the packages in its care is at the absolute core of the company's value. Furthermore, by making access to status information a basic expectation of its public information service, the company can concentrate on selling other offers to its markets.

FedEx's package tracker is a good example of downstreaming effort to the customer. It also sets a good example for partner inclusion. So far, we have dealt with the synchronization issue on the implicit assumption that collaborating companies need to reconcile their versions of each other's promises, particularly their promises about products, prices, and dates. A great deal of information traffic among partners, however, involves checking on the status of deliverables or projects currently in the ownership of the partner. This can be difficult to achieve on a weekly or daily basis, let alone in real time. Interrupting a project team to prepare a status report for an external party is likely to have a low priority. Such communications tend to be handled by account managers in the partner organizations, who summarize activities for their respective teams and swap updates with each other. Many opportunities occur where partners could usefully peer into each other's projects to check on status, without interrupting the flow of work.

The simplest example is the *Webcam,* a gimmick from the earliest days of the Web that continues to find neat applications in business. For example, setting up a simple video feed to a Website, perhaps limited to a sample taken every minute, can allow a project manager to track progress broadly on the fitting out of a store. The camera acts as a probe, relaying status information that is easy to interpret and doesn't require storage in any subsequent system.

Other status probes for business processes generally require some kind of action to create the status information. Where determining a set of discrete states for a deliverable is possible, this becomes a matter of the deliverable's current owner clicking the right button. If we go back to our marketing department and its media projects, we can imagine the commissioning company contracting with a design agency to produce an advertising campaign for a promotional campaign. The collaborating teams agree the agency will take the project through from creative brief to final artwork and up to three inter-mediate deliverables will exist, open to review by the client. In this case, the agency could allow the client to probe its project area and discover the marked status of any deliverable in the project. When a designer files a piece of work, she marks it with a draft number. Or the parties may have agreed on a scheme that marks each piece of work against a life cycle of client review 1, client review 2, client review 3, and approved.

Many collaborative business relationships contain status lookups of this kind and, often, the named states are already well understood by the partner companies. In transportation, container tracking is a good example. A company that supplies containers may rent or sell them to clients. In either case, its business operations rely on complete and accurate knowledge of the disposition of its assets. If a customer needs to rent eight containers to convey a shipment from Rotterdam to San Francisco, then the capability to recognize which containers are becoming free at the correct time and in the correct starting region is key to making the sale and striking the best price. Automating the entire allocation process may not be desirable because the container company may want to vary its offer to different customers. In this case, the company could decide to offer a container-status tracking service to those renting a container, thus downstreaming some effort to the customer. At the same time, it could make status information available on a wider basis to its agents using the same fundamental mechanism, giving them an up-to-date and comprehensive negotiating position.

Partner inclusion begins to deliver its greatest benefits when either substantial workloads are transferred to partners or when the collaborative relationship creates a business channel with a competitive edge. Both these effects can be seen with agent relationships. In the financial services industry of the United Kingdom (U.K.), Independent Financial Advisors (IFAs) are regulated to ensure that products are not mis-sold to customers. Assurance of an IFA's independence includes a limitation on the level of support a financial product company may give to the agent. If an insurance company, for example, were to install a terminal of its own sales system at the IFA's office, this could be deemed as affecting the level playing field.

Providing a URL and a password to a protected gateway Website, however, is less dramatic, but potentially more powerful in its effect on sales. By opening its sales system to the agent in this way, the company enables the agent to input new business to its systems, eradicating data transcription from forms by its own staff. The agent may well be tempted to channel more business through companies that offer this facility. Of course, as the practice becomes widespread, the competing companies have to seek further means of differentiation for competitive edge. Insurance is a good example of an industry where clerical demands are a deciding factor in the company's performance. Any reduction in bureaucratic effort can directly improve the price of the company's products or its returns to shareholders. By recruiting its agents as business system users, the company improves its relationships with its partners while accruing administrative cost savings.

> ## Simple Applications for Partner Inclusion
>
> The most common routine queries among collaborating companies—outside core systems lookup—include these seven applications:
>
> - price probe
> - delivery slot booking
> - time-sheet entry
> - company phone book
> - room booking
> - account status
> - calendar query

A New Map

Any off-world visitor using the U.K.'s Standard Industrial Classification (SIC) codes for insight into contemporary economic activity would form a strange picture. While the British authorities distinguish between the manufacture of knitted and crocheted fabrics and the manufacture of knitted and crocheted hosiery (SIC codes 1760 and 1771, respectively), the best match for a mass market ecommerce business would be 5263: Other nonstore retail sale. Six types of activity are listed under Computer and Related Activities, putting this category on a numerical par with Manufacture of Wood and Wood Products. But perhaps the SIC scheme is ahead of us: If ecommerce is just a channel, then maybe the traditional industry sectors continue to be valid.

We shouldn't read too much into the persistence of a coding scheme that has to cover the breadth of a nation's economic activities as they develop. The scheme will naturally grow to include new activities and just as naturally resist applications for new codes as it gets more unwieldy. It will also be affected by economic policy. If a government decides to encourage knitted and crocheted new media with special tax breaks, then a code for it must be created.

However, saying that ecommerce challenges the traditional sector models we have all internalized, to a greater or lesser extent, is true. As we have seen in discussing channel development, businesses embracing ecommerce have to challenge their own assumptions about whether they are in the communications business. If "the way we do things around here" excludes certain disciplines on a categorical basis, then change becomes hard indeed. And, while new practices may challenge ideas about old boundaries, many businesses would be more comfortable with change if they could substitute a new sectoral scheme for the old one. Most of us like to see an arrow labeled "you are here" when we arrive in a strange place.

Using FedEx's package-tracking facility as an example, a company could make core status information available to its partners and customers, thereby becoming a new kind of company altogether. Its partners and customers begin to expect a new level of core competency. Faultless execution of this core competency shines a new light on the other services the company can perform. The brand grows and begins to lap over the edges of its home sector. A strong portal offering isn't just a Yellow Pages resource; it becomes an ally in the fight to stay on top of the information explosion. A community-oriented retailer isn't just a place to go, it's a place to be. These are all qualitative differences that are hard to encapsulate in an industry sector model.

That being said, some traditional sectors may be better suited to the e-world than others. Surely a publishing business is a natural candidate for the ecommerce transition? Financial services seem well placed to make the change, as well. As we have seen, anybody in retail with a wide, complex, or niche-oriented stock list should be able to win on the Web. These are all fair assertions. When we analyze the reasons for such matches, however, we find the decisive features belong primarily to the target environment. In other words, ecommerce exercises its magnetism more strongly on certain types of business because they have obvious points of entry. If we can understand these, then we can create a generic model that enables us to discover nonobvious candidates for migration.

Publishing and financial business share one obvious characteristic: both are information-based businesses. Publishing deals in words, images, music, and software, all of which are predisposed to electronic transmission. Financial products are bundles of information about how money may be shifted around in time: Loan products represent the time-travel of money from future to present, while savings products represent the reverse flow. Whether we are attempting to push money into the future or pull it into the present, we are dealing with commitments that can only exist as information.

Retailers—including retailers of publishing and financial products—also share a common characteristic. All retailers are looking for markets and ecommerce acts as a channel to market. They may not be selling products and services that can themselves be digitized. In this case, they are selling messages about physical products, and undertaking to arrange their supply.

If we then consider the requirements of partner inclusion, we can see the ecommerce world can be mapped as a space with four principal sectors. This section forms a tour of the new map and its local characteristics. If we then consider the requirements of partner inclusion, we can see the ecommerce world can be mapped as a space with four principal sectors, as shown in Figure 2-2. This section forms a tour of the new map and its local characteristics.

FIGURE 2-2. A sectoral model for ecommerce.

	Physical	Informational
Business-to-Consumer	Books, CDs Tools Sports Equipment	Stocks and shares Premium news
Business-to-Business	Hardware Operating resources	Software Travel reservations

Physical/Informational

The sector model is divided into two main parts: physical and informational.

Nicholas Negroponte, of the influential MIT Media Lab and *Wired* magazine columnist, conceived and popularized the use of the words *atoms* and *bits* to mark this split. *Bits* are easy to shift around networks, while *atoms* are heavy and notoriously attached to neighboring atoms. Bits can be manufactured from thin air by knowledge workers, whereas atoms have to be won from the ground.

Confusing an atom business with a bit business can be bad for your back, but it's easier to do than it looks. We have already noted that Amazon.com is in the business of shifting atoms. Books and CDs may contain information, but they are themselves physical products. Yet Amazon is also heavily into bits because it relies on its catalog, recommendations, and reviews to enable and add value to the purchasing process.

On the other hand, take 1-800-FLOWERS, the world's largest florist with $300 million in sales. This company's online channel brings in ten percent of its annual sales and a four-year exclusive deal with AOL is expected to generate $250 million alone. Is this a physical or an informational business? Although flowers are indisputably made from atoms, they are consumed as information. Sending flowers is primarily a greetings service, not a transfer of physical assets. The recipient won't eat the flowers or build a patio out of them. And, although the flowers must be physically delivered to the recipient, the chief activity in ensuring delivery is issuing appropriate messages to local florists. A business such as 1-800-FLOWERS actuates a delivery network to create a social service, so it is more correctly a bits business than an atoms business.

The force of intellectualization implies more and more atom businesses will also find themselves in the bit business, wrapping services around their products and creating community-oriented ecommerce channels. From the point of view of the business manager, what is important to understand is where the major part of the business's weight rests in any phase of its development. For example, a physical business that wants to use the Internet to "go global" may need to concentrate on its distribution strategy alongside—or ahead of—its ecommerce channel development effort. The business may need to negotiate partnership deals in foreign territories and to clear any tariff barriers that apply to its goods crossing a particular border. A common mistake is for companies transitioning to ecommerce to consider ecommerce channel requirements without addressing the knock-on effects in fulfillment. In rushing to understand the bits side of the model, such companies neglect the physical problems of servicing a new demand stream—a stream which, on the ground, is still a dispersed collection of droplets.

This dimension of the model helps decision-makers to consider the physical and informational aspects of the ecommerce world together, and to allocate resources in line with a plan that maximizes their combination. For example, the figure uses sports equipment and premium news as examples of physical and informational products, respectively. These are shown side by side in the diagram, though they are not meant as opposites or complements of each other. Yet, a seller of sporting goods may also want to offer a specialist sports news service. He might seek sponsorship for the news service from one of his product suppliers. On the other hand, a sports news service might tie in with a set of sporting goods specialists, becoming a portal for active sports fans. None of these options may be attractive in the individual situation, yet too many ecommerce decisions have been taken without considering both ends of the physical-informational split.

Seeing the physical-informational split as a continuum is also possible. This requires some imagination because, in reality, flowers don't shade into greetings any more than words morph into books. Yet, as a technique for provoking creative thinking this can be useful. This is also not too far removed from the process of thinking in terms of benefits rather than features. "What does our product do for our customers?" is a good way to ignite thoughts about the service aspect of your offer and service elements are candidates for informational delivery. A company that makes fire alarms, for example, can see itself as offering security, rather than timely loud noises. Perhaps it should also offer information about fire safety, link with partners who supply fire-retardant materials, or even offer fire insurance. If an insurance company can sell devices that reduce the price of its own products, then why shouldn't a fire protection company sell policies that reduce the price of its products?

Business-to-Consumer (b2c)

Our model is also divided along another dimension into business-to-consumer and business-to-business.

Business-to-consumer (b2c) is the area usually identified with ecommerce as a whole. In fact, most people's understanding of ecommerce is concentrated in the physical business-to-consumer space, to the exclusion of other parts of the model.

Business-to-consumer is not, however, exactly equated with mass-market ecommerce, the loose phrase we have used so far. If we make this identification, then we are assuming the consumer market is the only location of volume business in ecommerce. Business-to-consumer, therefore, does not mean volume business. Rather, it denotes a type of customer relationship: one oriented to individuals acting in a personal or family capacity. The emphasis is on the customer role and, therefore, the types of products, services, relationships, and communications that match this role. In one sense, we are saying that sometimes people elect themselves into interactions of this type, where they wish to be addressed and to behave as leisured individuals servicing their personal needs.

The types of offer that fall into this category are, therefore, determined by consumer wants and needs, and a business's capability to target and fulfill them. If we aim at one-to-one relationship management, proactively predicting the needs of customers from their past interactions with us, then we may treat this category as a universe of possibilities without making further distinctions. On the other hand, we may look to break down the opportunity space into a set based on the other change drivers we explored in Chapter 1.

For example, globalization may lead us to posit a service that supports the shrinking of the average executive's world and the dedication of much of her time to air travel. We could provide entertainment itineraries and tickets to accompany business trips, recommending theatres and restaurants while booking seats. Note, although the executive travels on business and may be able to charge her use of our service as a business expense, we are still selling to her and not to the business that employs her.

In this case, travel is creating a set of personal pressures that opens a potential consumer business opportunity. No rule requires business travelers to fill every hour with work. The success of business-oriented hotels with sports facilities and fine dining shows that adequate relaxation is an important aspect of an effective business trip. The perceived need to organize her free time as effectively as she manages her work time is an example of work behavior spilling over into the executive's private life. Many of the opportunities for business-to-consumer applications, as we shall see in Chapter 3, take advantage of this rise in the professionalization of private life.

Business-to-consumer is also the space we look to for television-based ecommerce channels. As suggested earlier, the TV set isn't necessarily the natural locus for finding the ecommerce consumer. But because TV sets define family gatherings, they are perhaps the natural communications medium to the consumer family unit. Our feeling is the fragmentation of channels and of viewing units will degrade our concept of television as a mass market channel for anything other than the supreme cultural messages associated with world events.

Business-to-Business (b2b)

Over seven quarters from July 1996, Dell's sales via the Internet grew from zero to more than $5 million per day.[2] Suppliers like Dell and Cisco sell significant volumes over the Web, predominantly to companies. Computing and network equipment is sophisticated stuff. Product features change constantly and most products can be individually configured to the user's requirements. Although hardware represents a large and growing fraction of corporate assets, it is no longer seen as a special purchase. IT is bought on a commodity basis, with buying companies defining machine specifications for particular classes of user or application. This is serious ecommerce—and it is largely business-to-business ecommerce.

The Aberdeen Group, reporting in 1997, predicted 430,000 U.S. businesses would be involved in business-to-business ecommerce by the year 2000. In March 1999, Forrester estimated consumers would be spending $108 billion buying goods online by 2003. Businesses, on the other hand, would be spending $1.3 trillion on goods and a further $220 billion on services, by the same time horizon. In other words, the little-known area of informational business-to-business may be worth twice as much as the familiar land of physical business-to-consumer. The depths of partner inclusion are to be found in this corner of the model.

Most business is, in fact, business-to-business. While the end customer can be seen as pulling the value chain, clearly the majority of economic activity that goes on to satisfy consumer needs is bound up in the chain and its intermediary links, rather than its terminating node. The trading of inputs and outputs between neighbors in chains, and the supply of services to participants and groups of participants, make up a huge area of activity ripe for ecommerce.

Consider also which group is best adapted to adopt or exploit ecommerce. Looking from the customer side, clearly the corporation, heavily invested in technology and the skills to make it work, is better placed to enact the ecommerce purchaser role. As we have seen, the consumer, on the other hand, is still being chased to a determinate

---

2. Dell's Web site, May 1998.

location for her ecommerce behavior. We pursue the putative purchaser from desk to couch to car, attempting to find the "natural" home for a behavior, which is, thus far, unsupported in private life. Workers in offices know they use computers and networks to get work done, so no cultural or ergonomic problem exists in adding business-to-business ecommerce applications to their suites.

Businesses have several benefits additional to technical readiness that make business-to-business ecommerce a warm-start area. First, business has evolved a trading culture and associated legal framework, which makes intercompany trading somewhat simpler than transacting with consumers. The traditions of issuing purchase orders and invoices, respecting credit periods, and running persistent account relationships eases intercompany transactions. Once admitted to a trading relationship, an organization need only follow standard industry practice to effect transactions. In the consumer world, on the other hand, we are continually on the lookout for fraud and prefer our non-cash payments mediated by a trustworthy agent such as a credit card company. In business, we assume that standard business practice and the law will ensure that most transactions will complete successfully. When translated to the ecommerce environment, this means agreement to dispatch goods or payment is reduced to a check on the other party's identity, rather than an investigation into their ability and intention to honor the contract.

Second, a large proportion of business-to-business transactions are repeat orders. Despite the variability that build-to-order brings to a manufacturer, a high degree of stability persists in the range, quantity, and frequency of materials he will order from suppliers. Even where he seeks to reduce the volume of materials he keeps on hand, ordering more frequently from the supplier, he will most likely be varying the level of an order, rather than revising his entire rationale. The predicted pattern of transactions can, therefore, be built into the business-to-business ecommerce relationship in a way that is currently rare in the business-to-consumer world. A b2c analogue may be a regular savings e-plan, where an amount is debited from the customer every month and credited to a portfolio that he may amend online. Business-to-business scenarios include schedules for deliveries of materials and supplies, and performance of services, such as cleaning or recruitment.

Third, business-to-business ecommerce need concern itself less with the subtleties of consumer behavior, though we suggest b2b players will want to revisit this topic as they develop their services. In current business-to-business ecommerce relationships, little requirement exists to track customer behavior at a fine level or to create a high degree of personal rapport. Many users may enact the customer role at a purchasing business site; the seller will "see" one customer, whose behavior can only be analyzed as corporate and that is probably already defined by relationships inherited from pre-online days. Business-to-business ecommerce is business-as-usual: largely routine, largely impersonal.

This last characteristic of business-to-business ecommerce is likely to change as the industry matures. As the ecommerce channel becomes the natural place to enact business-to-business relationships, it will become more competitive. Supplier companies will be able to acquire new customers more easily than in the past, using online marketing. Buying companies will be able to switch allegiance more rapidly because they will be equally well connected to all potential suppliers. Furthermore, brands are already important in business-to-business relationships and competitive ecommerce channels will highlight brand values in their attempts to provide differentiation. In other words, business-to-business ecommerce will acquire many of the channel characteristics of business-to-consumer.

This prediction relies on two main factors. Culturally, or in terms of business process, business-to-business ecommerce has to be demonstrably efficient, frictionless, and nondisruptive. Technically, a competitive business-to-business ecommerce industry relies on the emergence and adoption of common standards for intercompany transactions. If channels are built using incompatible standards, then buyers will find themselves locked in to their suppliers and unable to choose alternatives. We can already see this happening as some suppliers begin to offer business-to-business ecommerce services with free hardware and connectivity offers.

The first application areas for business-to-business ecommerce are now coming into focus. We look at pathfinder applications in this area in Chapter 3.

Cross-Pollination

Business-to-consumer and business-to-business are useful distinctions that help us direct activities and investments in ecommerce. To think neither side of the model influences the other would be wrong, though. As we have seen, modes of communication and techniques of behavior analysis are likely to become as applicable in business-to-business as they are in business-to-consumer.

We also need to consider that private life is becoming more and more like work.

Out of Bounds: In-Business

We have deliberately excluded applications that impact solely within one organization from this model. While Internet technologies can certainly have a positive effect on the usability and reach of contained business systems, they seem to fall outside the bounds of ecommerce. An ebusiness is most likely to use such systems to support its internal processes, but little is distinctive about them from the point of view of the business decision maker.

For the sake of completeness, we could extend the user-group dimension of our model and map it to equivalent technical terms:

business-to-consumer
business-to-business
in-business

Internet
extranet
intranet

This may be a useful perspective for systems developers.

Searching for information and completing forms are clearly more work-like than leisure-like, yet this is the general consumer ecommerce experience to date. At the same time, the business of ordering one's personal life continues to impinge on work-life. Are employers right to crack down on employees using the Web for nonbusiness purposes? Some companies have introduced blanket bans on surfing the Web during work hours or make external access available only during certain hours of the day. Yet it is probably to the employer's advantage that employees do their shopping or arrange for services to be carried out from their desk. The more efficiently people order their private lives, the more bandwidth they have for their work—or, if we want to be more enlightened, the higher the quality of their free time and, therefore, the lower their level of stress at work. Buying groceries from work is no more disruptive than using the office phone line to call a plumber. Employers can still ban access to sites that have neither business nor domestic value.

The important point here is, while the generic business model can be used to clarify the nature of particular opportunities, applications, and solutions, it can also be used to suggest novel opportunities. Imitation is a strategy that can be applied at a structural level, as well as at the level of individual competition. Decision-makers do well to look for successes on the b2c side that may have analogues on the b2b side and vice versa. Similarly, they may want to consider transposing a putative ecommerce channel from one side to the other during the planning phase, if only to test assumptions about its natural home.

Consider, for example, a scheduling service conceived as a means of allowing consumers to organize themselves into car pools. The organizing company may look to make revenues from the commuters who use the site, but they are more likely to base their business model on advertising revenues and, potentially portalizing their site, with links to traffic and employment services. The site will need an underlying system that comprehends routes and times, as well as storing spaces, potential occupants, and the attributes against which they can be matched. The system will need scalability to cope with growing user bases. Growth may be staged by developing the service according to additional metropolitan areas.

Having created this scenario, what would it look like transported to the business-to-business world? Obviously we're no longer looking at car pooling, but there could be an analogue. How about those companies with fleets of vehicles making regular trips—perhaps we could match spaces in vehicles with companies whose packages need delivering. In rural areas of the U.K., the postal service carries small numbers of passengers in its vans; long-distance buses often carry packages; in Denmark, prescription drugs are delivered to patients via taxi cabs. The transport network suddenly begins to look like the

Internet. We can start to imagine shipping atoms around with the ease of bits.

The sale of moving space is one of the pathfinder application areas we look at further in Chapter 3, when we consider the topic of inventory exchange. Dislocating our sense of what is formally business-to-consumer and what is business-to-business is one way to discover such application areas. Much of the excitement for innovators in ecommerce comes not from the imagining of cool devices or cyber-style bonding between people and machines, but from twisting embryonic ideas in the new light that ecommerce sheds on the business world.

We have also seen how physical and informational applications may disguise each other: our information product is really a physical book, our physical flowers are really an informational greeting. Recasting your product or service from physical to informational is another way of creating new ecommerce opportunities. This principle can be hard to apply in real life if we use computing metaphors too rigorously. For example, making your product downloadable may not be possible (in this universe). But making your product updateable, assuming it already contains some modicum of intelligence, may be possible. One example would be a car that learns how to tune its engine more effectively by acquiring the distilled experience of its clones.

A less radical approach to transposing physical and informational applications lies in the intellectualization of products and the concretizing of services. As an example, we can consider the evolution of designer products. Couture designers discovered they could leverage their prestige brands into mass markets by moving into perfumes and accessories. A bottle of Chanel N⁰ 5 is considerably more affordable than a Chanel wardrobe. The customer is buying a lifestyle message that is embodied in scent. The Chanel symbol carries sufficient intellectual freight to make it a leading target for counterfeiters. Did Coco Chanel ever imagine the pirated Chanel logo T-shirt would become her most visible legacy? Yet even accounting for the loss in revenues attributable to the piracy of insecure information such as logos, the elevation of the Chanel mystique to a valuable asset is something ecommerce players can seek to emulate. The potential for building one-to-one relationships via ecommerce channels is great enough to suggest that pure brands may acquire commercial viability without straying into physical production of any kind. An early indicator of this development is Yahoo!'s slogan *Do you* Yahoo!*?* As a proposition, it defies all rational analysis, yet we know what it means. Yahoo! could be the world's first soft drink not to contain any soft drink.

ROLE TYPES

The map we have outlined creates some defined spaces where we can look for ecommerce opportunities and scope projects. We also need to consider what kinds of roles organizations can adopt with respect to the different areas of the map. This section looks at the main role types and relates them to ecommerce practice.

Intermediation, Disintermediation, and Reintermediation

Ecommerce has been responsible for popularizing some particularly strange words, but none stranger than disintermediation. *Disintermediation* refers to the removal of an established intermediary and replacement by a direct connection between the parties formerly serviced by the intermediary.

The Web was quickly identified as a profound source of disintermediation effects. In particular, product manufacturers would be able to sell directly to end consumers, cutting out wholesalers, retailers, and their margins. These middlemen supposedly only exist to distribute goods and to engage customers. The ecommerce channel appears to cut around them.

From the development of Web-based ecommerce to date, this clearly has not been the case. Ecommerce actually provides new types of intermediation opportunities and shows no sign of destroying retail. While ecommerce certainly threatens many of the practices and economics of physical retail, it does not erase the role of the retailer.

We can immediately notice that book and music publishers are not leading the sale of books and music on the Web. The leaders in sales of cars and travel services are not the auto manufacturers and airlines, but intermediaries in the shape of Autobytel and Travelocity.

Ecommerce dislocates traditional intermediary structures, but it strengthens the requirement for intermediation. In the case of cars, the traditional sales route is through a chain of showrooms. Vehicle stock is expensively shipped to neighborhood outlets, where prospective customers can look it over and book test drives. The sales representative is cast in a consultative role, targeted with helping customers to buy rather than pressure selling. A showroom generally only carries the products of one manufacturer, so a buyer looking to compare features and performance across manufacturers has some traveling to do.

When transposed to the Web, we have a situation where the buyer can access information about every available model of vehicle, including moving video and technical data. He may be able to register for a brochure or a call-back from his nearest stockist. He has not only saved some shoe leather, he has also been protected from registering his interest with a live sales representative.

His decision-making process has now become more complex, however. Without such easy access to information, the buyer may have restricted his search to showrooms in his local area, to manufacturers of models owned by his neighbors, or even to stockists who employ people he finds congenial. However nonscientific these methods of reducing the search space are, they still help to make the process more manageable. In the Web scenario, the buyer is likely to suffer from information overload.

We can help the prospective customer if we have two capabilities that we can deploy on his behalf. The first is the ability to compare candidate purchases so a smaller group of winners can emerge. The second is the ability not to care which manufacturer or model the customer buys, so long as he buys through us. Add these qualities to a welcoming, nonthreatening, and trustworthy environment, and we have a classic intermediary business. This business may not exist in bricks and glass, but it exhibits the key characteristic of a successful retail proposition: the closure of a sales process.

The term *intermediary* makes us think of a party interposed between transacting partners—someone who is somehow in the way, obscuring the buyer and seller from each other's view. But intermediaries play a creative and constructive role in the buyer-seller relationship. The intermediary holds both ends of the relationship and earns his turn from the provision of this sales route. Without intermediation of some kind, most sales relationships remain theoretical.

What happens to physical retail space when ecommerce channels take over the intermediation of consumer products? It is unlikely that physical retail real estate will lose all its value. Instead, we can expect to see retail spaces evolve into spaces where the search and transaction functions are de-emphasized in favor of service functions. Some spaces may be redeveloped as experiential facilities, where customers primarily learn about and sample goods, and obtain advice about their use. Buying computer equipment via the Web is already cheaper than buying from a physical store, yet the demand for computer hardware and software services to the domestic environment continues to grow. In this case, consumers may prefer to visit a space and talk to an expert, or even to interview an engineer to book a home visit.

The development of retail banking gives some clues as to how retail space may develop for other kinds of businesses. Once cash machines, telephone, and Internet banking, and easy access to credit remove the need for a sturdy building housing a safe, bank branches change their functions. Some become wine bars, particularly where bank consolidation dictates a reduction in combined branch representation. Others evolve into spaces where bank customers can book meetings with advisors to discuss their financial affairs. While a bank branch may not be the most efficient means of providing routine retail banking functions to a mass customer base, it remains the best opportunity for the company to develop a deeper relationship with a customer. Banks have increasingly integrated their routine functions into area-based service centers, gaining economies of scale at the area level and freeing their retail space for disposal or repurposing.

The generic retailer is a model intermediary because all other types of intermediary perform the same kind of structural function, whatever their title. An account manager for a venture capital fund may not look much like a branch of a consumer electronics chain, but his purpose is to sell money to customers who can pay the required price. A real estate agent matches housing stock with families looking to move, taking her fee from the seller. Intermediaries ensure matches are made and consummated.

Intermediation in the e-world is, therefore, first concerned with the definition and optimization of space. Intermediaries add value to the sales relationship by creating a space in which potential partners can meet and where their search costs are sure to be reduced.

Intermediaries also create liquidity; that is, they introduce a measure of tradability that otherwise might not be realized. As an example, we can imagine a seller has a quantity of machine parts it wants to sell. The seller's own searches reveal no one who wants to buy. An intermediary may offer to buy the stock and find his own buyer. Because evidently no present market exists, he requires a discount to cover his risk. The seller will be happy to liquidate his excess holding for ready money. The intermediary then holds the stock until he can sell it or he uses his superior search expertise and network connections to find a buyer.

As well as creating space and liquidity, intermediaries create meaning. By aggregating content from a wide range of sources and making it comparable, they help reduce friction in the buying process. In addition, an intermediary is well placed to enhance the value of the sale by adding service guarantees to the product or service being mediated. An online retailer who also arranges credit and shipping services as part of the sales transaction provides an attractive end-to-end service and stands to take commissions from two additional sources at no risk to himself.

Intermediation clearly provides opportunities for ecommerce players. The discovery that middlemen don't disappear in the e-world can also lead to misunderstandings about effective intermediary strategies. Merely interposing yourself in the marketplace or creating a space where buyers and sellers may trip over each other is no substitute for a business plan that describes how you will profit from either of these situations. The ABC model for intermediary roles shown in Figure 2-3 is a planning tool for would-be intermediary players.

FIGURE 2-3. The ABC of intermediation.

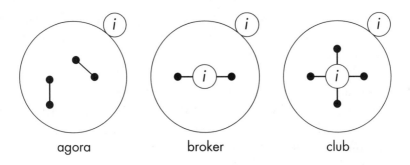

agora   broker   club

The first role is as owner of an *agora*, the assembly place of a Greek town. The agora quickly became the market place, as well as the social meeting place of the citizens. An intermediary may set up a community or a portal with the intention of deriving revenues from visits alone. That is, he may seek to charge a door fee, to sell advertising space, or, somehow, to sell his captured population to another power.

The second role is the *broker* role. This is the classic intermediary role, where the middleman acts as a matchmaker. Revenues can be derived in the same way as in the agora, but the broker can also take fees from one or both of the matched parties.

The third role is less well known than the first two. Unsurprisingly, this is a role identified with business-to-business ecommerce. The *club* is a set of parties that gathers with a common purpose. For example, they may all have an interest in obtaining reduced prices for goods by combining their buying power. The club is more tenuous than a virtual organization and generally requires a central coordinating function. Special interest groups, pressure groups, and fan organizations are further examples. The intermediary derives additional revenues by charging members for the maintenance of the club and its aims.

While the broker may superficially seem the most attractive intermediary posture to take, it is worth finishing this discussion with a member comment cited at a leading agora, Match.com:

"I will continue to pay you the nominal fee you request for membership to what I find the most successful, fun, and safe service I have found on the net. Thank you, for helping me find people."[3]

Transformation Agents

This ecommerce role type is sufficiently novel and compelling to consider separately from the intermediation roles we discussed previously. A *transformation agent* is an intermediary who gathers data, collates, and processes it, and then sells it to other users. Rather than being relationship- or transaction-focused, transformation agents concentrate on the opportunities of refinement. They approach data as a raw material and look for ways to cleanse and aggregate it, so the data can be applied to new uses. Principally a business-to-business phenomenon to date, transformation agency sees the data spoil of one community as the information raw material of another. The general process is illustrated in Figure 2-4.

The best way to understand this alchemy is to look at some examples.

A gasoline retailer runs a price-promise scheme throughout one of its territories. The scheme assures the customer that the company's branded gas will always match the best price for gas in the neighborhood. The program is promoted using images of vigilance, the implication being that the gas company's staff is constantly monitoring prices among its competitors and adjusting its own pump prices accordingly.

FIGURE 2-4. Transformation agency.

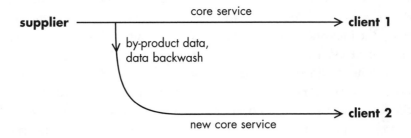

3. www.match.com, April 8, 1999.

In fact, the gas company monitors its competition with the help of a transformation agent. The agent is in a different core business: the servicing of corporate fuel cards. It supplies fuel cards issued to employees for their business use, acting as a traditional financial intermediary between the employer and the gasoline retailers. Essentially, it bridges the cash gap between the driver and the gas station and administers the employer's scheme on his behalf.

As a by-product of this core activity, the fuel card company amasses a vast amount of data. Every time a cardholder buys gas, the pump price is transmitted to the fuel card operator, often along with the driver's license plate and current mileage. Because this is a transaction that will be settled with real money, the date, time, and location must also be recorded. And, because the fuel cards are widely accepted, the card operator obtains a near-real-time representation of all gas prices across the territory. A little light sorting and summarization, and we have valuable, actionable business intelligence.

Notice the fuel card company has also acquired a mass of potentially useful data about vehicle performance. If it has records of the drivers' vehicle models, it could report to the manufacturers on average fuel consumption figures. Of course, this kind of activity may be illegal in some countries for reasons of privacy protection.

The value in this scenario results from altering our perspective on the transaction. From the driver's point of view, the fuel card is a convenient way of ensuring he doesn't have to expense his business mileage and then claim it back from his employer. From the employer's point of view, he has outsourced an administrative and policy area to a third party who can achieve economies of scale. But when the fuel card company casts itself as a transformation agent, it is seeing the fuel purchase transaction as a data sample, as well as a commissionable event.

Another business-to-business example is in the area of staff reward and recognition. Here the leading company in the field operates schemes on behalf of employers that allow employees to earn valued rewards for performance. The employer may issue points against sales made by customer representatives, for example. Points might be accrued in an account and redeemed against items from a catalog or travel brochure. The rewards company has a traditional intermediary business, providing a more flexible and efficient service than the employer could implement himself.

But in the process of carrying out this core business, the rewards company also acquires valuable data it can process and return to the employer. If the rewards company is recording reward points for staff in a distributed retail environment, it may well own a better representation of staff attendance than the employer does. After all, some staff may be more motivated to record their qualifying sales than to sign an attendance log. The reward records may also act as a check on the sales system's figures and a useful infill if the store's systems go down during the working day. Looking outward from the client-supplier relationship, the reward company also acquires proxy sales data for the items or events selected as rewards. The rewards company could feed back to its featured catalog suppliers on the volume and origin of sales, which otherwise will be masked by the intermediary's bulk purchasing practice. On the other hand, the rewards company may simply use this information for its own purposes in negotiating future deals.

Other opportunities emerge for organizations that enforce or monitor any kind of policy on behalf of a client. A company may tour retail outlets, checking on the positioning and stocking of branded food units. It has already invested in the costs of visiting stores and transmitting data back to a central point, so any other data collection it can perform will have a low incremental cost. The company could be reporting on refrigerator failure or damage to in-store promotional displays. Strictly speaking, this is perhaps an intelligence function rather than a transformation function.

Is all this activity ecommerce? It's a long way from selling products to customers via the Web. However, this is clearly a practice that fits in the informational business-to-business space on our model. These opportunities have been created jointly by business and technology change. The business influence is the growth of extended enterprises, with companies joining forces with specialist suppliers to enhance their own offerings or employee benefits. The technology influence is the growing connectedness of systems and the sense that regular data exchange can enhance a business's world view at an attractive service-priced cost.

Applying this strategy in the business-to-consumer world is equally attractive, though more closely regulated. Although information about customer behavior is valuable, it may be unacceptable or illegal to sell it to other parties. Where information is offered voluntarily by the customer in return for some kind of reward, however, it is usually possible to use that input more freely. This is established practice in consumer questionnaire processing. We have seen experiments where Web users have been offered reward points for reading ads and where phone users were offered free calls if they listen to a short commercial message. It would be a small step to issuing points to consumers who report on current data values. The used car industry has relied on this approach since the 1930s, with publishers gathering auction and dealer prices via attendees and issuing price guidelines in a strictly "trade only" regular edition. Extending the principle could see bar room habitués recruited to count and report sales of rival beers or drivers rewarded for hitting a button that sends a "traffic jam ahead" signal to their motoring organization. The intelligence strategy may be the main business-to-consumer analogue of the business-to-business transformation agent.

Pathfinder Application Areas

This chapter explores six key emerging application areas in electronic commerce. These pathfinder application areas are organized into business-to-consumer and business-to-business domains.

The accent in this chapter is on scoping and outlining types of application, with an eye to finding further opportunities for business and systems decision-makers to create successful new applications of each type. The application areas range from the expected—if commonly mismanaged—category of consumer retailing to the close embrace of real-time business-to-business collaboration.

The main purpose of this chapter is not to sing the praises of isolated ecommerce successes and their unique attributes, although each cited case deserves our respect and gratitude for showing the way, and usually for creating the way. Instead the aim is to extract lessons that can be applied by other ecommerce actors to enhance their own businesses and to extend the ecommerce field itself.

BUSINESS-TO-CONSUMER APPLICATIONS

Ecommerce used to mean business-to-consumer ecommerce and business-to-consumer ecommerce meant selling things over the Web. Since retailers first appeared on the Web in 1995, Web-based retail has become an established and substantial sector, but it is by no means the entire story of business-to-consumer ecommerce. One analyst noted in

February 1998 that for retail, "all of the low-hanging business-to-consumer fruit has been taken."[1] The aim of this section is to explore how ecommerce retail entrants can manage the orchard and to discover some other productive parts of the farm.

The three application areas discussed here are retail, auctions, and advice. Although each has its own distinguishing characteristics and dynamics, a consistent theme underlies the development of all three. This is the increasing "busy-ness" of consumer lifestyles: the extension from work life into private life of a culture of ever-decreasing time-frames and ever-increasing obligations. Lack of time and complexity of choice drive the growth of products and services in each of these areas.

Business-to-consumer is a term that stresses the direction of delivery: business-to-consumer ecommerce is supposedly something done *by* businesses *to* consumers. Yet this domain is founded on intense customer focus. Insight into the conflicting desires and pressures affecting consumers is a powerful ally in building successful strategies in this highly competitive arena.

Retail and the Lifestyle Crisis

The Web is becoming the average consumer's shop window on the world. Yet not all product categories are equally represented. As we have noted, specialty items perform well in the new channel, exploiting and aggregating geographically dispersed markets. Mass market items have been slower to make their mark. Clearly some barriers must exist to full scale business-to-consumer ecommerce success and some barrier-busters must also exist.

Two major ecommerce initiatives have currently launched themselves on the Web with the aim of establishing supremacy in the online pharmacy category. PlanetRx[2] and Drugstore.com[3] enable customers to fill prescriptions, purchase other drugstore items, and access health-related information. The pharmacy business has all the characteristics of an ideal ecommerce business. First, the range of products is

---

1. Bill Burnham of Piper Jaffray, *Red Herring* 51, February 1998.

2. www.planetrx.com

3. www.drugstore.com

wide and complex. Searching for the correct medication, delivery format, and pack size lends itself well to automated searching. Second, the expected economies of online retailing kick in quickly with the potential customer volumes, allowing such providers to consider discounts. Both of these factors are classically Amazonian and, indeed, Amazon acquired 40 percent of Drugstore.com. Pharmacy products easily outsell books in value and naturally apply to all parts of the community. While each purchase transaction could be said to be the fulfillment of a niche requirement—because nothing is more one-to-one than the relationship between an illness and its sufferer—in commerce terms we have the model of a persistent, pervasive, high-volume business.

Other characteristics of the pharmacy business take it beyond the Amazon baseline. First, repeat purchasing is built into one part of the business: many prescriptions require refilling at regular intervals. Physical pharmacies issue repeat-prescription cards to customers, so their orders can be met rapidly and discretely on subsequent occasions. When translated to the automated, territory-wide ecommerce channel, this service becomes even more convenient for the customer and even more valuable to the seller. The online pharmacies stand to gain significant and detailed knowledge about the buying habits of consumers. They can assess whether requests for repeat prescriptions are accompanied by other non-drug purchases and, if so, look for patterns. Perhaps they will discover some customers sweeten the pill by buying additional hair care products, for example. If either player manages to establish leadership in the domestic U.S. market, then it will have achieved a position unparalleled in the traditional pharmacy market, where no one retailer dominates. The breadth and depth of the information it will own alongside that market share will be equally unprecedented, and immensely valuable to pharmaceutical and healthcare companies.

Second, online pharmacies can deliver useful, targeted, and enriched health and medication information to their users. As we see in the section "Advice and Care," advice is a potentially lucrative application area in its own right. Allied to related product delivery, the dispensing of information that assists customers' decision-making is a powerful force. The pharmacy business has a particular specialized, yet rewarding, subcategory that should benefit immensely from such added information services; this is the herbal remedies sector. The efficacy of herbal remedies is a controversial topic; but it must be said that the consumption of prescription drugs is equally contested. What is certain is herbal remedies are not patentable and, therefore, not of immediate interest to pharmaceutical companies. At the same time, consumer interest in traditional plant-based remedies continues to grow. The information gap has damaged the growth of this market and we can expect sales of herbal remedies to improve as customers gain access to summaries of test results, guidance on dosages, and education about what we might call the items' heritages. Clearly, providers in this area will need to present such information as product detail, rather than individualized health consultancy.

In what way do PlanetRx and Drugstore.com lead the way in mass market business-to-consumer ecommerce? They confirm the Amazon rationale that wide, complex product ranges make good online subjects. The in-built repeat purchase aspect of prescription medicine should give them a head start in developing continuing customer relationships with their users, although healthcare regulators continue to stress the need for patients to visit their physician for repeat prescriptions. The intractability of healthcare information—its breadth, changeability, and sometimes obscurity—dovetails well with the Web's supremacy as a conveyer of complex information. Repeatability and decision support are, therefore, good candidates for persistent factors in these types of application.

Decision support is, in fact, the key value offered by traditional retail. Retailers often deemphasize their role in supporting customer decision-making and cast their real estate assets as outlets. Sales training must ultimately emphasize closure as the goal of customer interactions, yet closure is a state that can only exist in a wider context, which takes in attraction, learning, and comparison as its predecessors. Retailers need to consider the life cycle of a customer purchase when transitioning to ecommerce. Mistaking the outward form of successful traditional retail and replicating it in the online medium with poor results is too easy. Successful business-to-consumer ecommerce players deconstruct the retail process and reconstruct it for the new channel. One way of imagining this task is shown in Figure 3-1.

The easiest way to approach this task is to focus on the retail sale as a customer experience. What brings a customer into the retail space? This may be a blend of location and store brand. Once he is inside the retail space, what factors influence his browsing and selection behavior? Location and brand figure prominently here, too, though product information plays an important role in judging competing items.

Using this simplistic analysis, we can see how the first generation of commercial Websites arose. Store location was translated to presence in an online mall and latterly to a memorable URL. Malls soon fell from favor, as operators realized the simple grouping of online stores made no real sense on the Web. Arguably, the online mall is being reborn as the Web portal, a mechanism that offers guidance and comparison as well as co-location.

The concept of physical location needs to be unpacked before it can be assembled afresh for the ecommerce channel: we must understand what makes "location, location, location" the mantra of real estate. A good physical store location is one that superimposes a customer's

FIGURE 3-1. Unpacking the retail process.

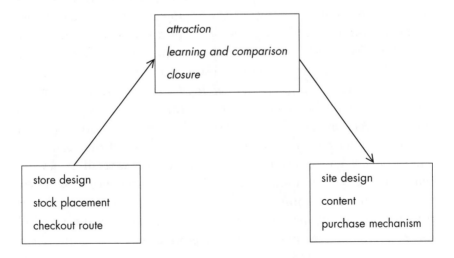

location. This means a successful store appears close to a user who is in purchase mode. Inevitably, this almost always means it is close to a pre-existing store and preferably one that appeals to the same type of customer without competing directly with the product. In the online world, this translates not to a particular address, but to a set of references. The capability to appear in the vicinity of a user who is prepared to consider purchasing something you offer is directly related to your level of connectedness in the online world. This is why click-through advertisements have been sold as premium spots at search engine sites. The site can use the input search terms to select an ad related to the inquirer's current concerns. Generating links in to your ecommerce channel from other sources is another important source of customer/seller collision. Reciprocal linking, sponsorship, and hyper-linked citations in editorial copy all provide virtual co-location opportunities. A further means of extending a site's reach to its potential users is to create explicit or covert funneling pages. These are sets of content that link in to the ecommerce channel, but that may not contain any particular branding. They rely on the inclusiveness of search engines to provide an extra level of potential awareness. In short, physical location translates to a kind of relevant accessibility. The store "happens to be going past" its potential customers.

Few translations from physical to virtual retail space are straight-forward mappings. For example, prescription pharmaceuticals act as a loss-leader for most U.S. drugstores, bringing customers into the store to buy other items. While waiting for her prescription to be filled, the customer may explore the store and buy other items. In the online world, delays do not stimulate the customer's further interest.

Retail store branding is another means of attracting customers. We mostly think of branded stores as mature entities, with each example leveraging the familiarity of its brethren to create a sense of homecoming for the customer. But, of course, much of the business of retail store design is concerned with introducing new retail names and concepts, and with guiding the evolution of existing ones toward new values. While establishing a pure Web brand is a new challenge, so is the creation of any new physical retailing brand. In the physical world, a retailer can, nevertheless, determine the type of effect she wishes to create by appealing to prevailing category standards. We can do the same for ecommerce channels.

By a *category standard,* I mean the bundle of design elements that suggests, in any one era, a particular type of store. So, a convenience food store may be characterized by glass areas adorned with icons and offers, and further complicated by freestanding displays of fresh flowers or newspapers. A convenience store has some kind of noticeable entry and exit control, such as automatic doors. A clothing store, on the other hand, may be designed with a wide entry aperture and discreet tag detectors. Island displays of folded apparel may be positioned to intrude into the external walkway, while greeters and music play their part in bringing the customer over the threshold. Many restaurants present their menus in small type, next to a door that is recessed into the property so potential customers must physically extract themselves from the restaurant's space if they decide to reject the offer.

While money is undoubtedly to be made from establishing pure ecommerce retailing brands that act as unmistakable signals to customer entry, we should not neglect the underlying design principles that traditionally animate such brands. When we talk about the importance of Web design for ecommerce channels, it is the discovery and implementation of such category standards we should be pursuing. Visual design for ecommerce channels is fundamentally concerned with communicating the retail offer, rationalizing the complexity of the choice on offer, and facilitating the customer's progress through the purchasing process. Fonts, colors, frames—these are the means. Engagement is the end.

How do these concerns relate to decision support? We can characterize all purchasing behavior as a decision-making process. We are usually wary of taking this approach because we associate decision-making with the supposedly rational patterns of work life rather than private life. The *consumer* has always been roughly sketched as a passive victim of economic activity, helplessly responding to impulses fired at him by business. Ecommerce strips these illusions away. The Web delivers vast amounts of product, service, and lifestyle information to its users, who are free to analyze it as best they can. They may perform their own comparison searches or use a shopping agent such as Excite's Jango facility to find the best price for a particular product. In effect, consumers are armed with knowledge, with opinions, and with secret doors that take them instantaneously to the premises of your competitors. In this context of consumer empowerment, it makes sense for the business-to-consumer player to use every means at her disposal to ensure the customer comes to her channel and completes his purchases there.

Repeatability may be built into the prescription drugs business, but for most ecommerce players it is a quality that needs to be manufactured or—more effectively—sought beyond the accepted retailing relationship. Manufactured repeatability may dictate the redesign of a product into a stable and an obsolescing component. This is the *refill* tactic, whereby a customer needs to recontact a supplier for continued use of an appliance—buying ink cartridges for a printer, for example. The dependency relationship ensures the customer revisits the store, with the attendant opportunities to learn about other products. The ink cartridge decommoditizes ink and creates a bond between owner and supplier. The purest informational ecommerce players deal in news of various sorts, which, by definition, becomes stale and requires refreshing. Opportunities clearly exist for business-to-consumer entrants of all kinds to exploit regularities in consumer lifestyles. A toothpaste brand may undertake to remind users of their dental appointments, while the direct marketing opportunities associated with family birthdays are obvious. These tactics may prove valuable to some players, but equally possible is that consumers will revolt against these relatively clumsy intrusions in their private life. Web users are already tiring of the levels of junk mail generated by the online services to which they subscribe. Indeed, some early users of Web ecommerce sites say they no longer use such services because of the unwanted inbound mail they tend to generate.

The shining lights on the business-to-consumer pathway have absorbed all these lessons—and gone beyond them. Two examples exist in this corner of our map, which together prefigure the future of business-to-consumer ecommerce: Peapod[4] and Streamline.[5] Intimate without being invasive, these players deliver the necessities of life to

4. www.peapod.com

5. www.streamline.com

their users and become colleagues in their customers' battle to stay on top of life.

Peapod offers a detailed online catalog of grocery products, but it isn't in the food retailing business. Peapod delivers something slightly different: personal shopping. It began its operation by sourcing goods directly from supermarkets. The user would choose items from the catalog and Peapod personnel would pick those items from the aisles of a food store. Peapod staff pick items as carefully as the customer would himself, honor discount coupons, and deliver the order at a time convenient to the customer. As the business has grown, the company has been able to put in place supplier agreements that allow it to centralize its operations by region, without sacrificing quality. Peapod currently serves 100,000 customers across eight metropolitan areas.

Peapod's distinguishing feature is the personal nature of its service. Its business model isn't predicated on complex systems integration or expensive stock purchasing policies. The proposition is Peapod will relieve you of the burden of shopping for groceries and it will perform this function with as much care as you would, if only you had the time. As its customer base grows, more complex processes, systems, and supply chain agreements will be demanded. The key insight, however, is not that technology can transform shopping, but that consumers regard shopping as a skill, as well as a burden. The weekly grocery shop is not something that can be entrusted to some inhuman supply process; it is intimately connected with our family duties and our responsibilities for their health and well-being.

Certainly Peapod is well positioned to take advantage of repeat purchasing behavior. But its significance as a pathfinder lies in its recognition that the primary factor in establishing a successful business-to-ecommerce offer in the future won't be product complexity, or disintermediation, or even product comparison. The key differentiator will be the extent to which the ecommerce channel makes sense of contemporary consumer life and resolves its tensions.

Streamline is an innovative ecommerce service, which has taken a slightly different execution approach to Peapod, but that also emphasizes personal service. Streamline has chosen to establish itself

The Power of Perceptions

Hollywood Stock Exchange (HSX) (www.hsx.com) gives its users $2 million in pretend money, in return for a little demographic information. Users then get to trade portfolios of movie stars.

What's going on here? Are the hosts of HSX giving the world some free and entertaining training in market capitalism or merely gathering demographic information to attract advertisers?

Advertising revenues and portal tie-ups have certainly helped to fuel HSX, but the owners also point to its potential value as a market research tool for film makers. Studios already use test screenings to determine the final shape of a movie, sometimes ordering reshoots if re-editing won't be enough to make the rough product successful with its target audience. Instant feedback on the perceived values of stars and movies could help the studios plan their creative processes with even greater accuracy.

by metropolitan area, starting with an area defined around its fulfillment center in Westwood, Massachusetts. The customer's relationship with Streamline begins with a home visit, when Streamline staff create a shopping list for the user. This list can be amended and actioned online, by phone, or by fax. An inducement to return to the Website regularly comes in the shape of special offers.

Streamline's home visit creates an initial bond, but it seals the customer relationship with a physical device: a $60'' \times 30'' \times 62''$ unit containing shelving and a refrigerator, with a keypad access control. The unit is installed in the customer's garage and is used as an exchange point between the customer and the company. Streamline delivers the order to the box, perhaps picking up the customer's dry-cleaning in exchange.

Remarkably, Streamline appears content to grow by word of mouth. However, the type of relationship the company is building with its customers is extraordinary. Streamline essentially owns a physical footprint in the customer's home and a logistical toehold in her life. The Streamline Box may not be the device any seer had in mind when he envisioned a wired world transacting effortlessly via the Internet. Yet it has the potential to control the commercial interactions of real families, taking over more and more of their domestic business. Streamline has noted that the ecommerce potential in the business-to-consumer space isn't confined to selling products to people. The bigger opportunity lies in being the family's faithful servant: efficient, reliable, flexible, discreet, economical.

Both Peapod and Streamline have business models that require their customers to pay premiums for their services. They both stress personal service and they both target the time pressures that assail contemporary family life. They align the technologies of the Web, its power to deliver information and take orders, with the emerging needs of consumers whose private lives are coming to resemble more and more their business lives. Fractured time, complex choices, multiplying commitments: these factors—more than beautiful catalogs and prestige addresses—will power the business-to-consumer ecommerce leaders of the next several years.

> HSX is an example of a transformation agent or intelligence approach. HSX is also a neat example of a phenomenon that would be impossible without the Web: a service that aggregates the niche obsessions of a dispersed audience and fashions a business model from the uptake. While players like Peapod and Streamline are benefiting from consumer perceptions about the scarcity of time, HSX is benefiting from its perception that popular culture is important and its icons are rankable. Of course, a contradiction exists here: how can there be no time to ensure the family is fed, but time enough to speculate in movie star bonds? Perhaps the potential user groups have no overlap. But that would be like betting no member of a gym drives a car to the gym.
>
> Consumer behavior is rational enough when viewed in pockets. New applications for business-to-consumer ecommerce have to concentrate on such bounded propositions. ∎

Auctions and the Emerging Electronic Marketplace

A lot more exists to physical consumer commerce than retail. Retail is easier to see when we walk around an urban center. But on the Web, every type of experience is only a few clicks away. Step slightly to the side of ecommerce retail and you enter a whole new world of frenzied activity: the online auction.

Auction sites, such as eBay,[6] make a huge range of items available to Web users who wish to bid against each other for their ownership. eBay members can buy and sell items, and make comments about the trustworthiness and efficiency of each other—comments that are

6. www.ebay.com

posted for all to see. At first sight, eBay has gone beyond business-to-consumer ecommerce: it seems actually to be facilitating consumer-to-consumer ecommerce.

Consider the list of functions eBay has devolved to its users. The company doesn't decide what product areas it should be in because the users define these with their offers. eBay doesn't have to describe the goods being exchanged. It certainly doesn't set their prices because value-setting is the prime user benefit of the service. And not only does eBay have zero stock, it doesn't undertake fulfillment. eBay users organize their own shipments.

eBay isn't a superfluous presence in this customer-created market, however. First, it is providing the physical servers and software that enable the auctions to function and allow the service to scale to growing demand. More important, from the point of view of generating a high-volume business, eBay provides the rules of the game, which it calls its *community guidelines.* The guidelines set out how auctions are run and advise on good manners. They also stress that the user is taking certain kinds of risk by joining in the auction. For example, "fraud is a reality of doing business, both on and off the Web, and you should report it to the authorities if it happens in our community."[7]

This hands-off stance is offset by eBay's SafeHarbor service line. SafeHarbor offers a number of value added services, including routes to insurance, escrow, and appraisal services. All these have the potential to generate revenues for the company.

eBay introduced insurance for items over $25 up to a maximum of $200 in March 1999, at no cost for the first six months. The insurance is backed by Lloyd's of London. For items over $200, eBay recommends users use an escrow service, which will act as an intermediary, holding the buyer's payment until the seller dispatches the item. The suggested escrow service is i-Escrow, which will take 5 percent commission, or $5 on each transaction, whichever sum is greater.

These are both clearly efficient routes to commission-related revenues for eBay. Also worth noting is the services are again implemented

7. www.ebay.com, 19 April 1999.

as outsourced capabilities. eBay is acting here as a classic broker. The same strategy is pursued with its appraisal services, which essentially route users to specialists who can help with the authentication, grading, and verification of various specialist items. Users trading baseball cards, for example, are referred to Professional Sports Authenticator[8] for assistance with assessing the physical condition of a card and its genuineness. Users who use the service receive a discount in recognition of their membership of eBay.

The supply of secondary services is likely to be eBay's chief generator of revenue and this is a model anyone can copy. Attracting volume traffic to an auction site is another matter, though. Why has eBay been successful in attracting users, when to the outsider, it appears to be nothing more than a gigantic flea market or garage sale? We believe eBay is compelling because it harnesses the Web's key customer differentiator—the capability of ordinary users to create content and dialogue—and yokes it to a timeless principle of progress: the desire of ordinary folks to live like kings. This is a powerful combination.

We have already seen the capability to form and engage in communities is a characteristic of the Web that distinguishes it from traditional media. In the auction setting, this empowers users to set values on items that have community significance, rather than general market visibility. In other words, collectibles treasured by a dispersed group become valued merchandise. Much sneering occurs at the values fetched by movie-related merchandise in the online auction world and some of it sounds like the noises made when Impressionist paintings started shifting for millions. We are witnessing an effect we could call *trickle-down royalty*. Those with disposable time and money are able to divert those resources into nonproductive activities that bring them pleasure. Once upon a time, only kings could command music to play for them during meals, but now we are used to summoning high-quality music at the touch of a button. In the same way, many of the items offered in online auctions play the role antiques played for the elite of previous generations.

---

8. www.pscard.com

The idea that auctions tap some kind of desire for conspicuous social betterment is not trivial. Those who prefer to concentrate on the speculative opportunities of auctions—because such opportunities are respectably calculable—forget the values they are computing rest entirely on emotions. Shifting dimensions, seeing the contemporary consumer obsession with time and its scarcity as stemming from a similar source is not unreasonable. As we saw in the cases of Peapod and Streamline, an important part of the proposition of each is the customer no longer has time to carry out the basic maintenance operations of life because he is too busy. He needs a virtual domestic staff to help him run the household. But what has happened to erode the consumer's day so drastically? The planet's rotation hasn't altered noticeably. In truth, activities once deemed exclusive have come within the reach of a larger population and become accepted as essentials in certain classes: these range from vacations to school management meetings. Our grandparents didn't need personal organizers, but then, most of them didn't own skis either.

The significance of the online auction as an ecommerce application type is its power to actualize the unrealized leisure desires of an upscale, leisured audience. As a pathfinder application, the auction demonstrates neatly that community spirit, when skillfully nourished and served, can generate attractive service revenues. The possibilities of this direction are far from played out.

First, current online auction sites predominantly trade in physical goods. Physical items are offered for transfer of ownership. Not all commerce is concerned with such transfers, however. Consumers also buy rights to enjoy certain benefits, usually over a specified time period that is used to help calculate the cost of the deal. In an auction setting, such items can become negotiable instruments.

Consider a service contract that has some time to run, such as a membership in a gym. The gym member moves to another city and cannot gain a refund on the outstanding balance of her annual membership. The gym will happily transfer the balance to another user because it loses nothing and, potentially, it gains another long-term member. The gym is not keen to let members use its bulletin boards to offer membership transfers, however, as this could create the impression of a dwindling membership base.

In this case, an auction site would enable the user to offload her remaining membership rights without offending the gym and with little search effort of her own. Perhaps the ideal site would be metro-based, serving the needs of city-based residents or newcomers, and affiliated to sites centered on other cities. The gym membership example extends to any kind of transferable pre-paid contract, including certain kinds of equipment lease. The agreement of the issuing party may be required in most cases, but few service providers are likely to turn away a new stream of potential customers willing to take up the obligations of their departing customers. Indeed, such traffic will provide better information on mid-term lapses. Such auctions could prove to be powerful tools in the control of churn, that is, the propensity of a service provider's customers to quit.

As auctions move beyond the transfer of ownership of physical items and toward time-based enjoyment of rights, they begin to become indistinguishable from financial markets. Three months of cell phone service on a defined call plan looks like a financial instrument and would surely behave like one in a market for phone service contracts. In fact, the Web's first share sale scandal—unwittingly mediated by an auction site—emerged at Amazon.com soon after the launch of its auction service in April 1999 (1,000 shares in a privately held software company were offered for sale and were rapidly removed by the site's operator). Amazon was unable to trace the identity of the seller. If it had gone ahead, the sale might have broken the Securities Act of 1933.[9]

Auction operators must take some responsibility for the business done through their sites, however hard they seek to distance themselves from the trades being carried out there. While financial law may not yet have addressed the sale of rights-based instruments, the onus is on any auction site that moves into this business to police the channel rigorously.

Another potential direction for online auctions takes us away from trade in used goods to reservation of new goods. Amazon's initial auction strategy is to channel users toward participating merchants, who

9. http://www.news.com/News/Item/0,4,34844,00html?st.ne.fd.gif.d

behave more like traditional retailers. A merchant may offer exclusive, unique items through this channel, though some merchants also make the same offers through their own Websites. The potential to engineer rarity and to recruit the market to establish prices for such rarities, is tantalizing. A manufacturer could invite bids for products he proposes to build. On the strength of the bids received, he may be able to secure funding for the actual manufacture of the goods. The focus of the auction is on the right to enjoy use of a rare product or the right to be among the first to enjoy a new product. This means of releasing products could also generate mass market demand for the second-wave release of the product. The online auctioning of, for example, the first 500 examples of a new model sports car, could simultaneously finance the manufacture of the car and stimulate general consumer demand more cost-effectively than entering it in high-profile races or letting favored journalists drive it across remote deserts.

It may be counter-intuitive to envisage an ecommerce channel as a means of creating scarcity because perceptions of ecommerce's role are generally trained on volume. Yet trickle-down royalty has enabled the jewelry industry to put a diamond on the finger of every fiancé, while ensuring diamonds don't become *too* affordable. By auctioning a desirable product, perhaps in a limited edition, a company can establish the high-water value for its goods and so determine an appropriate mass market price for its fixed-price retail channel.

Online auctions, therefore, offer a combination of beguiling capabilities to the ecommerce player. In the first place, the auction can be the ultimate in downstreaming, with the customer setting prices, describing offers, and arranging transfer of ownership. In the second place, the ecommerce channel has the opportunity to offer related services to those using the auction. Finally, the auction enables producers to control the desirability of their offers. Taken together, these characteristics represent the evolution of a true electronic marketplace. What effects will this development have on other businesses?

If auctions evolve to become the main means of determining prices, then all businesses will be affected. Those using auctions to engineer scarcity or to offload loss-leaders will inevitably upset the plans of those players who have stuck to price planning. In effect, auctions create a real-time pricing environment that changes the market rules for everyone. Regional pricing is already under intense pressure from fixed-price online retailing because little defense now exists for a CD, for example, that is priced differently in two different geographical territories. Auctions may strip away analogous certainties about what makes one type of product or service a luxury or a commodity.

Furthermore, auctions represent a stunning boost to shipping companies. The opportunities for consolidating consumer-to-consumer trades and guaranteeing their fulfillment are immense. The history of the logistics industry is of continued extension into integrated transport solutions and end-to-end service. The online auction is a bit business with great implications for such atom-shifting companies. As auctions grow to embrace greater volumes of trade in rights, we can imagine a related growth in intermediary services, perhaps developing from the type of escrow service already associated with eBay.

The implications for fixed-price retailers and physical retailers of all kinds, are more difficult to see. But it would be wrong to sound the death-knell of such businesses. We believe both ecommerce and physical business-to-consumer players will need to invest in the quality of experience they offer the customer. Both will need to maximize the entertainment value of their spaces and continue to add ancillary services to their offers.

More fundamentally, retailers will need to consider the potential for strengthening the guardianship values of their brands. The sense of security that goes with an established brand will act as an important counterbalance to the sense of risk that inevitably attaches itself to auctions. Many consumers will not want to engage in competitive purchasing. Some will regard the ability to bid as a burden rather than a benefit. After all, productization, branding, and pricing all reduce the complexity of acquiring new goods and services. Some users may prefer to bid for discretionary purchase items, but regard the pricing of their utilities as values that should be fixed. Others may be keen to get the best possible deals for their utility supplies, but would be unnerved by the shifting price of a luxury branded product they had previously regarded as inviolable.

Retailers can respond to this situation by stressing values that are the inverse of those associated with auctions. Where auctions emphasize scarcity, retailers can emphasize abundance. The turbulence of the auction's pricing mechanism is countered by the retailer's guarantee of a fixed price. While auctions celebrate competition, retailers can embody consumer equality. In the final analysis, the consumer's choice of purchasing location will often be determined by a trade-off between price and quality of experience. Companies could possibly play in both of these spaces. British Airways, for example, runs its low-cost airline Go in apparent competition to its regular branded services. As an ecommerce application type, the online auction allows companies to stream different offers to different consumers. For some players, the self-regulation of the online auction will be a more attractive means of reaching individual customers than creating a responsive one-to-one marketing capability within a standard retail site.

Auctions also have lessons for players who are active in more traditional broking activities, particularly where market values have tended to remain industry secrets. Most Web-based job recruitment sites, for example, are composed of static ads. Operators who add value through related services could build commanding volume in this market. Such services include structuring résumé and job description information, and performing intelligent matches. Smarter services would include holding auctions for job opportunities. In this case, some auctions would focus on applicants competing for jobs, while others would focus on recruiters competing for applicants. A player who built credibility in providing this service, perhaps using some system of sealed bidding, would be well placed to create further lucrative services, including underwriting deals. An ecommerce channel that brought together buyers and sellers, established their values to each other on a real-time, case-by-case basis, and offered to guarantee—for a premium—the success of deals made through it, would be the paradigm of a successful, full-service, business-to-consumer ecommerce channel.

Advice and Care

Before the Web became synonymous with the Internet and before the Internet became confounded with the term *online,* online services established themselves as tools for creating communities of interest among the connected. Bulletin board systems (BBSs) catered largely for those seeking to exchange software with each other, while online conferencing systems served groups who wanted to share topic-based information and opinions. AOL, a major pre-Internet player, remains a dominant online force and its organization and shaping of the online experience continues to be one strength of its brand.

The Web itself was originally conceived as a tool for collaborative research groups. The online world has always been one where people *help* each other. Many early users of the Internet resented the coming of commerce to the Web, fearing their world would become one where people simply helped themselves to easy earnings. As ecommerce develops, however, it is becoming apparent that help is itself a commercial quantity and one that can be both colonized and leveraged by innovative businesses.

When Merrill Lynch launched its online stock trading service in January 1999, its competitors had a head-start of some two years. But the heavyweight, full-service broker is arguably in a different business from the discount brokers that had already opened for business on the Web. The factor that discriminates a discount broker from a traditional broker is "execute only." Discount brokers offer reduced commissions because they only carry out customer instructions. Full-service brokers offer advice, which comes as the result of expensive research.

Merrill Lynch offered free research at its site during the launch period of its broking service. In the meantime, the discount brokers started to improve their research offerings. On the face of it, it looks as if both types of provider are heading for the middle ground. The reality is a little more subtle. The finance players are essentially betting on the distribution of different types of investment behavior. Transaction-oriented brokers such as e*Trade attract customers who want to play the markets on a daily basis, perhaps building and liquidating a position within a single trading day. Relationship-oriented brokers, such as Merrill Lynch, are more concerned to attract customers who already have substantial assets and who wish to invest their portfolios wisely.

A well-attested fact is the more assets someone owns, the more she fears a loss. Those with few assets take more risks, but become more risk-averse as they accumulate assets. On the whole, investors will mature from short-term risk-takers to long-term asset-protectors. From the point-of-view of a transaction-oriented broker, adding advice services helps him to retain customers whose entire investment experience has potentially been with the one company. The relationship-oriented broker, on the other hand, has the opportunity to pick up newer investors by offering an online brokerage service, attracting them to a long-term home with an affordable, branded execution service.

Consumers' varying attitude to investment risk mirrors their divergent attitudes to auctions and fixed-price retail. When we considered the tactics a retail player could use to counter the threat of auctions, we essentially called on the comfort factors a retailer can deploy to minimize the customer's exposure to risk. In this scenario, the retailer's guaranteed price stability and, possibly, the values of her established brand, reassure the customer about her transaction. Advice can also be seen as a comfort factor. In time, the quality of its advice could become the chief competitive competency of the successful business-to-consumer ecommerce provider, surpassing its technical capability to complete commercial transactions or deliver the associated products or services.

Advice has been overlooked as a business-to-consumer ecommerce application type, yet as the user base of ecommerce channels continues to grow, investment in this area is bound to follow. The main reason advice has lagged behind the other application types we have discussed is intimately connected with the character of the Web's early adopters. Subsidiary issues exist with the labor required to give good advice and the litigation arising from giving bad advice.

Although the public Web is around five years old and has penetrated the consumer consciousness with incredible speed, most sites are designed for inquisitive folks who persevere. Web users need to be goal-oriented to get satisfaction from the Web. Certainly, today's users are pampered compared to the true pioneers who navigated the Web with text-based browsers, such as Lynx, and searched the Internet's resources with tools such as Gopher, Archie, and Veronica—all now consigned to the history books by search engines such as AltaVista, Excite, and Hotbot. Yet, despite the improvement in graphics, page layout schemes, and, above all, download speeds, the Web user still needs to be able to model his information requirement as either a system query or as a branch of some explicit knowledge structure.

To understand this problem—and why it is a problem for the development of ecommerce—we can consider someone using a public library to help him fix a leaking faucet. Most libraries are organized according to some structuring of knowledge, which groups resources by subject. If the library is well labeled, the user may be able to head directly for the "plumbing" section, and then thumb through the index sections of the books on those shelves. Alternatively, if the library's catalog has been automated, he may enter "fix faucet" in the system and see what items are suggested.[10] If he is not sure what section he should look in and if he is unsure how to frame his query to the catalog, he might just wander around until he finds the answer he needs.

This is how users habitually approach the Web. A resource like Yahoo! offers both a library structure and a search engine, to cater for those who want to express their requirement as a branch of knowledge or as a search term. Both these preparatory activities can be complex, but they have a higher success rate than random surfing. But no matter how comprehensive a catalog is or how large and efficient a search engine is, neither is a complete answer to the problem of successfully working the Web for ecommerce purposes. This is because getting a faucet fixed isn't the same thing as learning about how to fix a faucet. Commerce is about satisfying needs and, while the need for knowledge is an important commercial area, it should not be confused with the whole space. That would be like mistaking a city's Yellow Pages for its aggregated business community when, in reality, it is one tool for gaining access to that community.

10. As a speaker of British English, I'm likely to enter "fix tap" and be offered a course of remedial dancing lessons.

The Web, then, is well suited to people who have research skills. Some politicians and business leaders argue that the teaching of research skills should be prioritized in schools so the next generation will be adequately prepared for a life of electronic shopping, form-filling, and employment. Although research skills are clearly important in empowering people to make use of the information environment, relying on the development of such skills for the future of ecommerce is foolhardy. Expecting the entire population to approach ecommerce as a mental puzzle is like insisting that traffic signs are rewritten as riddles.

While developers will continue to search for better ways of presenting and delivering information to users, the complex search problem can be cut down radically with the use of advice services. Creating advice is labor-intensive, though. If all advice has to be delivered one-to-one by humans, then advice as an application cannot scale to mass-market ecommerce proportions. We need a means of creating, structuring, and delivering device that exploits computing capabilities to assist users. An early example of such a device is AskJeeves.[11]

AskJeeves looks superficially like a standard search engine, with an input text box at the top of the page, but the site doesn't ask you for keywords or Boolean search strings. It takes standard questions written in natural language. When asked "How do I fix a leaking faucet?" the site replies with a list of possible answers. At the top of the returned list is the construction "How can I learn to . . ." joined to a drop-down list with the entry "fix a leaky faucet?" highlighted. If I select this option, I am taken to a relevant page from learn2.com, which is embraced within the AskJeeves frameset. A range of alternative options exists, as well, including the leading hits from a group of standard search engines.

When I ran this example,[12] I was not offered any commercial service or targeted advertising. I put the same question to AltaVista, which incorporates AskJeeves's technology. It returned the same suggestions, although it naturally excluded results from other search engines and its default display for the learn2.com resource is full-page

11. www.askjeeves.com

12. 24 April 1999.

rather than framed. However, when I asked both sites "What is Wireless Application Protocol?" the results differed in one interesting respect. AskJeeves offered general help on the meaning of the term *protocol*, but specific matches to Wireless Application Protocol only appeared in its search engine summaries. AltaVista, on the other hand, went straight to a listing of Web pages based on the phrase "Wireless Application Protocol" and displayed an ad from Nokia on that very topic, with a click-through to Nokia's WAP site.

The success of AskJeeves, not least in its deal with AltaVista, indicates first that better ways exist of making the Web's resources available to users than demanding they learn Boolean logic. More significantly, AskJeeves reminds us the commercialization of the Web has created a population seeking solutions—initially to problems of information but, increasingly, to problems related to their daily concerns. In other words, use of the Web as a channel is evolving from the satisfaction of secondary problems concerned with knowledge to the supply of primary needs requiring action.

To clarify this distinction, consider the area of healthcare. Information about illnesses and cures abounds on the Internet. Newsgroups and Websites are dedicated to the support of all kinds of conditions. This wealth of information is distributed and highly variable in its quality. A search for information about one disease may yield medical teaching materials, newsgroup messages comparing symptoms and treatments, and advertising material for herbal remedies. Little of this mass of information amounts to advice and the fraction that does cannot be tailored to an individual's needs. As we saw when considering the potential for online drugstores, general healthcare advice can support sales of healthcare products, but healthcare consultancy needs to be one-to-one. Healthcare professionals rely crucially on patient history and examination. In other words, the sought queries the seeker. Information flows in both directions.

The bidirectional nature of the advice relationship is the key to solving the remaining two problems associated with advice as an ecommerce application: the labor required to create it and the legal ramifications of poor advice. In short, online advice applications need to be designed as contracted services between client and supplier. In this way, the labor element is a chargeable consulting activity, rather than a content-creation task. The scope and applicability of the advice proffered, and the client's obligations in implementing it in accordance with any detailed instructions, can also form part of the contract.

In other words, online advice applications have to embody professional standards. Mediconsult.com charges $195 for a report and advice based on a client's submitted history and query. Although the advice is not claimed to be a diagnosis, the company is ensured against malpractice claims. CyberAnalysis.com, "the Internet's first and only source for one-to-one online psychiatric therapy,"[13] implements a traditional patient-therapist model using the Internet as a communications channel. Fees for initial consultation and follow-up sessions are comparable to those for physical sessions. Run by an accredited British psychiatrist, CyberAnalysis.com claims that for some clients, the distancing created by the online channel actually assists its cognitive therapy techniques.

Few businesses transitioning to ecommerce currently see themselves as being in the advice business. Engaging in advice relationships, however, can be seen as a natural development from one-to-one marketing. Both involve intimate communications and both are focused on the satisfaction of individual needs, rather than generic solutions. As businesses develop their ecommerce channels, the capability to advise customers effectively will become an important competitive factor. The next challenge will be to reintroduce some form of automation as the demand for individual advice scales beyond the capability of all-human systems to supply it.

Expert systems—the once-glamorous corner of 1980s IT that has lost visibility during the rise of the Internet—will play a key role here. The technology underlying AskJeeves, the personalization engines embedded in some one-to-one marketing systems, and the language translation facilities built into AltaVista are all species of expert systems. Expert systems rely on the collection and processing of rules to suggest possible courses of action. Knowledge engineering is the process of soliciting collections of rules within a professional

---

13. Press Release, 1 December 1998.

domain and rendering them intelligibly to an expert system. Expert systems have found many applications in healthcare and, arguably, most useful advice in any setting is the result of a diagnostic procedure.

The initial technical challenge for organizations implementing advice applications in their ecommerce channel will be the integration of the service with other communications modes. Just as the availability of basic product information on the Web needs to be taken into account in the staffing and training of call center teams, so the availability of online advice needs to be factored into the company's other communications channels. Specifically, maintaining comparable standards across competing channels will be vital to credibility. If a company representative offers guidance that deviates from that delivered by "the system" and both outcomes are based on identical customer-provided information, then one or other source will suffer, to the detriment of the company as a whole. Any expansion in a business's routes to market creates the potential for inconsistency and advice services bid for a supreme position of trust in the customer's mind.

Further technical challenges will arise with the development of the "intelligence" of systems supporting advice services. The first shopping agents, which compare prices of items offered at ecommerce sites, are well established and now integrated in the services of the leading search engines. The potential for roaming agents, licensed to travel the Internet looking for intelligence, has yet to be tapped. It is not hard to imagine services that log a customer's interests and then actively patrol information resources in search of information that may fulfill those needs, developing a model of the interest areas it researches as it progresses. Perhaps customer agents will be lured by commerce agents that draw them toward particular commercial solutions, just as ad servers pop up relevant advertising messages to today's search engine user. In other words, our research behavior will devolve to software avatars—a billion invisible Jeeveses, living on their wits.

This may seem a long way from contemporary business-to-consumer ecommerce. But the speed of change online suggests that advice applications will assume major importance over the next few years. As we have seen, the enduring power of retailing on the Web is connected with consumer choices about their allocation of time. The power of the online auction rests in its capability to generate real-time electronic marketplaces, where prices and availability are directly determined by consumers, rather than by market seers. As both of these application types come to dominate large areas of commerce, the growing complexity of the active consumer's life is increasingly exposed. Some may take refuge in the comfort of simplified, branded services that rationalize some of the complexity and exact a fee in return. Others will prefer to arm themselves with the best advice they can find to make sense of their choices themselves. In a world awash with more and more information, the creation of actionable knowledge attains a higher value. Caring for the customer, guarding her best interests, fetching her solutions rather than offers—these will be among the most distinctive applications in the business-to-consumer ecommerce space.

BUSINESS-TO-BUSINESS APPLICATIONS

The business-to-business application types gathered together in this section represent a three-lane route to a radically modified business landscape. Procurement, inventory exchange, and real-time collaboration are relatively obscure categories of application, which have the potential to flip many businesses inside-out.

Procurement introduces process improvements in the buying functions of organizations and also points the way to a more competitive environment in intercompany trading. Inventory exchange introduces the mechanism of the market to smooth out supply and demand inefficiencies across entire industries, and potentially unpicks traditional buyer-supplier relationships. Real-time collaboration allows organizations to cooperate as fluid colonies of actors, undermining the stability of companies who prefer hands-off relationships or who prefer their reality-checks to be presented monthly.

Procurement and Its Impact on Competition

Procurement is the fastest growing business-to-business ecommerce application area. Labeled "Operating Resources Management" by one of its proponents, Ariba,[14] a major area of procurement is concerned with the acquisition of nonproduction supplies within an organization. This isn't the most glamorous area in business, but it is one ripe for automation and one that benefits especially from the capabilities of ecommerce.

All organizations purchase resources that are not directly used in making their product or service. These resources include office supplies like pens and binders, as well as essential technical supplies like test tubes and modeling materials. Capital goods, such as desktop PCs and other office equipment, qualify for inclusion. At the high end of the scale, procurement also applies to outsourced infrastructure and professional services. Everything from paper clips to building security, via the carpeting of the reception area and the care of its potted plants, must go through a procurement process. Ariba estimates the typical manufacturing company spends around 35 percent of its revenue on operating resources.

Buying just about anything is possible on the Web in the consumer space, but this doesn't add up to a solution for the procurement activity. The additional requirements serve to demonstrate the key differences between the business-to-consumer and the business-to-business domains.

First, businesses purchase resources in bulk and on repeated occasions. A structure exists to their requirements that demands a level of forward planning. The planning function allows the organization to concentrate its buying activities and to obtain economies of scale in both process and price. In other words, if a procurement department can enforce acquisition of stationery supplies from a limited menu carried by one supplier, then it can simultaneously reduce the number of suppliers and product lines with which the organization deals and bulk up its orders for improved prices. Procurement is different

---

14. www.ariba.com

from consumer purchasing because it is rationalized according to business policies.

Second, the invocation of the procurement process is a distributed activity. This means, while a procurement department may be tasked with creating policies, negotiating deals, and making orders, the actual procurement requests are generated at the operational level. Traditionally, staff fill in requisition forms, which then go through a process of approval before being put into action. Consumer purchasing is generally considered to be impulsive or, at best, subjected to an unwritten approval process within the family. Certainly, consumers neither perceive themselves as being locked in a hierarchy of authority when it comes to making a purchase nor do they see themselves as part of a collective that could demand better prices from retailers.

Both these characteristics make procurement an ideal target for automation. Procurement departments have been automated for some time, at least to the extent of maintaining databases of suppliers, products, and contracts. The invocation and approval part of the equation has not been addressed before, but it is peculiarly well suited to the intranet. We need to provide a controlled catalog of items throughout the organization—what better way than as a Website? The procurement department can produce its own catalogs or adopt catalogs from its suppliers. Either way, it removes the expense of printing and distributing catalogs, as well as solving the problem of out-of-date catalogs remaining in circulation. Using physical catalogs, high-production costs usually mean only departmental heads are sent catalogs. Using the intranet, any user can see what is available.

So far, this is shaping up to be a classic intranet application: an internal publishing project that creates some savings in printing and distribution. We can easily go to the next stage of automation, however, which is to make the catalog actionable. We can implement checkboxes and shopping baskets on the procurement site, so users can choose their own resources. The approach is fundamentally the same as that used for business-to-consumer retailing, without the need to take payment.

The intranet then adds the next important element: approval by policy. A user's shopping basket is not regarded as an order, but as a proposed requisition. The completed request is routed through a pre-defined chain of approval nodes. These nodes may be people or rules. For example, a user may fill out a request for five boxes of printer paper. The system recognizes the request type, the total cost of the request, and the authority level of the user. The system may pass the request directly to the procurement department for conversion into an order. If the user requests five photocopiers, on the other hand, the total cost of the request causes the item to be routed to a depart-mental budget-holder for his explicit consideration. This can be achieved by a system-generated email or the system may simply create its own alert flag, which the relevant budget-holder will see when he next logs into the procurement system.

The design of approval routes is theoretically without limit. Steps in the chain can happen in serial and parallel, as shown in Figure 3-2. A unique route may be designed for every resource that can be requested or generic paths can be designed for classes of request. From the point-of-view of application design, including the capability to define and modify approval networks in an intuitive manner is important.

Automating the procurement function, therefore, gives us an ideal intranet application. It exploits the ubiquity and ease of use of the

FIGURE 3-2. Procurement approval routes.

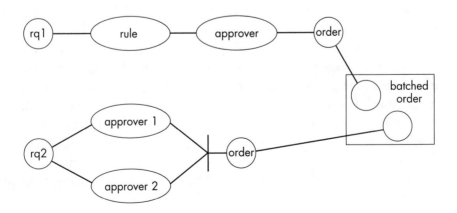

corporate Web and its underlying infrastructure to improve a necessary business process and to devolve part of it to the individual requester. It captures important business rules about how resources may be purchased within the organization and turns those rules into functioning parts of a system: in other words, procurement systems take policy and implement it. Finally, the automated procurement function introduces a workflow element to the process, ensuring requests are carried efficiently to the points where decisions need to be made.

All these are beneficial effects, but they all occur *inside* the organization. Given that many organizations have implemented intranets, but have done little with them—except for putting the internal phone book online—a procurement system like the one we just outlined may be justified simply on its capability to earn back some of the investment made in the corporate intranet. But procurement is promoted to an ecommerce application the moment the system reaches beyond the corporate boundary and connects with the supplier world.

First, the purchasing company can place orders electronically with its suppliers. It may use existing EDI links, feeding EDI documents with content pulled from the consolidated orders produced by its intranet procurement system. Second, organizations can source their catalog information electronically, downloading product and price information for reformatting in its internal Web pages. Of course, the purchasing company can choose to outsource the catalog function completely to the supplier, merely linking to the relevant pages at the supplier's Website.

Once the external business-to-business channel is established, interesting things begin to happen. We are now no longer merely improving the internal purchasing process. We have joined a vibrant and dynamic marketplace, in which buyers and suppliers may coalesce in various shifting combinations to create new opportunities. Think of it this way: If you are a buyer and you can trade electronically with your existing suppliers, you can also trade electronically with new suppliers. If you are a supplier trading electronically, then every buying organization that implements an ecommerce procurement system is a potential new customer. The procurement playing field has become much more open.

The initial effect of the move toward ecommerce procurement is a growing battle among suppliers to capture customers and to lock out competitors. Technology can be an ally here because a supplier of, for example, office stationery may offer to install a dedicated PC and communications link free-of-charge to a buying organization. It creates a direct channel into that organization and one that cannot be infiltrated by competitors. The problems arrive when the customer wants to source more items than the supplier offers and, crucially, when it wants to integrate its purchasing process across the board. The procurement system outlined in this section is an ideal, end-to-end system where user requests flow effortlessly into company orders and supplier shipments. If a supplier gets to the party first, however, she may well automate only the part of benefit to herself, which is the ordering mechanism. Indeed, an external supplier will be poorly placed to propose the deployment of an intranet approval system and the procurement department may not be any better positioned. As it adds in new supplier terminals, the buying organization may end up with a mass of point solutions to its ordering requirements, no commonality of function, and no backward reach into the request and approval process. This is a pattern that tends to repeat across every application area in every business. Individual automation opportunities are grasped in isolation and each generates benefits in a limited domain but, as the number of point solutions grows, the need for integration and flexibility grows.

Businesses should be able to learn from prior experiences in building islands of automation and subsequent bridge-building projects. The business will be best served by an ecommerce solution that links across from requester to shipment, welcomes new supplier entrants, and can be integrated with other business systems. Procurement is a classic case of an application type that benefits from architectural planning, rather than short-term opportunism. The industry is insufficiently mature, however, to have created the kinds of standards that would reassure buying organizations looking to implement ecommerce procurement strategies. Despite initiatives like Open Buying on the Internet (OBI), which describes a data and process model for making these kinds of transactions, no definitive, universally supported standard exists that defines, for example, the structure of an item in a catalog. Without some kind of common currency in this area, suppliers cannot simply switch their own catalogs in to buyer sites in place of their competitors or in addition to suppliers in other industry sectors. Potentially, each time the marketplace grows, a new systems integration project is required. Every buyer system needs to understand every supplier system and vice versa. Looking within the buying organization, integration with the company's Enterprise Resource Planning (ERP) systems may take priority when considering a procurement solution. Until standards emerge in the business-to-business arena, adopters need to make careful tradeoffs between potential breadth of supply and internal process efficiency. Meanwhile, we can expect to see procurement solution providers continuing to improve their offers to build market share and, thereby, create de facto standards. CommerceOne,[15] for example, quickly focused on acquiring the widest possible set of supplier catalogs for use with its system. Ariba concentrated on "closing the loop" of the procurement process by partnering with the purchasing card function of VISA and also with FedEx for delivery.

Procurement will continue to grow in significance as a business-to-business ecommerce application, despite the growing pains associated with standardization and integration. As ecommerce comes to control the larger part of intercompany trading, several new forces will emerge. Looking inward, an efficient and accessible request and approval system will expose more resources to tighter management control. Ariba identifies internal services as a type of resource that can be managed using its solution, so the configuration and installation of a desktop PC by the systems department, for example, could be included within the formal procurement process. Immediately, the cost and quality of internal services are pulled out of obscurity and potentially set against external competition. The chargeout of internal services continues to be a contentious issue in many organizations and bringing the requisition and billing of such services within the remit of a procurement system can help to impose additional management discipline on them.

Extensity[16] has targeted the travel and expenses area for similar treatment. Many organizations struggle to service travel purchasing

---

15. www.commerceone.com
16. www.extensity.com

and expenses administration. Some suspect they have insufficient control over these expenditures, yet cannot see how to improve the situation. Bringing these items within the orbit of the procurement solution allows for better control of premeditated purchases.

Looking outward, buying companies may find themselves allying with other buyers to shape favorable deals with suppliers. The Web gives companies a simple means of discovering the other customers of a supplier. For example, one buying company—or a new intermediary—could set up a Website to facilitate discussion about the services of a target supplier. Users of the discussion site could thereby become members of a buyer's club, dedicated to negotiating the best terms for all its members with that supplier.[17] Here again, we have an echo of one of the major differentiators of ecommerce applications: the capability to aggregate dispersed interests into a powerful commercial actor.

We have characterized procurement as a combination of internal business process efficiency and smart external trading. Where does this leave the majority of "normal" business-to-business trading applications that continue to appear? Software and services companies pushing packaged procurement solutions make a noise in the market but, in the meantime, individual, unique solutions are quietly being put in place to handle intercompany electronic trading. Many are relatively simple gateways into corporate systems that allow checking of prices and placing of orders. Finding the larger manufacturers fronting their EDI systems with Web-enabled gateways is common, so non-EDI customers can use the same facilities as their brethren. Mobil, for example, introduced such a facility for its lubricants distributors in early 1997, enabling them to exchange orders, buy-backs, and invoices. As an evolution of existing systems and a measure of downstreaming, this is a successful strategy. We return to this subject in the sectrion "Real-Time Collaboration and Real-World Change," when we consider the powerful effects of real-time collaboration.

---

17. This strategy could also be used by private individuals to create "consumer unions" with favorable purchasing terms. We believe this application would also require the leadership and support of an intermediary, so it is included as a business-to-business opportunity.

Inventory Exchange and the Market Mechanism

All businesses acquire resources, modify them in some way, and then dispose of them. As we have seen in the area of Operating Resources Management, a large part of business-to-business trade is concerned with goods and services that facilitate a company's operations, rather than contributing directly to its end product or service. The core of business is concerned with some of the same issues—acquiring parts, tools and services of the correct specification, quality and quantity at the optimum time. Authorization processes are likely to be less convoluted and greater restrictions may apply to the range of resources that can be ordered. Most obviously, specialists will be responsible for sourcing particular resources.

For the sake of simplicity, we can consider a manufacturing business that uses standard components to build electronic products. Buyers purchase against parts catalogs and aim to stock the lowest levels of inventory compatible with manufacturing throughput. Inventory that is not moving is a wasting asset. Ideally, inventory should be constantly flowing from load bay to production line.

Large manufacturers, led by the automotive companies, have invested heavily in making such Just In Time (JIT) processes a reality. Many companies can demonstrate savings derived from insisting their suppliers take responsibility for timely delivery. On closer inspection, however, the suppliers often can only meet their JIT delivery obligations by relocating closer to the buyer. At the macro level, the problem of stationary stock has, in many cases, been lobbed over the factory wall to the supplier, who now bears that economic burden. If he is in a chain, he may seek to pass that burden on to his suppliers. Inevitably, JIT displaces supply pressures around the community.

Any manufacturing process proceeds through discrete states and, while IT may help to improve its pipeline characteristics, inevitably mismatches will occur between supply and demand. While systems efforts may continue to pare away at these discrepancies, business-to-business ecommerce offers a complementary route to solving the problem of excess inventory. Rather than striving to improve the fluidity of the supply pipeline through, for example, predictive algorithms, we employ market principles to redirect resources. Market mechanisms divert over-supply to areas of demand. By looking outside the principal value chain to the industrial environment within which it is located, we can alleviate the problems of excess inventory. Inventory exchange is, therefore, a leading application area in business-to-business ecommerce. As we shall see, it can be applied to all kinds of supply mismatch, but it is, perhaps, best approached via its success in the manufacturing arena.

FastParts.com[18] was launched in 1996 to serve users of electronic components. It deals solely in brand-new components and is membership based. Membership criteria are nontrivial and include current membership of a recognized industry body. The company describes itself as a trading exchange, modeled on the NASDAQ securities exchange. FastParts.com doesn't act as a broker and it takes no financial interest in any lot being traded. As an exchange, FastParts.com operates and maintains the communications mechanisms that allow deals to be made. It does arrange physical delivery, however, and charges a fee for successful deals. The fee is shared both by buyer and seller.

Compared to a public online auction site like eBay, this may seem like an overly rigorous regime. FastParts's undertaking to deliver also looks, at first sight, like an unnecessary intervention. Two key differences are at work here. First, components traded via FastParts must be genuine, unused, and provably so. These components will be used to manufacturer new products and they must be, in every sense, identical to factory orders. The components traded at FastParts are not curiosities, they are inventory, resting before finding its correct home.

FastParts's role in delivery is connected with the most important feature of the trading exchange: anonymity. Buyers and sellers are not identified on the site. The major reason for anonymity is to preserve the integrity of FastParts's market prices. Component lots find their transaction value in the normal market way, depending on buyers' interest in acquiring the parts. If a small company were seen to be offering a large quantity of parts, larger companies might assume they

---

18. www.fastparts.com

could force a lower price. At the same time, large companies offloading inventory would be sending intelligence signals to their competitors. The success of the inventory exchange relies on a guarantee of anonymity. Transacting members know in principle they may be helping out their competitors; anonymity ensures they are playing in a win-win game. Because buyers and sellers remain anonymous, FastParts acts as a physical clearing house for transacted items. This ensures lots are stripped of any indication as to the identity of their previous owner before shipping.

FastParts uses the Web to create its trading exchange, but it is worth noting that FastParts is more than its Website. As well as its roles in qualifying members and operating a neutral parts depository, FastParts holds funds during the physical exchange period. Its ability to deliver lots to participating members also puts it in a prime position to bid for core supply business in its business. In other words, FastParts could develop from being a market mechanism for correcting excess inventory problems to being a mainstream provider of inventory.

Inventory exchange is a strategy that can be applied to any situation where excesses occur and discretion is required for their removal. Identifying unused physical inventory and calculating its cost to the business has always been easy. But what about the other resources a business potentially has in over-supply? Two main classes of asset exist that repay attention: slots and people.

We touched on the potential for trading in moving space when we considered porting a car-pooling service to the business-to-business domain in Chapter 2. Spaces in vehicles are a type of *slot,* defined as a bounded, atomic, and historical value opportunity. A slot is *bounded* because it has a predetermined size and shape: it may be an ocean-going container or a seat on an airplane. A slot is *atomic* in the sense that it is the smallest possible unit of aggregation in a scheme that exploits slots. So, for example, an airplane seat cannot be divided into parts for sale to a potential customer. If you want the seat, you have to buy the whole seat. On the other hand, a container may be an atom in one scheme and an aggregation in another. One company may rent containers, while another company factors space inside rented containers. In this case, the factoring company would determine a within-container slot, possibly using a measure, such as the cubic meter, or using another industry slot such as a pallet.

A slot is only fully defined when the time dimension is added. A slot is *historical* because every slot has a predetermined lifetime. Our airplane seat isn't just H3 in a particular 747. It is H3 on that 747 flying from London to New York on October 10TH, 2005 at 11:50 A.M. The date may be in the future, but it is, nevertheless, historical. The slot will be consumed at that time and never be repeated. If the seat flies across the Atlantic without an occupying passenger, then that revenue is lost for ever.

Many business activities create slots of one kind or another. They are most noticeable in manufacturing production lines. In this case, unused slots in a subprocess can bring an entire production process to a halt. But slots are being generated in all types of businesses. Distribution space is a key example. As we have already noted, nonprofessional logistics processes run the risk of freighting large quantities of air around the planet.

Accommodation space is also slot-like. Companies build or hire accommodation space on a footage basis, using projections of likely use patterns and headcount growth to guide their decisions. Once purchased, much of this space sits idle while other portions are overcrowded. It may be hard to imagine how such imbalances could be smoothed out during the day, but it is possible to imagine companies trading day-long slots with each other. If a company has a meeting suite in a business center location, then it makes sense to sell or trade its spare capacity to others who may need it.

Slots are a neutral commodity in business and, once they are recognized as tradable items, they make excellent candidates for business-to-business ecommerce applications. Each potential match represents a win for both parties. Technology provides the meeting place that aggregates a fragmented field—a vast mass of small, dispersed opportunities with complex characteristics which, rationalized by a market mechanism, yield up hidden value. The slot is a generalization of many types of opportunity, including the advertising spot.

It is interesting that advertising space is known to its sellers as "inventory."

Can we really also say people are inventory? It may be a corporate cliché to say "our people are our greatest asset," but many CEOs would think twice about offering them for sale on the Web. In a business environment increasingly aware of the role of knowledge workers in creating value, many leaders balk at treating their people as tradable assets, at least in public. Service representatives, team leaders, designers—these are all skilled roles that seem naturally unslotlike. How could you slot a team leader from a white collar factory into a project management role in an industrial concern? The pegs don't match the holes.

The trend toward portfolio careers suggests that some, if not all, of us are capable of precisely these kinds of transformation. Career changes are becoming more and more common as the fabled "job for life" becomes extinct in most cultures. Of course, the motivations for such translations are intimate and profound. Sudden redundancy or a strong personal urge to change lifestyle are at the roots of many portfolio careers. Is importing these forces into the business possible or sensible?

This has already happened. The effect is most noticeable in the engineering professions and, above all, in the IT sector. Here, recruitment and executive search services drive the human resourcing of an entire industry. In a world where five years at one company is a lifetime, those with employee status are hard to distinguish from contractors passing through. Changes in technology inspire some to change direction and others to hunker down and maximize their existing opportunities before the axe falls. But everyone, employer and employed alike, treats the environment as a market. IT consulting organizations make this the explicit dynamic of their business: they match supply and demand.

The issue here is whether any business at random can emulate a consulting organization. Can it make its people available to work elsewhere? And is it open to using expertise from other companies? Many leading organizations manage to create this permeability when it comes to charitable or community involvement on the part of their people. The fear of giving away commercial secrets or losing the best people to a competitor, make it hard for many to imagine a similar free flow with other companies. Businesses continue to assess business units in this way, however, acquiring and disposing of teams or constituent companies to assist the development of the overall mission. The inventory exchange model would enable them to do this at a finer level of detail.

For example, a company may have a first-class research and development team, but a temporary inability to fund them. It can fire the team or dissolve it into other functions within the company. Either way, the company is destroying a carefully nurtured and expensively built capability. An enlightened organization might find a way to spin the unit out of the main company and even seek external funding to contribute to its maintenance.

These are all structural decisions. What if the business were able to take opportunity decisions instead? If it could find the right partner, then it could consider lending the team to another company. This might be a company in a noncompeting sector, but it is not unreasonable to imagine its being a competitor as well, especially if shared rights in any resulting intellectual property form part of the deal. Our putative R&D team could be outplaced on elastic. It would be respected as a team, retained as an asset of the business that invested in its development, and accorded a public value underwritten by the engaging parties.

Of course, if we follow this line of reasoning, then nothing exists to stop individuals from managing their own career trajectories, using exactly the same means. The Web could be used as a giant talent exchange, with consumers trading directly with consumers. This situation is analogous to that of the online auction in the business-to-consumer space. In that case, the added services supplied by the auctioneer create the ecommerce opportunity. The same is true in this business-to-business analog, the inventory exchange. Intermediaries can supply additional services alongside the maintenance of the exchange, including evaluation and insurance services—and these can be applied to people as easily as they can be applied to physical inventory or slots. Like a Hollywood studio, the inventory exchange operator defines and organizes project spaces, gathering resources to fulfill particular goals. Like a studio's movie projects, some inventory exchanges terminate at a set point and, with luck, continue to repay their investment after that point.

The broad significance of inventory exchange as a type of business-to-business ecommerce application is it brings market mechanisms into the foreground of systems planning. Most current business-to-business applications are built to service dedicated relationships between two parties. Typically, a supplier enacts a facility that a group of his clients can use, as Mobil did with its lubricants solution. As the number of such facilities grows, so the complexity at the client end increases. On the surface, this is not a problem. Just as a consumer can choose from any number of online retailers, so a business can navigate to its partners. The difference is, in the business-to-business domain, the relationships are privileged. While a consumer may use a robot at a portal site to indulge in a little comparison shopping, such a robot deployed in the business-to-business space will merely bump its nose on a lot of closed doors. Terms of supply and payment, and their technical implementation, will remain hidden to the general searcher.

The inventory exchange approach could melt this rigid situation. No conceptual reason exists why a company should not direct its mainstream inputs and outputs to a suitably credible exchange. An energy company, for example, could sell all its capacity in this way. Smart companies might operate a dual-channel policy, buying and selling as a branded entity with some partners and as an anonymous player on the exchange.

As we saw in the business-to-consumer domain, auctions and exchanges create a means of rapidly establishing values for all kinds of things, including items as slippery as the bankability of a movie star. Applying the same principles and technology in the business-to-business domain will bring the fluidity of the established commodity exchanges to all areas of business. The proliferation of inventory exchange applications will force the commoditization of an increasing range of goods and services, and redefine the competitive climate within many industries.

Real-Time Collaboration and Real-World Change

The business-to-business application types we have looked at so far and the future paths we have outlined for them, trace a steady increase in the level of intercompany intimacy associated with ecommerce practices. Attacking procurement with an ecommerce mindset enables a company to improve internal processes, to trade electronically with its suppliers, and, ultimately, to combine with other buyers. Inventory exchange enables companies to train external market mechanisms on their internal demand/supply discrepancies and, thereby, cooperate with a wider range of partner companies than before. How intimate can business-to-business ecommerce relationships become? And how do loyalty—and promiscuity—pan out in a world of heightened electronic business interaction?

As we saw in Chapter 2, status inquiries promote the principle of partner inclusion: collaborating organizations peer into each other's operational systems to check the progress of items in which they have a common interest. This type of collaboration is the basis of the category of applications in this section and the harbinger of a new era of business practice.

We can use an innovative service of telecommunications provider Teligent[19] as a starting point for this trail. Teligent is a competitive local exchange carrier (CLEC), competing to provide services to business customers in 34 U.S. states. The company builds microwave networks to act as the local connection to its customers, who are based in metropolitan areas. A receiver located in a customer building relays calls to handsets and also communicates with other Teligent network nodes. The company connects to the long-distance network as a reseller. Teligent's relevance to our story is its e-magine service, launched in early 1999. E-magine enables customers to query their bills online, to download the data used to calculate the bill, and to pay online. Most important, the billing data is real-time.

Presenting invoices for payment via the Web is becoming an option for customers of many services. But the chief beneficiary of this practice is the service provider. She saves on invoice printing and

---

19. www.teligent.com

dispatch, and can track when customers check their bills. From the point-of-view of the customer, the Web invoice is little improvement on the traditional format. He may need to print the invoice, so it can be routed for payment within the organization. If he wants to analyze an itemized bill, then he needs to find some way of stripping the data from the HTML page and importing it to a spreadsheet or other analysis tool.

Teligent's service shows a finer understanding of its business customers' motivations. Some may want to pay their bills electronically, in which case the bundled payment mechanism is a distinct benefit. The capability to download raw usage data shows consideration for users' priorities: Businesses don't just want to pay their bills, they want to know how the charges are being generated. Access to real-time data is the clearest indicator that Teligent recognizes the dynamic nature of the telco-customer relationship. In this highly competitive environment, the telecommunications partner needs to position itself as a business ally, rather than a source of some commodity.

A monthly bill may give some clues as to a company's phone use, but it may raise alarms long after action can be taken. With access to a real-time analysis capability, Teligent's customers can monitor call patterns as they develop. Some may want to build monitoring systems that feed on the billing information and take, as it were, evasive action—implementing a call-bar, issuing an email reminding a user of call length policies for international calls, even switching calls through an alternative service provider.

A frankness occurs in this relationship that suggests this level of intimacy could be usefully applied elsewhere. In one sense, the telco is merely echoing the customer's call behavior back to her, so it could be argued no novel information relationship is involved here. According to this argument, the customer is outsourcing the task of call monitoring, which she might choose otherwise to implement in a local exchange. But whether you regard the customer as accessing privileged information from the telco or as outsourcing the monitoring function, both amount to the same thing: the two parties are collaborating around the optimization of the customer's use of telecommunications facilities. The customer is seeking to save money on the service, while the telco is seeking to attract and retain the customer. This is a refined form of ecommerce that is light years away from the common conception of ecommerce as another name for retailing to consumers over the Web.

Real-time collaboration can also apply to groups of players, particularly virtual organizations. Companies that team up together to undertake complex construction projects are prime examples, as are those dedicated to staging a major event. The common factor is the role of feedback mechanisms in determining corrective behavior. So, for example, a building project management company monitors the types, costs, and locations of different building materials across a range of potential suppliers, making orders as the market changes but, potentially, also changing the materials requirements of the building.

Traditionally, the larger and more complex a project is, the harder it is to change the project in mid-flight. Each commitment to action reduces the options available for the next step, with architectural decisions precluding entire classes of potential solutions. This effect is understandable in physical construction projects, but it applies equally in business projects. Few complex, multiparty business projects retain any flexibility after the initial scoping phase. Inevitably, when the partners disengage to go about their allotted tasks, realigning them according to a new strategy becomes hard. Put simply, multiparty organizations find adapting to change difficult. The key to vitalizing such organizations is not to pour on the balm of "better communications"—a mantra universally used whenever virtual organizations or consortia succumb to rigidity. The solution lies in real-time information relationships: systems speaking with systems and negotiating agreements with each other.

Take a scenario where one company hires another to carry out building maintenance for it. The service company contracts to look after the cleaning, heating, lighting, and decoration of every room the client company uses, on a per-room rate. The rooms could be in any building. In this case, the service company's systems could collaborate with the client company's systems to determine optimum use for the rooms. The service company could rearrange meetings or decant meetings of small groups into smaller rooms, creating space in its schedule for maintenance. The service company could even shift entire teams temporarily into other serviced buildings, just as medieval courts moved from castle to castle to allow each residence to be cleaned in turn. At the same time, the client company could be trading room slots with other companies. This might require the service company to create an instant affiliation with a similar service provider in the foreign city to carry out its obligations and bill its per-room fee. At the same time, it might find itself cleaning up after visiting delegations and negotiating compensation with the company who booked the slot.

Of course, this is crazily complicated, even before we start to examine some of the wrinkles. But for communicating systems, these kinds of interaction are simple. And if it becomes simple to create real-time collaborating business systems, then businesses will be able to implement this kind of complex intercompany behavior. The speed with which companies embrace the real-time mode depends crucially on their capability to see themselves as already being in real-time businesses.

One company that recognized the central role of real-time response in its success is Cemex,[20] the number three cement producer in the world. Cemex is based in Mexico and the combination of product and home market conditions make it an apparently unlikely source of business-to-business ecommerce leadership. Yet Cemex is an object lesson in applying innovative business thinking in the Internet age.

In the first place, Cemex realized that while delivery timing is crucial to its business, changing requirements and logistical problems will frustrate any over-designed delivery method. Concrete is mixed en route to construction sites because only a short window exists within which it is usable. Get the timing wrong and the load must be written off. Rather than struggle with this dilemma, Cemex moved to an operational model that, essentially, puts cement in perpetual motion. Cemex trucks are constantly on the road, being directed to customer sites by phone and reporting their own positions back to base via automatic satellite positioning systems. It's as if the company's product is patrolling the territory: cement has become a

20. www.cemex.com

service. Cemex now guarantees delivery within 20 minutes of the agreed time.

To facilitate this change, Cemex adopted technology enthusiastically. Hand-in-hand with the real-time operational revolution, the company invested in systems to make real-time data available to its managers. The principle has been extended steadily to Cemex's partners so, from mid-1999, all its clients, distributors, and suppliers will be connected in real-time. Clients will be able to view the disposition of Cemex's trucks and plan their own requirements accordingly. Cemex will be able to view a client's payment status in real-time and monitor deliveries made by distributors. Online sales will be added in the year 2000.

The Cemex case is a remarkable story of a company transforming itself from a commodity supplier into the hub of a global, collaborative, construction enterprise. All the contributing parties gain in its business-to-business ecommerce strategy and competitors are left scrambling to catch up. Cemex is building loyalty via intimacy. As other companies catch up, then collaborating parties can be more promiscuous, switching between partners. This level of flexibility will only arrive with standards, though. Just as we saw in the ecommerce procurement area, companies that pioneer standards—particularly data format standards—stand to gain as the marketplace grows.

A Checklist for Moving Into Real-Time

1. How are the time dependencies in our business masked by existing processes?
   —by artificial reporting cycles?
   —by poor workflow?
   —by prevailing service standards?

2. What variables can we expose to our partners?

3. What variables in our environment affect our behavior?

4. How can we reorganize to react to real-time signals?

5. What extra services can we wrap around a real-time collaborative relationship?

4 The Technology Landscape

This chapter is necessarily selective. As we have seen, ecommerce has a potential breadth of application that potentially allows any and every technology to be recruited to its ends. Attempting to survey the whole technology field in a book like this would be neither practical nor illuminating. We have, therefore, scoped this account using two principles that should hold true for the majority of managers working in ecommerce related projects over the next few years:

- Ecommerce applications will continue to exploit Internet technologies and their spin-offs.

- Ecommerce applications will be architected to migrate easily to alternative technology layers, especially new network and client application options.

The primary boundary for this chapter is, therefore, based on Internet technologies. The formal architectural considerations associated with defining and implementing technology layers are discussed in Chapter 5. This chapter outlines some of the technology types that play layer roles.

The other drivers for inclusion in the survey are derived from the commercial and management concerns peculiar to ecommerce: security and payment. We also tried to focus on mainstream technologies and standards, and to guess intelligently at those technologies and standards that will become mainstream in the next few years. This survey looks out to around the year 2003. Technological and commercial events in the intervening period will, doubtless, modify or replace some of the technologies highlighted here, but we believe the focus of the discussion will remain broadly correct.

This chapter is divided into six main sections. "Data on the Web: From Publishing to Processing" deals with how data is represented on the Web and explains how the addition of semantic information to the Web is an important step toward the realization of credible and robust ecommerce channels. "Moving Data and Dynamic Networks" looks at how data moves around networks, while "Implementing Security" examines techniques and strategies for providing security in the ecommerce setting.

"Network Options" outlines a range of network technologies in the fixed and wireless spheres that promise to improve both ubiquity and service levels for ecommerce channels. "Payment Solutions" summarizes the main payment mechanism types available to ecommerce players and "Ecommerce Standards" explores several ecommerce technology standards proposed as frameworks for building interoperable ecommerce systems.

DATA ON THE WEB: FROM PUBLISHING TO PROCESSING

The Web is generally perceived as a static medium: a kind of gigantic magazine, with some neat navigation methods. Interactivity is fairly low and most users experience the Web as a passive experience. Bending the Web away from its surfing associations and investing it with an active, responsive character are key to the success of ecommerce in the mass market setting. In the business-to-business ecommerce world, the Web is a handy way of displaying information, but a poor way of connecting business systems.

Despite its appearance as a sophisticated, interlinked magic lantern show, the Web is a computing medium. This section looks behind the user experience to find the data that creates it. If we can locate and understand the role of data in the Web medium, then we can begin to see the Web as a medium for transacting business. Once we have an understanding of the data issue, we are then in a better position to imagine ecommerce floating free of its current confinement in a publishing-oriented system.

HTML and Adornments

Our tour of ecommerce technologies starts on the surface—with HTML, the language of Web pages. HTML is a scheme for embedding instructions about how text should be rendered within the text itself. Although a Web browser appears to present a prebuilt page, it actually builds that representation by first processing the document that represents the page for information about style and formatting, and then uses this information to render the document within the Web browser. Every HTML page contains hidden instructions called *tags,* which the browser interprets. A tag may indicate a particular word should be in boldface, for example. In the HTML text, the word to be emboldened is preceded by a <b> tag and followed by a matching </b> tag. The browser software switches to boldface font when it reaches <b> and switches back when it reaches </b>. Any text in the document encased in angle brackets is not part of the content of the document but, instead, it represents an instruction to the browser about representing content. These tags are known as *markup*— the M in HTML—and are not seen by the end user.

HTML is a simple in-line means of causing pages to be rendered on a client device. As well as adding styling to text, HTML can cause images to be included in the rendered page. Most important, HTML can be used to create hyperlinks within documents. Although hyperlinks enable the user to move around efficiently within a page via anchors or to move to another page of content anywhere on the Web, they do not make HTML a programming language. You cannot, for example, write conditional routines within HTML. And, although you can use HTML to implement forms that take input from the user, you cannot handle this incoming data using HTML itself.

HTML acts purely in the presentation layer of Web-based systems. That is, HTML is responsible for conveying the visual structure and styling of a document, and for enabling navigation to other resources. Although this sounds like a minor accomplishment, it has had a profound effect on systems development. The practical outcome of the "operating system wars" of the early 1990s for software developers was a dilemma about which proprietary system they should target. Systems designed for the maximum possible user base had to be developed in parallel versions that ran on the competing operating systems. HTML doesn't wipe away this entire problem, but at least it removes some presentation burdens from a large number of systems. Systems that deal primarily with data presentation, particularly documentation systems, immediately benefit from using a presentation medium that can run on any platform. Wherever a Web browser can be persuaded to run, HTML can be viewed.

Special HTML tags enable the document author to include various kinds of content other than text. Graphics in gif or jpeg format are the most obvious adornments. Animated features can be added using animated gifs, plug-in devices like Macromedia Flash, or simple Java applets. Sound can also be added to the document experience, as well as full-motion video.

Each of these additions increases the complexity of the document being processed by the browser software, however. Features like Flash require a plug-in to be installed in browsers prior to generation 4.0, many of which are still being used. Plug-ins are client-specific, meaning a different version must be discovered, downloaded, and installed, depending on which platform the user has. Any content provider using plug-ins has to assume the plug-in is available for the platforms used by the bulk of its intended audience. This is a major step away from the platform independence of HTML. The leading information-oriented sites have tended to reduce their use of nonbasic content types, so a site like Yahoo! appears quite stark.

For applications that entail publication of electronic documents faithful to an original, Adobe's PDF format is the most-often used solution. PDF documents represent colors and spacing with a high degree of accuracy and have been accepted as true document representations in legal proceedings. The files are created with Adobe's Acrobat software. They can be read by any user with the Acrobat reader utility, which is probably one of the most widely installed pieces of "helper" software. The standard Acrobat reader runs outside the browser environment.

These are the basic presentation technologies that today's page designer has in her toolkit. Design tools like Macromedia's Dreamweaver 2 enable designers to layout competent pages without learning HTML.

Scripting for Web Page Behavior

The first step in making Web pages truly active is scripting. Simple languages, such as JavaScript, can be used to add programming behavior to HTML pages by embedding pieces of code within the page. These embedded scripts are interpreted by the browser and executed, rather than being parsed as styling information.

JavaScript is not the same as Java, and the similarity in the names has led to much confusion in the gray area where new media and systems development companies overlap. Java, as we shall see, is a fully fledged programming language, which can be used to build any kind of computer system, large or small. Java's early association with Web pages now looks like an accident of history, especially now that the Web is an integral part of the mainstream systems development world. *JavaScript,* on the other hand, is a general purpose scripting language that can be embedded in Web pages, where it is typically used to enable user interaction in the Web browser.

JavaScript can be used to add bells and whistles to Web pages, in the form of moving text or buttons that change when the mouse rolls over them. One of JavaScript's more useful business applications is in field validation.

When a user fills in an HTML form, the contents of each field are sent to a backend process. Neither HTML nor the HTTP protocol concern themselves with the makeup of the field contents. The program that handles the incoming data first must check if it has received input with which it can deal. If the data received is not in the correct format, then it must return an error message for display in the user's Web browser and ask him to go back and resubmit the form. This adds a further set of transactions that slows the overall process of satisfying the user's needs.

As a more efficient alternative, JavaScript code that checks the input values can be embedded in the form and executed by the browser. For example, if we wish to ensure a user inputs his email address, we can check that the input value contains at least a @ character and one dot. Our backend application may go on to perform a more rigorous check on the email address, such as sending it some test mail. In this case, the field level validation will catch basic errors of input and require the user to rekey the field before the page's data is sent.

JavaScript, and its Microsoft variant JScript, are supported by most browsers, but with inconsistencies. JavaScript was originally introduced by Netscape and was, for a time, a distinguishing feature in the browser wars. The inconsistencies between implementations arose from independent development by teams at Netscape and Microsoft. Because neither had direct sight of the other's implementation, they naturally tended to diverge. Once out in the marketplace, these different feature sets can start to converge again as each team tries to make its browser "more compatible" than the other. This has also affected the development of style sheets for defining Web page layouts.[1] JavaScript has been standardized in the form of ECMAScript,[2] however, and the World Wide Web Consortium is trying to standardize a Document Object Model for browsers.[3] The main browser manufacturers are expected to adopt these standards as they continue to enhance their products.

Many Web site designers build pages for the latest browser generation and it is broadly true that whatever type of HTML extension is being used, later browsers support it better. Not all users upgrade their browsers as frequently as people in the programming and design

---

1. The table at http://webreview.com/wr/pub/guides/style/mastergrid.html compares different implementations of style sheets by different browsers and gives some flavor of the pitfalls lying in wait for the developer who strays beyond basic HTML.

2. See http://www.ecma.ch/stand/ecma-262.htm

3. See http://www.w3.org/DOM/

industries tend to do, though. A huge installed base of Internet Explorer 3.01 browsers still exists, the generation that coincided with the adoption of intranets in many corporations and the establishment of the free browser principle. Designers who depart from standard HTML risk losing portions of their potential audience, and exhortations to "download the latest browser now!" tend not to win many friends.

Designers can get around the problem of inconsistency in handling scripts and, indeed, in laying out page elements, by including different routines for different browsers within the same page. An initial call to determine the browser being used to display the page controls which scripts are run in this execution of the page. This technique is sometimes called *content negotiation* because the content of the delivered page is controlled by a recognition process. Strictly speaking, content negotiation refers to the sending of content based on the HTTP headers received by the Web server. Content negotiation more loosely refers to strategies for displaying content relevant to a particular user or group of users and is initiated by more explicit means. For example, a site may register a user's preference for language, and then subsequently display pages composed in that language.

Server-Side Functionality

So far in this discussion, we have concentrated on the client side of the Web. But Web pages come from somewhere and, as we saw when we looked at using scripting for field validation, POSTed form contents go somewhere. This "somewhere" is the server. The server is where serious computing is carried out in ecommerce applications. The server is where content originates and it is the home of business systems.

The easiest way to start exploiting the power of the server is Common Gateway Interface (CGI). *CGI* is a protocol for taking data from Web forms and processing it. CGI is the simplest extension to a Web server, allowing HTML code to be generated on the fly and returned to the client. With CGI, any programming language can be used to process data coming from the standard input and send results to standard output. The most common language used with CGI is Practical Extraction and Report Language (Perl), although practically any programming language may be used. Perl has become the most popular language for CGI applications, largely due to the ease and speed with which new Perl scripts can be developed. Perl's text processing capabilities also make it eminently suited to the generation of HTML pages.

CGI programs simply parse an incoming stream of data into its name and value pairs, and then based on that data, generate a stream of HTML. In the interim, the CGI program can perform any server process it requires, including database access. For example, a simple catalog shopping application could use CGI to collect checkmarks entered against listed items, use the associated product code as a key for querying the sales system, and compose a page listing the availability and pricing of the items.

CGI is a simple scheme that brings backend processing power to the Web, but it is limited by its simplicity. CGI routines only persist for a single transaction. This means, in our catalog example, every time a user wants to order a set of items, the backend routine starts a database session, runs a query, closes the database, and outputs a page. For repeated uses, this is clearly inefficient.

More robust and scalable server-side solutions have, therefore, arisen to improve on CGI's performance. Microsoft's solution is Active Server Pages (ASP). ASP pages are HTML documents that contain code to be run at the server. Although it was designed to work natively with Microsoft's IIS Web server, third-party products now enable other Web servers to process ASP. On the Java side of the street, servlets act as server-side objects that cooperate with a Web server to get work done. *Servlets* are Java components installed on the server, which can be called from HTML pages. Servlets often act as gateways to more extensive server-side functionality, particularly business system functions that have been given a Java coating.

Java and Objects

The introduction of Java has been arguably the most successful launch of a programming language to date. Java was marketed heavily at the developer community, and it acquired much of the cachet of the Web as a "cool" technology. Sun Microsystems, its begetters, fueled the messianic flavor of Java with its dedicated evangelists and massive annual JavaOne conference. By the time of its official fourth birthday in June 1999, Java was variously understood as a "simple" programming language, a means of producing animations on Web pages, and sometimes the entire future of IT. There is also a vague feeling around that Java is the technology counterpart to ecommerce—some kind of magic wand that produces profits out of the Web.

For all its perceived coolness, Java is a serious, extensive, object-oriented programming language, which is not readily accessible to the beginning programmer. Many Java tutorial books take the would-be programmer through the famous HelloWorld applet and enable her to achieve some interesting effects in Web pages. But the concepts and applications of object technology, which lie at the heart of Java's significance, are usually covered in a few pages about software reuse. The myth that Java expertise is somehow easy to acquire and apply derives from the fact that, in comparison to C++, Java has fewer traps for the unwary, especially in memory management.

Object technology (or object orientation [OO]) is a wide subject and implying it didn't exist before Java would be wrong. For our purposes here, however, it is worth understanding that object technology helps to split systems up into cooperating collections of modules, which may be located anywhere on a network. An *object* is a package of data and function that does some coherent job, and one or many objects may be collected into a component. An object can offer services to other objects or it can be the subject of operations by objects. So, for example, we might have a customer object that contains data about the customer's financial history, together with a function that produces a credit score for the customer. This object could be passed to an object that makes loan decisions. In this scenario, the customer object has no knowledge of the criteria required for obtaining a loan and the lender object has no knowledge of the customer's personal details. The objects communicate through strictly defined interfaces and cannot directly inspect each other's contents.

The encapsulation of data and function (or state and behavior) behind object interfaces is the key to object technology's association with software reuse. The theory of software reuse is systems should ideally be composed from prebuilt parts that have tried and tested functions. Building systems entirely from components is still some way off, though Java has helped by becoming established as the most commonly discussed object-oriented language. The Common Object Request Broker Architecture (CORBA) movement is another influence in the realization of reusability.

In the ecommerce context, the value of object technology lies less in the ability to reuse pieces of functionality, but in the ability to *replace* them. So, if our lender object proves inefficient, we can replace it with another implementation that adheres to the interface we have established for it. In other words, as long as the new lender object recognizes the same requests and replies with the same kind of answers, it can slot into our distributed system without any other changes being required to other objects. We can even build a small object that communicates with a large legacy system that processes loan requests, acting as a wrapper to the legacy system. CORBA is a standardized technology for wrapping objects on different platforms and is discussed further in Chapter 5.

Some technologists argue whether Java is a language or a platform, but this is largely a theological question. This question arises because Java is primarily a two-step language, where responsibility for the program's compilation and execution is distributed. Java source statements are converted into a kind of base currency, known as *Java bytecode.* Java bytecode is interpreted by a piece of software called a Java Virtual Machine (JVM). As the name suggests, a *JVM* is a notional computer that runs Java bytecode. JVMs are created to run on particular platforms, but they can all read Java bytecode. This is the basis of Java's "write once, run anywhere" promise.[4]

The bytecode-JVM strategy suggests Java is not simply a means of describing instructions to a computer, but also a restatement of responsibilities at the execution platform. With JVMs available for every conceivable hardware platform and operating system, and with versions of the core Java language available for devices as small as

---

4. Java can also be compiled to machine code for a specific platform.

smart cards, Java can be thought of as an entire implementation environment. Whether a developer chooses to think in this way is largely a matter of inclination.

Outside the developer community, some of the lingering confusion about Java's role is undoubtedly due to its early success in the Web page context. Originally developed as a platform-independent language for networks of heterogeneous devices, Java was repurposed as a Web tool that would bring real computing functionality within HTML pages. The Java applet is, therefore, the best known use of Java.

An *applet* is, as the name suggests, a little application. An applet is a set of Java classes that can only be run within some larger, more complex environment—an *applet runner* such as a Java-enabled Web browser. In this case, the applet is downloaded alongside the HTML page that refers to it. It then resides temporarily on the client machine, where it is kept in the JVM's "sandbox." This means the applet cannot by default gain access to any machine resources. The applet may run an animation or take input from the user and process it. As a way of implementing limited client-side functionality, such as calculators and graphing tools, Java applets are a useful feature. A level of interactivity can be provided that does not require repeated calls to the server. An applet can also communicate with the host from which it was downloaded, giving it (but not necessarily the user) access to backend resources. Amendments to Java's security scheme allow trusted applets to access client resources—to play outside the sandbox.[5]

Java's association with ecommerce is mostly a matter of coincidence. Each term is associated with the excitement of the Internet, but one tends to belong to technologists and the other to nontechnologists. While some business people mistakenly assume ecommerce equates to Java, some technologists believe Java equates to ecommerce.

From the business-decision maker's point of view, Java is significant for a number of reasons. First, it enables the creation of distributed, object-oriented systems, which, in turn, supports the need for dynamic collections of business services and partners. Second, it encourages the openness of systems, that is, the capability to run any

5. ActiveX components play a similar role to applets in Web pages. ActiveX is a Microsoft technology.

software on any platform and to make subsequent changes to the software without requiring proprietary skills. Third, and perhaps most important, commitment to Java has become a badge of merit among software development organizations. This doesn't mean "and it's in Java" is a generic seal of approval for a software component, but this does mean it should be easier to replace that piece of functionality if it underperforms or if a more suitable solution becomes available.

For the technologist, I believe Java is the inevitable mainstream language for business systems that need to be distributed and object oriented. For this reason, Java must be a central part of any developer's strategy if she wants to play in ecommerce. This is not strictly a requirement for ecommerce, but XML, today's other hot technology, definitely is a core ecommerce technology.

XML and the Retention of Meaning

HTML has become the de facto common language of our technology age but, as we have seen, it is merely a means of describing Web pages to Web browsers. HTML is itself based on Standard Generalized Markup Language (SGML). *SGML* is a way of describing the treatment of any kind of document in a processing system. A classic use of SGML would be for preparing the text of a dictionary, where different fonts, weights, and markings are used to denote foreign language words, derivatives, and pronunciations. Strictly speaking, HTML is a specialization of SGML, formalized within a Document Type Definition (DTD). The creators of HTML started with SGML as the best basis for creating their scheme, inheriting generic features such as its parents' angle brackets for enclosing tags to ensure HTML documents can be read by any text processing system, but adding new features, such as the capability to indicate hyperlinks. HTML can be thought of as a species of SGML: an adaptation that has split off from the parent language and that now follows its own evolutionary path.

HTML's heritage is important because the rapid rise of the Web as a means of doing business has made HTML one of the most significant forms of expression and presentation yet devised. HTML is being bent, stretched, and probed to force it to behave as a medium for exchanging business information, even though its strengths are in rendering and linking documents competently, regardless of client platform. HTML has been the Web's apparent building material for most of its first five years in the public eye, but it is not adaptable enough to serve adequately all the requirements ecommerce now places on the Web. XML—a simplified version of SGML—will be its successor.

Consider the situation where a buyer wishes to monitor the price of a particular item. The supplier publishes a catalog to the Web. The pages of the catalog are, of course, in HTML, but they have been automatically generated on the fly by querying a database. In effect, the supplier's product information has been selected, ordered, and flattened into a presentational structure, and then decorated with HTML tags to make it renderable on a Web browser. The monitoring buyer can access that Web page, and then cut and paste the relevant price information, perhaps dumping it into a spreadsheet, which is itself uploaded into a corporate market intelligence system.

The buyer's information gathering process can be improved by further automation. By examining the structure of the target HTML document, he can write code that parses the document to extract the relevant items and then write these to a file. This strategy is sometimes called *Web scraping* because it enables the user to remove only what he wants from a Web page and insert it in another system, rather than displaying the entire resource on a Web browser.

We have, therefore, gone through a number of intermediate steps to transfer a business data item from one party to another. The item has been pulled from a database, wrapped in HTML, sent over the Internet, scraped from its HTML backing, and pushed into another database. Although this works, some problems occur with it.

The buyer who is using the Web page as a data source has to trust the source document will not change its structure. His ability to locate the relevant data item in the page will rely on some combination of its positioning and styling, and, possibly, on a subsequent check on its data type. So, when analyzing the catalog page that contains the price, he may have noted all the information is presented in a table, the price information is in the third column, and the product of interest in the tenth row. His scraping program then peers through the incoming document, counting instances of <tr> and <td> tags, which indicate the presence of table rows and table data, and extracts the string it finds at the relevant place. Clearly, all the supplier must do is to introduce a new product at the top of the list and the wrong item price will be extracted. The buyer's scraping program is blind to the semantics of the data contained in the HTML document—and HTML is, likewise, blind to the meaning of the strings embraced by its tags.

Unless the buyer and supplier can agree on a page composition they will adhere to or a process whereby the supplier can inform the buyer of changes, the two parties' systems will soon be out of step. If the situation exists where the partners can agree on such a relationship, then they should, in any case, probably abandon the Web as a method of data exchange. Wrapping and scraping data from HTML pages makes little sense if the business relationship is close enough to allow the buyer to "slurp" directly on the supplier's data. Presumably, the pricing data is made available publicly on the Web because the supplier wants it to be available to a multitude of buyers, each of whom may have different preferences for its layout.

HTML is adding little business value in this scenario. It is simply the most readily available vehicle for transporting character data around the Web. XML can also be rendered by Web browsers, but unlike HTML, XML can be made to represent and preserve any type of coherent knowledge structure. So while HTML is limited to describing the layout, styling, and linkage of documents, XML can also take a view on what the elements of a document *mean*. Of course, no piece of data means anything without a defining context, so XML provides that, too.

XML stands for eXtensible Markup Language, but thinking of the X as standing for *anything* is helpful. *XML* is a purer descendant of SGML, in that XML documents are associated with their own specially designed information contexts. We can then define our own document tags, which have meanings within that context. While the HTML tag <b> is silently understood to refer to the meaning "render the following text in bold weight," we can define XML tags whose meaning can be looked up in a explicit dictionary. For example, we could define an XML tag <customer> and define it within a related DTD as a piece of character data of a certain maximum length. We can even define XML elements that contain other XML elements; so our <customer> could contain an <address> with its own definition in the DTD. Elements can also contain attributes, so we could define "name" as an attribute of <customer>.

When an XML-equipped browser meets an XML document, it can use the associated DTD and a style sheet to render the document as HTML. So, our browser might choose to replace XML

```
<customer>
    <name>Paul May</name>
    <contact>555-1000</contact>
</customer>
```

with HTML

```
<b>Customer<b>:<tt>Paul May, 555-1000</tt><p>
```

We could attach any styling scheme we like, effectively removing the document designer's sole control over the rendering of the document. But the principal power of XML is it enables us to process documents as data sources without rendering them at all. The client program can parse the XML document for <name> tags and fire their contents into the associated records in a customer database. We no longer need to concern ourselves with the positioning of content, the number of items of a particular type contained in a document, or their data types. In fact, the capability to relay and inspect DTDs makes human interaction at the time of transaction superfluous. Most XML documents will not see the light of day.

XML brings semantics to the Web and is rapidly being embraced as a superior substrate for ecommerce interactions on the Web. Perhaps its deepest significance is that a DTD can be used to define a data standard for an entire industry or class of applications. A DTD can act as a means of expressing and enabling any preexisting data model, as well as a vehicle for novel structures. EDI standards, for example, can be drafted into DTD format, allowing existing EDI systems to transact via the Web. DTDs themselves look superficially like comment entries in an HTML document and are quite accessible to human readers and writers.

Of course, if everyone involved in ecommerce chooses to define their own DTD, then we merely have a more sophisticated version of the semantic challenge currently posed by the use of HTML. Rather than seeking to interpret documents stripped of their semantics for the sake of convenient rendering, we will negotiate among different competing dictionaries, each proposing a standard solution to the domain. Whose dictionary will we choose to use when implementing an ecommerce system? How any one model of a domain could be superior to another is hard to see, assuming basic competence in data analysis on the part of its designers. Who is to say, for example, that specifying 32 characters for a name is any more correct or useful than specifying the same item in 30 characters? More important, who is to decide on the structure of an order, a receipt, or a credit note?

Without intrinsic differentiators among the competing ecommerce DTDs, the winners that emerge likely will do so via ancillary services and market share. Currently,[6] Microsoft's BizTalk is being promoted as an XML standard for ecommerce, but then so is Hewlett-Packard's Fremont initiative. Meanwhile, consortia such as CommerceNet and Rosetta Net are evolving their own standards and, in some cases, porting earlier standards definitions into XML. So far, little evidence exists to suggest any contender is any more true-to-life as a universal ecommerce standard than the others. Each is likely to gain strength, not through partner endorsement, but through signed-up customers—and these may need to be acquired with free products or services. In any case, while vendors like Microsoft and Hewlett-Packard have an interest in the overall growth of the ecommerce pie, they have a much more acute interest in their control of a portion of the pie. Industry experience suggests every "once and forever" standard exists in proliferating versions: it has happened with UNIX, and, to a lesser extent, with Java. Decision makers can be reassured,

---

6. May 1999.

however, that whatever standard does emerge as the leader in this field, it will be a competent standard. XML is an open and legible technology, and it is hard to introduce willful obscurity. Whichever standard wins, it is likely to do so to the benefit of the whole ecommerce community.

MOVING DATA AND DYNAMIC NETWORKS

The capability to move data around networks efficiently is at the heart of the Internet's domination of contemporary systems development. This section briefly surveys the basic protocols of the Internet. It also introduces Sun's Jini initiative as an example of how networks are evolving beyond the role of passive carriers of data and acquiring the capability to grow in scale and scope in line with demand.

The Basic Protocols

HyperText Transmission Protocol (HTTP) is the means whereby HTML resources are fetched across network connections. At its simplest, a link to a resource is translated into the HTTP message GET URL, where URL is the address of the required resource. The message is sent over a TCP connection, which, by default, is port 80. A client may also send a POST or GET message, which allows data to be appended to message; this is how HTML forms are implemented.

The Internet Protocol (IP) is the workhorse protocol of the contemporary network, slavishly toting data of all kinds across public and private networks the world over. In use for more than 20 years, IP is a packet-forwarding protocol. An IP packet is a *datagram,* that is, a collection of data accompanied by some addressing data. The IP packet header contains 32-bit addresses that identify the sending and receiving hosts, and the protocol performs a checksum calculation on the headers to ensure their integrity before transporting them onward. IP can split and reassemble packets automatically to squeeze large messages through narrow pathways. In addition, every IP packet has a number of "lives" that it can spend one-by-one at the routers it passes through. When a packet runs out of lives, it is discarded, ensuring networks do not become choked with packets that cannot find their destination.

Carrying voice traffic over IP networks is attractive for users wishing to avoid long distance and international call charges, though call quality is not as good as with traditional methods. Traditional phone connections create a dedicated channel between the users. The full bandwidth is rarely used during a conversation, yet it is reserved for the duration of the call. By splitting voice traffic into packets, more efficient use can be made of the network, with voice calls sharing capacity with other types of traffic.

The Jini Initiative

As we noted, Sun's Java language was originally developed for use in networked devices, rather than for Web pages. The Jini initiative brings Java home. *Jini* is an architecture that enables all kinds of devices to collaborate, whether they are desktop computers, mobile phones, Personal Digital Assistants (PDAs), or any kind of dedicated appliance. Jini is a federated operating system, where Java virtual machines communicate with each other to achieve useful functions.

Jini also supplies so-called *JavaTones,* the network equivalent of the telephone's dial tone. Just as the dial tone signals network availability to any device that can be attached to the phone network, so Jini extends a welcome to any compliant device that attaches to the network. A Jini network is, therefore, a device-aware system, recognizing and enabling resources as they announce themselves. So attaching a new disk resource to the network, for example, simply entails making the physical connection; thereafter, the device cooperates with its environment in a dynamic extension of the whole system's capabilities.

Jini is, therefore, a way of enabling impromptu systems. Most of the visions and scenarios published around the Jini topic relate to the value of impromptu systems in the workplace and in the consumer home environment. Jini also has a significant role to play in the development of ecommerce, but to understand why, we need to know a little about how it works.

Jini incorporates lookup services, which allow resources to discover one other, and to gain access to each other's interfaces. For example, a digital camera joins the community by registering its services and interfaces with the lookup service, effectively announcing its availability as an image-capture device and declaring the terms under which it is open for business. The digital camera now has a lease with the lookup service, which it must occasionally renew. If the device fails to renew its lease, then it is no longer part of the community. Devices that break down or are physically detached from the network will obviously fail to renew their leases. The addition or removal of devices from the network has no effect on any other device because no co-dependency is built into the scheme.

Effectively, all collaborations across the network are mediated by active, cooperative calls, whereby objects respect each other's integrity and can only invoke the services exposed by an object's interface. A device uses a lookup service to find resources and then ships the required objects directly from the target resources. Objects are shipped around the Jini community using Remote Method Invocation (RMI), Java's mechanism for implementing distributed object systems. Using Jini, device drivers are not globally shared in a platform space, but encapsulated within their owning services in a truly distributed object-oriented architecture. Resources self-organize via Jini, rather than being the subjects of isolated installation procedures.

This is different from a traditional desktop environment, where the installation of supporting libraries, drivers, and helper applications is crucial to the performance of a "peripheral." In the Jini environment, center and periphery have no meaning because system responsibilities are shared across a dynamically shaped collection of resources. One of Jini's immediate benefits is its positive impact on the system's administration workload in organizations. Jini pushes the system administration task into the network itself, thereby reducing reliance on expert human intervention. Outside the corporate setting, Jini provides a means of excusing consumers from the responsibility of becoming expert network managers.

The broader implication of the Jini vision is the techno-tools of contemporary life lose their distinct visibility and merge into an

Bluetooth

Bluetooth is a specification for short-range radio communications among mobile devices. Bluetooth-enabled devices discover each other when they come within range of one another and establish a networking relationship. Bluetooth is, therefore, conceptually similar to the dynamically adaptive Jini environment. While Jini removes the need for devices to be explicitly installed on a network, Bluetooth allows devices to connect with each other in an ad hoc manner, without the need for cabling. Of course, Jini and Bluetooth are each aimed at a different level of the adaptive environment problem. Indeed, Jini can run over a Bluetooth network.

Bluetooth is more than a cable replacement option for devices in the same locale. It has integrated encryption and authentication functions, ensuring commerce transactions can be secured at the semantic level. Bluetooth also uses a transmission scheme that "hops" around a range of frequencies 1,600 times per second, making it hard for any uninvited device to log a message. The power of a Bluetooth transmission is automatically choked back to the optimum requirement for any connection, which helps to insulate transactions from external monitoring. ◼

"intelligent" environment. Printers, drives, phones, PDAs, TVs, set-top boxes—anything with what Sun eerily terms *digital heartbeat*—can be recruited as a means of communicating with a user. This effectively extends the customer engagement opportunity to any networked device. In a world immersed in self-organizing Jini communities, an ecommerce channel can follow a customer across various devices in her environment, maintaining dialogue as she shifts from cell phone to car dashboard to home TV set.

To date, most concentration in the Jini world is on devices, yet a Jini service can also be pure software. At the technical level, software services include transaction monitors. At the application level, we can imagine commerce services joining a pervasive Jini community. The most obvious are services for billing, authentication, and special offers. For example, a billing engine can be written in Java—or, if necessary, cloaked in a Java wrapper that makes it comprehensible to the Java world—and adapted for Jini by adding the appropriate "announcing" behavior to it. The billing engine can then announce its capabilities to a potentially global clientele and act as a pay-per-use service to vendors of online services. Even more striking, creating Jini services that acted as sources of finance would be possible. Government or corporate debt could be packaged in this way and "placed" on a virtual market for consumption by other software agents.

IMPLEMENTING SECURITY

Security is the issue most often cited as a barrier to ecommerce. In many people's minds, security is a binary quality: it either exists or it doesn't. But, in reality, security is concerned with the management of risk, and particularly with trade-offs between accessibility and vulnerability. This is as true in traditional settings as it is online. A physical retail store, for example, must balance easy access to the trading area with the possibility of theft. We are habituated to the many security trade-offs in our traditional business dealings, but less sure about where to locate them in the ecommerce setting.

Security in the ecommerce setting is principally concerned with protecting the privacy of transactional information and authenticating the credentials of transacting parties. This section explains how both these aims are achieved.

Cryptography Basics

Like all the topics in this chapter, cryptography is a vast field in its own right and one with a fascinating history. People have been attempting to disguise the content of messages from the prying eyes of interceptors since human conversation moved out of range of the hearth. *Cryptography* is the science of rendering communications meaningless to all but their senders and receivers.

Every cryptography system uses a specific method or algorithm for transforming messages. This could be, for example, the substitution of each letter of the alphabet by another letter, based on a resequencing of the alphabet. An interloper who captured a message that contained words written in no known human language could conclude that such a substitution had been made, but would be unable to determine the revised alphabetical sequence immediately. Of course, this is a trivial example that is easily broken. If the interloper suspects the original text was in English, he can count the most frequently occurring character and guess that character is *e,* look for repeating two-character sequences, and so on. In effect, he can deduce the key that has been used to generate the text.

We could make the interloper's task a little harder by making the substitution rule more complex and making it dependent upon a more complex key. So, for example, we could say characters should be shifted along the resequenced alphabet by varying amounts and derive the revised alphabetic sequence from the first letter appearing on the first 26 pages of this book (adding the necessary number of pages to account for duplicated letters). The key has become obscure because both sender and receiver need to know which book is being used to drive the revised alphabetic sequence, though the shifting rule is still fairly regular and open to detection. The more transformational information we can shift into the key, the better; however, the more powerful the key becomes, the more vulnerable we are to its capture by an interloper. We may even have to disguise the key itself.

Contemporary cryptographic systems enable computationally secure communications over networks, together with the secure transmission of keys. This is accomplished through the technique of public key cryptography. Using this technique, each party uses encryption software to generate a pair of keys, known as the *public and private keys.* The remarkable property of this key pair is that neither can be transformed into the other. The keys are generated by multiplying large prime numbers together. Finding the original factors of the resulting product is computationally intensive, whereas knowing one of the factors will reveal the other readily.

A user can publish her public key and then anyone wishing to send a message to that person uses the public key to encrypt it. Only she can decrypt the message, using her private key, which remains securely on her own machine. If she wants to send a secret message to another user, she can obtain his public key directly by email or from a database dedicated to holding public keys.

This description of public key cryptography is based on Pretty Good Privacy (PGP), software available in both free and commercial versions. The security software most Web users will have employed, albeit, without knowing they have, is Secure Sockets Layer (SSL). SSL was originally developed by Netscape and has been widely adopted as a means of securely transporting messages across HTTP. SSL uses port 443 and amends the URL from http:// to https://. An SSL-enabled server can use a digital certificate to authenticate a transaction, obtaining the certificate contents from the client. Credit card details, protected by SSL, form the basis of most business-to-consumer ecommerce transactions.

SET

If SSL ensures that no intercepting third party can read a message, then isn't it enough to implement ecommerce transactions? After all, the supposed public fear of using credit cards for making purchases over the Web rested on the worry that credit card details could be intercepted. And it now appears users are becoming habituated to using credit cards for Web shopping. In fact, the success of the credit card as a payment mechanism exposes its flaws as a general ecommerce mechanism. In April 1999, Visa revealed research showing that 47 percent of online transactions went unpaid, with 22 percent of that proportion failing due to fraudulent card use.[7] It seems that, if anything, trust in the efficacy of credit cards on the Web is *too* high. Both buyers and sellers are using them without considering the basic rules by which credit cards enact successful transactions: the card user is who he says he is and the card acceptor is a bona fide retailer. This situation is no different to any traditional mail-order business that takes orders over the phone. Stories abound of companies being defrauded by users buying quantities of goods with repeated uses of stolen card numbers. At the same time, many users have been burned by using their cards to buy from unknown sellers.

Secure Electronic Transaction (SET) is a payment mechanism that performs authentication of both parties to a transaction. Buyer and seller each obtain a digital certificate from a trusted certification

---

7. *IT Week*, 19 April 1999. The research covered 15 banks operating in 12 European countries.

authority. Each certificate rests in a "wallet" at the relevant machine and the credit card details contained within it can only be decrypted by the issuing card company. SET is backed by Visa and MasterCard, and was launched in 1996.

Technically, SET introduces a dynamic intermediate process into the ecommerce transaction, while adding further software installation burdens on all the participating parties. Encryption and decryption require processing power and time, and transactions involve banks and card companies, as well as the buyer and seller. In addition, users have to acquire and install certificates on their client machine, which, as well as being an administrative barrier to use, restricts their ecommerce activities to one device.

SET is a sensible solution to the authentication problem. Indeed, a correctly designed credit card payment mechanism that only uses SSL still needs to implement features of the SET architecture. A seller can eliminate fraudulent card attacks by integrating with the credit card company's systems, so card details are checked before the transaction is closed. SET's effective limitation is its lack of portability at the client end and even this could be alleviated by its encapsulation in a smart card. Smart card support is planned for version 2.0 of SET.

The current competition between SSL and SET comes down to the allocation of risk. SET makes the buyer responsible for proving his credentials whereas, with plain SSL, it is up to the seller to check the buyer's ability to pay—and to assume the credit card account being referenced belongs to the user initiating the transaction. Without SET protection, sellers are faced with users denying they have made particular transactions and cannot prove that they did so.

PKI: A Generic Solution to the Security Issue

Public Key Infrastructure (PKI) is an ecommerce architecture that combines specialist authorities, digital certificate management systems, and directory facilities to create secure networks on top of unsecured networks such as the Internet. PKI combines three aspects of security: confidentiality, authentication, and nonrepudiation. As we have seen, confidentiality is the basic property of disguising a message's contents from an unintended recipient, while authentication refers to the ability to validate the identities of the communicating parties. Nonrepudiation means completed transactions cannot legally be denied by either party. The technique of public key cryptography provides confidentiality. Authentication is supplied by digital certificates, while the PKI's management system ensures nonrepudiation.

PKI's significant addition to the techniques of public key cryptography and digital certificates is, therefore, the capability to manage reliably and credibly the distribution of keys and certificates. This is achieved using Certification Authorities (CAs) and Registration Authorities (RAs). A *CA* is a software service that creates and issues certificates to users who have been registered with the CA. Qualifying users must have been pre-approved by an *RA*. The PKI also manages the entire life cycle of a certificate, from creation and issuing to revocation and archiving.

PKI can be implemented as a standalone function within the company's systems or as a distributed function shared with an external partner such as VeriSign. VeriSign's OnSite product locates the CA within the enterprise, but links to VeriSign's secure data center for running hardware-based cryptographic routines. This implementation avoids using software-based cryptography—a potential target for attack—at the enterprise's site and adds off-site archiving into the package.

Within an organization, registration of users is reasonably straightforward. Approved users can be drawn directly from a human resources database, for example, and fed to the RA module. As soon as we reach the ecommerce world, however, we can no longer rely on such a simple source of preapproval. Industry standards for PKI are under development and, as these reach widespread adoption, barriers to interworking between PKI systems will ease. A requirement will still exist to control the admittance of users into secure systems, however, and this is where initiatives like SET score. SET is a PKI scoped to financial transactions via banking industry intermediaries. Its authorities have the credibility to assure the admittance of parties on a dynamic basis.

The preapproval role that credit card companies play in the context of SET can be generalized into that of the trusted third party (TTP). A *TTP* is essentially an RA that runs a CA on behalf of other companies. The British Post Office, for example, offers an email signature and encryption service called ViaCode, which uses PKI software from Entrust. The backing of a postal authority provides assurance that users have been adequately checked before they are registered. The British Post Office is well known for its strict approval processes, which require physical proofs of identity. Presumably the organization hopes that customers' experience of its rigor in checking identity will help its brand to stretch to ensuring electronic identities. Indeed, its certificate policy[8] includes "face to face authentication" as the starting point of every relationship.

NETWORK OPTIONS

Communications technologies continue to evolve at bewildering speed. The physical properties of cables, fibers, and radio waves are combined with innovative transmission and encoding schemes to increase network options and offer enhanced capacity, performance, and value. Our business world developed largely in a regulated environment, where service quality and reliability were won at the expense of differentiation.

The spread of telecoms deregulation throughout the 1980s and 1990s has radically changed the role of communications in computing. We now expect systems to be connected to other systems, regardless of their geographical location. We are coming to expect Internet access from the desktop, from mobile devices, and even within dedicated devices embedded within other products. Indeed, the unspoken premise of ecommerce is that we live in a world of connections.

This section outlines some of the latest network options available to ecommerce players and falls into two parts. The first part deals with

---

8. *Certificate Policy for Medium Assurance Certificates*, 1999, www.viacode.com

fixed-line connectivity. In the short-term, efficient, high-capacity access to homes and businesses is a key driver for high-volume ecommerce applications. The second part deals with emerging wireless technologies—the network options that are propelling ecommerce away from the desk and into our lifestyles.

The Last Mile

While telecommunications networks have been revolutionized by the installation of fiber-optic backbones, the "last mile" or the "local loop" has remained a bottleneck. The connection between a user's premises and the local exchange is a pair of copper wires. The cost of replacing this piece of infrastructure with a faster medium is immense. Companies laying cables for television services in virgin territories have the opportunity to start with high-bandwidth connections. Wireless operators use radio to implement the last mile. The established telecoms operators have hit back with *Digital Subscriber Line (DSL),* a means of wringing more bandwidth out of existing copper wiring.

DSL works by using a greater range of frequencies than traditional telephony. Bandwidth can be increased by enlarging the number of distinct coding elements a channel can carry. The sounds generated by a Touch-Tone phone are one example. By using a mass of frequencies for encoding data, DSL can currently achieve bandwidths up to 1.5Mbps over ordinary copper wiring. The slowest DSL connection runs at 144kbps, in comparison to the best analog modems, which run at 56kbps.

DSL achieves this radical upgrading in bandwidth by singing at frequencies above the range of human hearing. Different ways exist of encoding those frequencies, however, and this is the basis of standards divergence in the DSL field. *Asymmetric DSL (ADSL)* implements a faster channel in one direction than the other, so that, for example, Web pages are delivered from an ISP to a user via a large virtual pipe, with the user's clicks returned via a narrower path. ADSL is also popular because it minimizes a form of interference called near end crosstalk (NEXT). NEXT is a kind of crossed-line effect, whereby signals in groups of cables interfere with each other, causing degradation of the encoded data. Bundles of cables are more likely to be located at the exchange than at the user's premises, so it makes sense to bias the high bandwidth channel in the direction of the user.

Worth noting is that DSL is a dedicated link, rather than a dialed service. This means DSL is connected all the time, enabling the user to run outbound services, as well as consuming inbound ones. Any user with DSL can now run her own public Web server at minimal cost, though with some configurations of ADSL, the server gives less than stunning response times to its visitors.

DSL solutions are offered by most telecoms companies. Telecoms companies traditionally own the last mile to the customer, but cable companies can also claim that connection. Cable modems can offer bandwidths of 1.5Mbps to 3Mbps. In other words, cable modem speed starts where DSL—and the vanilla T1 service—ends. Consumer prices for DSL and cable modem services are roughly comparable at the time of writing. However, cable companies have little visibility with business customers, who are, therefore, more likely to buy DSL services from their telecoms service supplier. The merger of Comcast and MediaOne in March 1999, and the earlier purchase of TCI by AT&T, demonstrate the cable industry is very much alive to the promise of delivering digital services to consumers. Success in the mass market may well lead to greater credibility in the business arena and the sales resources to convert that credibility into relationships.

Emerging Wireless Standards

Wireless Application Protocol (WAP) was due for rollout in late 1999. WAP is aimed at conveying data between wireless devices, including mobile phones and PDAs. WAP is similar to the HTTP-plus-HTML scheme of the Web, but designed specifically for devices with limited resources and small displays. WAP is also ready for today's relatively low-bandwidth networks.

WAP's Wireless Markup Language (WML) is a stripped-down version of HTML, optimized for rendering on small displays with limited graphics capabilities. WML can be used to write "pages" that render on two-line mobile phone displays that would have no way of coping with full-blown HTML. WMLScript is a similarly lightened-up analog of JavaScript.

The WAP initiative adapts the Web idiom to the growing population of mobile devices. WML addresses the restrictions in the display component, but WAP also deals with other characteristics of wireless networks that make them inimical to standard Internet technologies. Wireless networks are inherently less robust than fixed networks and improvements in one dimension of their performance must trade off against other dimensions. For example, bandwidth to mobile devices can be increased, but only at the expense of battery life. In addition, HTTP's simplicity begins to look like rambling inefficiency when put in the context of wireless communications. As we have seen, HTTP messages are written in human-readable text, making for a system that can be implemented at the simplest possible level in a system—by a human typing in real-time at a terminal. Text is a relatively bulky quantity, poorly suited to wireless communications, where devices can fall in and out of coverage as they move or as nearby network nodes come in and out of service. WAP uses a compressed binary format that better exploits connection availability.

WAP is driven by telecoms companies including Nokia, Motorola, and Ericsson. WAP

From GSM to UMTS

The standard digital mobile phone operates on the GSM standard, which can provide data transmission at only 9.6kbps. Some U.S. GSM networks use an enhanced encoding scheme, which allows bandwidth up to 14.4kbps. By aggregating channels in a scheme known as High Speed Circuit Switched Data (HSCSD), GSM can achieve 64kbps, which is equivalent to the fixed network backbone.

General Packet Radio Service (GPRS) uses the GSM channel in a different way. Rather than maintaining a switched circuit for the duration of the connection, it combines packets of data from different calls to make optimum use of capacity. Bandwidth in the range 64kbps to 170kbps is possible with this technique, though 100kbps is the figure most often quoted.

GSM is set to evolve via Enhanced Data rate for GSM Evolution (EDGE) at 384kbps into UMTS, the third generation of cellular communications—the Universal Mobile Telecommunications System (UMTS). UMTS is designed to scale to 2Mbps, though this top rate can only be achieved in static situations. The system is likely to become available in Europe in 2003 and in the U.S. in 2005. By that timeframe, satellite systems will be providing 64Mbps downlink and 2Mbps uplink channels. ◼

represents a way of upscaling the role of the mobile phone into a true commerce device. With its bias toward short messages, WAP is useful for transactional relationships, such as purchasing and banking. WAP is also suitable for alert-type services, which could encompass anything from product price updates to customer complaints. The mobile phone has already taken its place in business and consumer culture as a "live update" device, with many users deploying it to create fluidity in their daily schedules, reallocating time with others as business events unfold. Information services delivered via WAP will similarly liberate (or confuse, depending on your point of view) other aspects of business life. Distributing decision-making throughout a mobile team will be possible, turning the team meeting from a scheduled event into a channel. Consumers will be able to react to incoming sales messages by making purchases. They may even profile their phones to listen for particular sales items and to bid for them at prices below a set threshold.

PAYMENT SOLUTIONS

Extracting payment from an online customer has been an acute concern for businesses since the Web first welcomed commercial users. The need to channel payments through the Web medium has led to a proliferation of payment mechanisms competing for the customer's dollar—or fraction of a cent. The first few years of Web-based ecommerce have seen some solutions complete their entire life cycle, flowering briefly in trials and then fading away. The leading payment mechanism on the Web remains the credit card number, packed in an SSL transaction.

The main barriers to new types of payment mechanisms do not primarily include security. As we have seen, public key cryptography, the generic PKI architecture and specific implementations, such as SET, all combine to make secure online transactions technically possible. Yet intrusive elements at the client side tend to undermine the fortunes of these well-crafted solutions. Users balk at downloading and installing special client software. Users don't necessarily want to manage certificates on their machines and they don't want to add new brand names to their burgeoning virtual wallets. The successful payment solutions for mass market ecommerce combine implicit security with transparent invocation. We want to spend as we go—and we're not especially beguiled by the thought of novel, online currencies.

Micropayments

Part of the promise of the Web and a prime engine of the "new media" movement, is the notion that digital goods and services represent a market in themselves. As we have noted, expectations for the commercial use of the Web originally tended to focus on the sale of pure information, while the leading success of mass market ecommerce has majored in selling information printed on paper. Magazine and newspaper titles that moved to the Web, and attempted to charge subscriptions for content, soon abandoned their attempts in the face of user indifference, opting to fund their online ventures through banner advertising sales and, often, subsidies from traditional media business streams.

The key to enabling the sale of digital content is finding a mechanism that enables users to buy relatively tiny amounts of value: the few cents or fractions of a cent that represent a page of technical data or a current stock market price. Traditional card payment methods make subdollar transactions prohibitively expensive.

MilliCent is a system developed by Digital (and, subsequently, owned by Compaq) to enable payment of values under $5, including amounts less than one cent. It is aimed principally at content providers, who are looking for ways of charging users on a pay-per-use rather than subscription basis. MilliCent can be used to sell any kind of digital content, including software, either for download or on a metered use basis.

MilliCent uses prepaid "scrip" that is valid only for a specified vendor. Liquidity is achieved through a broker strategy. Brokers sell blocks of scrip in return for standard value transactions, such as credit card purchases. Holders of scrip can exchange it via a broker for other scrip.

MilliCent is a kind of coupon economy, using a lightweight security approach geared to the small unit value of scrip. Receipts are not issued and, because scrip is prepaid, no need for certification exists. The company asserts the system contains natural antifraud mechanisms: For vendors, the amounts involved are so small, it's unlikely any vendor would fail to provide the goods purchased, and brokers are unlikely to risk their reputations for easily traceable thefts. MilliCent customers must install a client wallet program to handle their scrip, while vendors and brokers each need to run their own MilliCent servers.

MilliCent completed its trials in late 1998 and was due to be rolled out in Japan during the summer of 1999. Meanwhile, the early digital cash company, Digicash, filed for bankruptcy in late 1998, while CyberCash closed its CyberCoin service in April 1999. Pushing the unfashionable cyber prefix to the background, the company refocused its small transaction value business in its new InstaBuy[9] offering. InstaBuy is a much simpler proposition, being a service that essentially stores a secure record of a user's payment details for subsequent transactions. InstaBuy is like an outsourced cookie service—a radically different approach from digital currency.

Meanwhile, Qpass[10] launched its Content Transaction Network in March 1999, attracting members, including the *Wall Street Journal* and the Corbis picture library. Although Qpass allows users to pay small amounts for digital content, it is designed to behave more like a passport than a currency. Qpass has also been designed to be easy to acquire. The first time a user visits a Qpass-enabled site, she can register for the service. She then has access to all sites that use the service. There is no client software to download.

Qpass avoids two of the problems associated with earlier micropayment schemes. First, users meet Qpass at credible, content-oriented sites, whose brands are already associated with paid-for information, such as Bloomberg. The users are then presented with a means of paying for information they are actively seeking. With currency-type

---

9. www.instabuy.com

10. www.qpass.com

applications, the user has to acquire a fund of currency—fill her purse or wallet—before setting out to spend it. Yet she will meet few sites that accept her currency because the currency is not yet generally accepted. We have a chicken-and-egg situation, where the customer is being asked to take the lead in innovation. With the Qpass approach, sites can sign up to the scheme with little effort and then discover the extent of customer uptake as users decide to join the service. This is a much more attractive option for buyers and sellers alike because neither is being asked to invest heavily in a unproven, general payment mechanism.

Second, Qpass does not require users to download any software, to run any kind of encryption software, or to understand the type of complex business architecture that underpins MilliCent. Essentially, MilliCent is a credit card purchase reseller. Users charge a particular amount to their Qpass account via credit card. The balance is then decremented according to use at Qpass sites. Qpass handles billing on behalf of all the sites in the network as a service to the seller sites. The company takes a commission on each transaction and requires sellers to install Qpass server software.

Packaged Services

Open Market's Transact is one of the most successful and widely used packaged ecommerce technologies. Transact enables vendors to create online stores and chargeable services using fairly unobtrusive mechanisms, and to outsource the transaction authentication function.

The system includes a set of standardized commerce objects, which can be used to create services. These objects include types such as offers and receipts. An *offer,* for example, is represented as a concatenation of data elements representing item identifier, price, and so on. The commerce object is composed of this data payload, together with an authenticating digest, and wrapped up as a URL. The *digest* is a value computed using a 128-bit key on the data payload. A digest can be thought of as a digital signature that can be checked to ensure the message contents have not been altered since their original creation. The entire object is, therefore, able to identify a server, trigger an action at the server, deliver a data payload, and authenticate the payload:

http://payment.icoms.com:80/tms-ts/bin/payment.

cgi?b8dde449d7fc8de58f5d4d6e5813413d:ss=env&domain=

nci-47209&kid=400014.9&goodstype=h&cc=USD&amt=9.88&curl=

http%3a%2f%2fwww.newbury.com%3a80%2fsku%2f47209.htm&op=

add&desc=47209%3a%20APPLE,FIONA%20-%20TIDAL%20CD%20[11]

In this example, http://payment.icoms.com:80 identifies the server and the port on which it is running. /tms-ts/bin/payment.cgi is a call to a server-side process, implemented using a CGI script. Everything after payment.cgi? acts as parameter data to the CGI program. The first part of this is the authenticating digest, represented as a hexadecimal string. Finally, we have the data items of the commerce transaction itself, identified as name and value pairs; cc=USD&amt=9.88, for example, is two data items indicating the price of the item is $9.88. The server process parses the argument to produce the discrete data items, just as any CGI script must do. It then checks the digest against the content. Finally, it can pass the authenticated data onto a backend order system.

Open Market's commerce objects make it relatively easy for a vendor to commerce-enable a site and do not require the user to install any client software. The mechanism is exposed within the URL, which is potentially off-putting to users who understand URLs merely as addresses of information resources, rather than as strings that can contain lengthy instructions and parameters. Adding ecommerce capabilities to a product catalog is a matter of embedding the

---

11. From *Internet Commerce: The Open Market Solution,* Open Market Technical White Paper, November 14, 1997.

correct URLs within the HTML, so user clicks are converted into commerce objects.

The use of the URL allows Transact great implementation flexibility. Because a commerce object is a URL, the Transact server can be located anywhere. A vendor can choose to implement his own Transact server or to outsource that service. Transact enables a range of payment methods and links in real-time to payment processors who, in turn, mediate on behalf of card-issuing banks. Smaller vendors can make a wide variety of payment methods available to their customers by using an outsourced Transact server, removing the need for the smaller vendor to maintain business and technical relationships with each payment processor. Another approach to packaging ecommerce objects comes from Actinic, which uses a Java applet to encrypt the customer's credit card details and transmit them onward to a card processor.

Open Market is positioned as an ecommerce enabler, a provider of ecommerce infrastructure that can be acquired as a product or a service. For players entering the business-to-consumer ecommerce arena, buying into an infrastructure is an efficient means of moving to the Web. This tactic makes the most of tried-and-trusted mechanisms and architectures, and reduces the need for the new player to develop her own expertise in low-level ecommerce technologies. iCat has followed this strategy, shifting its strategy from one of selling a boxed online catalog software solution to the provision of a complete ecommerce enablement and hosting service.

Using iCat's Web Store, users can create an online storefront interactively via the company's Web site. The Commerce Cart offering enables users to commerce-enable an existing Web site in a similar fashion. The chief difference between the two options is in the blank-sheet case, Web Store creates new storefronts from templates whereas, when an existing site is involved, the user must add in specific pieces of iCat HTML code. Both options are distinctly easier for small businesses to understand. Before discontinuing its boxed software line, iCat was tasked with reaching a large audience of small ticket customers, educating them about online stores, and helping them understand the systems relationships between online and backend catalogs. The natural way to reach such an audience is, of course, through the Web. So why not deliver the value through the Web, as well? iCat's rethink and its acquisition by Intel at the end of 1998, mark an evolutionary stage in the breadth and maturity of the business-to-consumer ecommerce domain. Portals and ISPs now see themselves as providers of ecommerce services; Yahoo!, for example, will build a catalog, inventory system, and Web site for $100.

ECOMMERCE STANDARDS

Rosetta Net[12] is an ecommerce standards initiative for the IT industry. Working from the basis that standards typically drive economic efficiencies in industries, Rosetta Net is a cooperative organization of companies from across the IT supply chain. The goal is to build business interface standards, enabling users to save money and improve productivity throughout the industry.

The speed of change in the IT industry adds an extraordinary pressure to Rosetta Net's activities. Specifications for a PC, for example, become outdated soon after a purchaser orders one. Unless the supply chain is fast and responsive, customer requirements will either be frustrated by the need to respecify purchases as offered inventory changes or be forced to select from outmoded products in an artificial slowing-down of product innovation.

The technology industry is an acute example of the potential for inefficient supply chain processes to inhibit the collective and individual success of industry players. Rosetta Net's high-level model for improving what it terms "eBusiness exchange" is applicable to all kinds of business-to-business ecommerce and memorably straightforward. This layered model is also a good introduction to layered architectures, a subject to which we return in the next chapter.

The model works by analogy with human commerce, as shown in Figure 4-1.

---

12. www.rosettanet.org

FIGURE 4-1. Rosetta Net model of eBusiness exchange.

Telephone	⟷	**Application**
Business Process	⟷	**eBusiness Process**
Dialogue	⟷	**Partner Interface Process (PIP)**
Grammar	⟷	**Framework**
Words	⟷	**Dictionaries**
Alphabet	⟷	**HTML/XML**
Sound	⟷	**Internet**

human-to-human	system-to-system
business exchange	eBusiness exchange

In human commerce, a basic carrier layer enables us to communicate with each other: sound. We have a general means of componentizing sound, which the model terms an *alphabet.*[13] Once we have an alphabet, we can compose words or units of reference. A grammar enables us to assemble words correctly, so they convey meaning to others who share our language. We communicate through dialogues, which are themselves tied to business processes. A device, such as a telephone, is an application that enables us to enact the underlying layers at a specific instance.

When systems talk to systems, the universal carrier is the Internet. The alphabet of the Internet, as we have seen, is HTML and its successor XML. At the top layer, any kind of application plays the role of the telephone in human commerce. The intermediate layers comprise Rosetta Net's focus. The organization's approach is, therefore, fairly sophisticated when compared with some proprietary solutions. Indeed, Rosetta Net's approach is generic and architectural, rather than opportunistic. In summary, its concentration in these layers is on the creation of a "master dictionary," which defines products, partners, and business processes. The result will be a kind of

13. Linguists would doubtless take issue with this term. An alphabet is a system for making marks; human speech is not dependent on the composition of letters into words. Rosetta Net's model is not meant to be academically correct, but a means of understanding interoperability issues in business-to-business ecommerce.

combined dictionary, grammar, phrase book, and etiquette guide for the new state of business-to-business ecommerce in the chosen domain.

Rosetta Net announced the first implementation of a Partner Interface Process (PIP) in a test with IBM and Microsoft in April 1999. The implementation enables manufacturers to insert new product details into partner catalogs without any intervention. Using XML to embody the standards and the Unified Modeling Language (UML) to conduct the underlying analysis, Rosetta Net is a state-of-the-art ecommerce standards initiative that can serve as a template for other industries.

Meanwhile, over at CommerceNet,[14] the accent is on providing global standards and proving interoperability step-by-step across the generic supply chain. Achieving catalog interoperability within a sound security framework has been a particular concern, with concentration on federal procurement processes. Familiar technologies—such as XML and PKI—play their parts in the CommerceNet scheme.

The most complete, publicly available ecommerce standard is Open Buying on the Internet (OBI),[15] a consortium formed in late 1996 and managed since June 1998 by CommerceNet. OBI is aimed squarely at business-to-business procurement, and seeks to provide an open and neutral architecture that benefits sellers and buyers alike. In other words, OBI is neither biased toward any technology provider nor does it favor sellers over buyers when it comes to ease of integration or access to partners. OBI is intended to support the high-volume, low-value transactions that make up the majority of a business's purchasing activity. Version 2.0 is due during 1999, but the existing 1.1 version is detailed, comprehensive, and implementable. OBI uses ANSI X12 EDI standards for Order Requests and Orders, wrapping these data formats within digitally signed OBI objects. XML is not used at present, though it has not been ruled out.

Despite its maturity, OBI has not been taken up as widely as it might be and most observers now consider OBI a stillborn effort. The

---

14. www.commercenet.com
15. www.openbuy.org

reason may be that interoperability in the procurement arena comes down to catalog interoperability—a characteristic few sellers find attractive. As we noted when we looked at this area in Chapter 3, aggregating catalog content enables buyers to compare offers and to substitute products, while sellers prefer to build and own customer relationships. Standards initiatives in business-to-business ecommerce inevitably bump into this problem, yet it's in business-to-business that the need for system-to-system collaboration mechanisms is most acute.

On the business-to-consumer side of our map, the leading contender for a general standard is the Open Trading Protocol (OTP). OTP[16] was launched in 1997 by Mondex, a smart card digital money player whose offering predates the public take-off of the Web. OTP was submitted to the IETF in June 1998, making it a candidate standard for the Internet developer community. OTP is intended to create a complete virtual analog of the traditional trading environment from trade negotiation to receipt of goods, as well as supporting new forms of electronic business.

OTP's model is strong at the analysis area, recognizing that parties can play a number of different types of role in a transaction, including those of payment handler and "merchant customer care provider" (a party that represents a merchant in the resolution of a dispute with a customer). Four atomic types of trading exchange exist, which can be combined into transactions. These types are Offer, Payment, Delivery, and Authentication. A Purchase transaction, for example, includes an Offer, a Payment, and a Delivery. A Value Exchange (for example, a currency conversion) involves an Offer and two Payments. OTP messages themselves are XML documents and use digital signatures. The full XML DTD is included in the specification.

OTP maintains a neutral stance toward payment mechanisms, supporting a range including SET and Mondex. This means a consumer can maintain a collection of different branded payment mechanisms in his wallet, while vendors can run promotions tied to particular mechanisms. A vendor could, for example, offer a lower price to users electing to use one brand of Visa card.

---

16. www.otp.org

Architectures for Electronic Commerce

This chapter explores the fundamental architectures that support electronic commerce applications. The chapter is organized in three parts, dealing in turn with architectures for the logic of the enterprise's ecommerce applications, the technologies that enable the applications, and the design of the supporting organization.

The models presented here draw on a number of practices from software engineering, systems design, and team building. They recognize most ecommerce initiatives are launched from within existing organizations and only a rare startup does not contain one or more subteams formed inside another company. The issue of legacy assets, therefore, underlies much of the discussion. Legacy practices, attitudes, and habits lie behind the organizational pitfalls, while the positive and negative values of legacy systems determine much of the logical and technological architecture material.

LOGICAL ARCHITECTURE

Ecommerce is a transformative phenomenon that crosses many boundaries within an enterprise, including system boundaries. The architectural concerns explored in this section are all relevant to the challenge of building complex, changeable, and scalable systems that rapidly become mission-critical.

We use the term "logical architecture" to refer to types of generic systems model: well-tried, standardized approaches to building successful systems. This section, therefore, deals with styles of construction and categories of capability, rather than specific branded technologies.

The main part of this section describes layered architectures in generic terms and focuses on their benefits. It also looks at application services, the capabilities that inhabit the middle layers of an n-tier architecture. Finally, it outlines the key requirements of the underlying technical platforms that must deliver such architectures.

Layered Architectures: Client/Server and n-tier Applications

Client/server systems have come to be called *two tier applications* in recent times. To understand this shift in terminology, consider the weight of the original term. The term *client/server* often refers to a pair of machines; but it can also refer to a pair of role designations.

In this interpretation, a software component can play one or both roles in a system. Usually the role is fixed for each component; that is, a component is either a client or a server. A client component requests services and a server component provides services. The client/server model is essentially a many-to-many, collaborative model. A server may serve many clients and a client may use the services of many servers.

Clients and servers, therefore, are reliant upon a communications mechanism and a protocol with which to communicate without loss or degradation of messages. Such protocols may be defined uniquely for an application or they may be defined by a standard mechanism. The communications protocol is a means of virtual systems integration. Clients and servers share nothing but an agreement about how to converse.

One implication of this communication-centric model is that clients need not share any platform characteristics with the server. Another implication is clients and servers may be distributed remotely from each other. Client/server creates a separation of computing elements with far-reaching consequences (see Figure 5-1).

FIGURE 5-1. From standalone to thin client.

 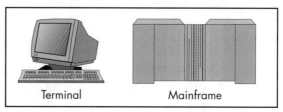

PC · Terminal · Mainframe

Standalone: user has total responsibility for installation, maintenance and upgrade — or none at all.

 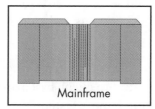

PC · Mainframe

Two-tier Client/Server: user has application, data is delivered by the network.

  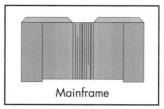

PC · Server · Mainframe

Three-tier Client/Server: applications are shared on the network as client becomes thinner.

  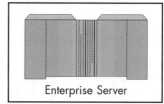

Server · Enterprise Server

Web-Enabled: user owns nothing physically, owns everything virtually.

Basic two-tier client/server architectures have had widely differing splits of functionality between the client and the server. Within this continuum, most systems cluster around a number of identifiable models:

- *screen-scraping*—where the client purely provides a user interface, normally a GUI, linking to a server application.

- *data validation*—an extension of screen-scraping, where the client has responsibility for performing an initial degree of data validation (for example, checking that fields are numeric or check digits are correct).

- *split application logic*—application functionality is truly split between client and server. Most systems that use database techniques, such as triggers and stored procedures, fall into this category.

- *specific server functionality*—systems where a number of servers provide functionality to client-based applications (for example, printing, accessing remote systems).

- *backend database*—all application functionality is contained in the client and the server is used purely as a data storage/retrieval device. Such systems are now frequently referred to as *fat client* and tend to be the type of two-tier client/server systems most often discussed in connection with n-tier, *thin client* approaches.

A common business constraint associated with two-tier systems arises from screen-scraping techniques. *Screen-scraping* is a minimally invasive technique for creating simple two-tier client/server systems, where a screen-scraping program mimics the actions of a user, playing keystroke scripts to a mainframe session. The screen-scraping program intercepts characters and control codes being directed to the user's terminal and uses them to populate its own screens.

Screen-scraping can be used to hide the functionality of a mainframe system and is particularly useful for standardizing screen layouts across a set of legacy applications. By its very nature, however, screen-scraping cannot improve the functionality or flow of an application. It may be used to create a new web front-end to an application, but truly new functions will only be implementable as sequences of existing ones. From the design point of view, screen-scraping limits the flexibility and maintainability of a system because it is tightly coupled to previous solutions. Screen-scraping can, therefore, be an expensive veneer that adds little lasting value apart from cosmetic updating of the user interface and some comfort that the legacy systems have been left untouched. From the business point of view, simple screen-scraping commits the organization to legacy automations of legacy business processes.

Another technical issue is the data traffic involved in fat client, two-tier client/server systems. Where many clients are dispersed across a large area, such systems involve large data transfers across networks with limited bandwidths. This can create performance problems, which may be addressed by locating the application logic on servers with high-capacity links to the database engines. From the business point of view, the point of separation between back end and front end is often dangerously arbitrary. For example, the fat client may consume large amounts of data irrelevant to its user. In addition, supporting multiple fat client systems and their various versions can create a significant systems management burden for the IT department, with clashes between libraries causing systems to fail in unpredictable ways.

The increasing use of object technology in application development, alongside relational or hierarchical databases, has also been a source of pressure on two-tier design. This mismatch between the application and the data representation has forced a logical separation of the two aspects, and this, in turn, has highlighted advantages of physical separation.

In summary, a two-tier architecture's lower layer is a database holding shared corporate data, while the upper layer contains any number of applications that work concurrently with this data. These solutions rely on a tight coupling between the user interface and the physical data it uses. This restricts the adaptability of the system to change, and constrains the number of business processes to which the system's components can be applied. In terms of the generic layered architecture, too few levels of abstraction are incorporated to make the approach useful as more than a point solution.

To break the tight coupling of the two-tier approach, an intermediate level is introduced that models the conceptual relationship between the user interface and the physical data structure. This creates a three-tier architecture.

In a traditional data-driven methodology, this layer equates to the logical data model. While monolithic development dispensed with logical data models once tables and code had been designed, the three-tier approach incorporates the logical model within the resulting software. Application code accesses physical data by its logical names and relationships; the intermediate layer translates this into meaningful physical actions and their result sets. This middle layer is, therefore, also responsible for constructing queries in some way that is shielded from the client application.

A typical approach is to bury objects that compose and execute SQL in this intermediate layer. As soon as developers make a design decision of this kind, they are, in fact, defining a new layer of service. The separation of data from applications via the composition of SQL is directly comparable to tasks undertaken by discrete layers in the OSI model, for example. Black-boxing SQL in this way brings many of the standard benefits of layering, notably by allowing specialists to concentrate on the development of relevant functionality. It also designs in the capability to change data access strategy at a later date by demarcating its scope.

The introduction of a specialized data access layer alongside the "conceptual middle" has been one factor in the market's confusion over three-tier, four-tier, and so-on-tier architectures. A further attack on the appealing simplicity of the three-tier model comes from the business analysis end of the architecture. The architecture we have described so far makes no distinction between a general logical model of shared data and the many disparate application uses we may want to make of that general model. Applications are, by their nature, specialized views and manipulations of data, and this needs to be recognized separately from the general model and also from their representation in a user interface.

Many ostensibly three-tiered systems are, therefore, five-tier systems, where the layers are

- ■ User Interface
- ■ Application
- ■ Business
- ■ Data access
- ■ Database

In simple terms, three-plus-tier architectures apply wherever a development team recognizes the need for an intermediary "middle" between shared data and its users. Organizations that additionally recognize the intrinsic value of building sharable business objects or services separable from underlying databases or windowing environments are continuing to invest heavily in this middle tier. Those achieving success recognize the layering principle applies equally within the middle tier itself and no absolute definition exists of a correct granularity for such systems.

Tiered or layered architectures have an honorable history in the technology world. The best-known layered architectures

Advantages and Disadvantages of the n-tier Approach

At the most basic level, the trade off between two-tier and multitier client/server architectures is complexity against performance and flexibility. In other words, multitier systems provide the opportunity for more scaleable performance and more responsiveness to change at the cost of systems that are more complex and, thus, harder to implement. This complexity can mean the benefits in performance and flexibility are not gained due to a poor system design.

These are the main advantages of the n-tier model:

■ **Separation of concerns—both physically and logically:** Data and functionality is partitioned according to meaningful areas. This limits the impact of change across a system. For example, if the application contains a data access layer, then changes to the way in which data access is implemented will not affect client modules that ultimately use the data. It also makes the system easier to understand, and therefore to maintain, optimize, and to integrate with other systems.

■ **Supports management of complexity without fragmenting the business process:** Large problems must be broken down into some manageable set of subproblems, if only to enable allocation of work items to developers. Multitier architectures are nonarbitrary and derive from analysis of the domain being addressed. Business process is preserved into the application architecture, which also supports the future reengineering of business processes.

■ **Share common services:** In two-tier systems, sharing of services or capabilities is restricted to basic client and server modules. Typically, the back-end database is shared among a number of application front-ends, all of which are constrained by the database's original design. The middle tiers of a multitier application contain services that can be supplied by many data sources and can, in turn, serve many clients. The generalization of services represented by the layering ensures new types of clients or data sources can be added to the application with little application reengineering. A good example is the rapid extension into Web browser user interfaces enabled by a strictly demarcated user interface layer. In addition, the more a service is reused across different processes, the greater the saving on maintenance compared to supporting individual, slightly different, modules.

■ **Helps migration:** Separating the application logic from the database enables a development team to switch database technologies during the lifetime of the system with minimal effect on other activities. This helps to ensure vendor independence and scope for using best of breed products. In particular, layering promotes the "cloaking" of legacy systems for use in ecommerce applications.

■ **Scalability:** A multitier application enables the addition of new processes within tiers, replication of processes within tiers, distribution of tiers across more processors, and improved communication strategies between tiers. This flexibility to design around bottlenecks is a key feature of this type of architecture.

in the IT arena are those used for physical computer networks. This approach partitions a communications protocol into a set of abstraction levels, with each level addressing a different scale of detail. The lowest level in such an architecture specifies how bits are encoded and transmitted across a physical link, while higher levels deal with concerns such as the packaging of bits into packets, the synchronizing of dialogues, and the structuring of information for presentation. The ISO's Open Systems Interconnection (OSI) model specifies seven such layers and has influenced the development of layered architectures in the related field of software systems design. As we have seen, the display of a simple Web page involves layering, with the HTTP protocol acting as a higher level of organization above IP.

The layered approach has several development benefits associated with the theme of abstraction. First, the layering organizes a complex problem that might otherwise be implemented as a monolithic solution.

Second, the clear separation of concerns at each level allows development to be carried on in parallel by different teams. In turn, this allows some parts of a system to be developed before other parts are finished because the interfaces of inter-acting objects are defined as part of the layering.

These development bene-fits can be extended into the runtime environment. If func-tionality is organized in defined levels of service, then it can be partitioned and located opti-mally for the organization. This allows, for example, database access to be performed on a platform tuned for disc access, while leaving user interface functionality on a multipurpose client PC.

The key requirements of a sound layered architecture are

■ defined responsibilities

■ stable interfaces

■ encapsulation within level

From the point of view of contemporary business sys-tems design and of special importance for ecommerce

The main disadvantages of the n-tier model are:

■ Additional complexity that requires addi-tional effort in all stages of develop-ment and increases the risk profile of projects. The use of multitier architec-tures introduces further layers of abstrac-tion, requiring greater attention to design issues. In many cases, the allocation of logic to specific tiers requires a deep understanding of business requirements, which is not always present in system architects and designers.

■ Needs a disciplined development approach associated more with main-frame development than with front-end development tools. Informal rapid appli-cation development (RAD) techniques can lead to piecemeal and poorly designed systems that fail to produce the benefits of scalability.

■ The relative lack of experience of large-scale multitier implementations makes it hard to form teams with suitable experi-ence and means a solid body of knowl-edge for educational and training purposes does not exist.

■ Testing of multitier systems is necessarily more complex. Because this is frequently an area of project development that is underestimated and skimped even with simple architectures, it is easy for multi-tier projects to slip badly during the testing phase and/or to be delivered in an unstable form.

■

application developers, the key benefit of the n-tier architecture is the intermediate layers interposed between the user interface and the data storage layer. The most valuable reusable components and services can be located in the intermediate business objects layer. Most significantly, layering allows enterprises to cast a functional wrapper around legacy systems, exposing their useful data and behaviors to new application components without requiring complete systems rewrites.

Application Services

One of the benefits of layered architectures is their provision of a home for common application services. Ecommerce systems of many types share requirements for services, such as:

- personalization
- billing
- authentication
- profiling
- order aggregation

At a more fundamental level, there will also be requirements for services, such as security and transaction management. Transaction management is worth looking at in more detail.

Transaction processing (TP) monitors have existed for almost as long as online processing. The original purpose of such software was both to provide a framework in which terminals could communicate with mainframe systems and to provide some degree of data consistency within the files or database on the mainframe system.

The TP monitor is a tool for undoing the effects of an operation that has previously taken place. If some event occurs in the application's processing that causes the application to be in an inconsistent state, then the application's state must be repaired. Because it cannot guess what the successful outcome should have been, the best the application can do is to undo each step taken until it regains its starting state.

This capability to retrace steps implies logical units of work must be declared within the application. Each of these units is a transaction and is explicitly marked by some begin/end convention. An example is the transfer of funds from one account to another. This requires operations to debit one account and credit another. Although these are separate operations, which may take place on separate data sources in disparate locations, the transaction brackets them together. If one of the operations fails, the successful operation must be reversed to preserve a meaningful state.

Although transactions focus on recovery from operational error, they are clearly derived from analysis of the business process. A transaction encapsulates a business rule in the time dimension, just as an object encapsulates the knowledge and capabilities of entities in the business. This encapsulation characteristic is known as *atomicity*. A transaction is atomic in the sense it is the smallest unit of work that has meaning in the real world.

Careful, defensive programming could ensure an application builds its own progress log and retains knowledge about what type of remedial action to take on the failure of each possible step taken by the application. This would place a huge burden on application development and it would equate to the development of a unique transaction processing system specifically for the application. TP monitors provide a framework solution, enabling the developer to bracket the application by transaction, secure in the knowledge that the monitor maintains a progress log and a strategy for reversal.

The transactional style is appropriate for any system where one or more components may fail. Distributed systems have the effect of distributing points of failure. With multitier client/server systems that often incorporate middleware and databases with some form of transaction control, an issue exists of providing an overall level of transaction processing that ensures consistency in processing and data across the complete system. This is done by including visibility of transaction scope within the application's messaging strategy. In this way the application can extend appropriate transactional scope to all the contributing processes.

Applying transactions in a distributed environment requires a degree of automated system management be built into the application by the framework. This management is represented by Resource Managers and Transaction Managers. A *Resource Manager* is an API to a file system, database management system, or other data source. Resource Managers enforce transaction integrity in the resources they control. The responsibility for extending transaction scope lies with the *Transaction Manager,* a module that delimits transaction boundaries, propagates transactions in the distributed environment, and collaborates with Resource Managers. The Transaction Manager, therefore, has a coordinating responsibility, while the Resource Manager ensures that transactions are consistent.

Early TP monitors enforced single-threading of transactions. This avoids problems of data-locking and potential deadly embraces between transactions. However, it clearly provides a bottleneck that severely limits the scalability of the system and is difficult to enforce in multitier systems, where the processing of a single transaction may be distributed over a number of processes.

A variety of solutions exist to this problem. One of the most common is to allow multiple processes, each of which single-threads transactions. This approach also allows load balancing and, if processes can be started automatically in response to increased loads, it allows dynamic reconfiguration of the system to meet peak demands. Where performance is a key issue, this subject must be addressed carefully in the choice of middleware. Approaches that make the best use of the environment (for example, using operating system native threads) and avoid synchronous communications wherever possible have clear advantages in this area.

Transaction management is clearly important in an ecommerce environment because it is crucial that any customer transaction is not left in an impossible commercial state.

Platform Criteria

The quality criteria that influence the choice of a technical platform to support ecommerce are often obscured by political and marketing issues. As we have noted, most ecommerce initiatives occur in heterogeneous environments, where legacy systems are recruited for their contributing functionality or data, and where incumbent machines, operating systems, and networks are still working to justify their installation costs. Although few developments occur in greenfield environments, vendors naturally have an interest in retaining or acquiring customers for their platforms. We cannot eradicate these effects in this discussion, but we can outline and prioritize the issues that should be shaping purchase and support decisions in the platform arena.

The criterion most often cited as a determinant of ecommerce success and the one that has the greatest apparent impact on platform choice, is scalability. On examination, scalability is often used to mean something more like availability, with which it has an intimate relationship.

Availability is simply a measure of a system's effective user uptime. It is set as close as possible to *always*—or *twenty-four seven* in the jazzier language of IT people. Online brokers have faced criticism for the occasional unavailability of their services and have had to compensate customers for trades made at unfavorable rates once the systems returned to life. The news of a site's sudden closure spreads like wildfire on the net and can create enduring dents in an ecommerce offering's credibility. Sometimes an ecommerce site fails because a backend process, possibly running in a complex mainframe environment, fails. This legacy function may have a history of occasional failure that was acceptable in its former inhouse life.

Scalability refers to the capability of a system to grow in size to service an increasing number of clients. Clearly, this is not entirely a platform concern, though it is often couched as one. One of the reasons for using an n-tier architecture is to create an efficient means of replicating crucial services, so bottlenecks do not occur. For example, we can create a pool of database connections in our data management layer that are ready to service data requests as they arrive. We can maintain a degree of redundancy in the pool without impeding the completion of other processes in the system.

From the point of view of platform, scalability is a flashpoint for vendor comparisons. The capability of an operating system to spawn new threads and processes without degradation is one measure of its enterprise strength. At the same time, the capability of the operating system's hardware environment to execute instructions efficiently, and to do so in harmony with the operating system, is another factor.

Scalability is a worrisome issue for ecommerce players. Everyone hopes their ecommerce channel will vastly outperform the usage estimates made for it and the relative immaturity of the field ensures reliable guidance on predictable user loads continues to be elusive. By the same token, no one wants to overspend on a technical platform. Some of this anxiety can be reduced by setting a context for scalability levels. While infinite, graceful scalability is the ideal, implementing a more realistic, and perhaps discontinuous, strategy is possible.

First, consider that a failure to scale does not necessarily imply complete loss of business from an unserved population. It may just mean some customers wait longer for service. The rhetoric of the e-age has it that customers want instant satisfaction, but instantaneousness is a matter of customer perception rather than absolute measurement. Ecommerce systems designed to release resources when they are no longer required are self-correcting with respect to scale, albeit over an unpredictable time period. Put simply, we can design ecommerce systems that serve known population sizes at known response levels and monitor how often they are asked to work outside these boundaries.

Second, no ecommerce player should regard scalability as an entirely systems-level issue. At least one line of fallback, if not several lines, must exist. The first may be a fire-fighting call center that fields complaints and captures instructions for later entry to the target system. Subsequent lines of retreat may include refund and compensation policies.

Availability and scalability are joined by response time as the third major criterion for platform choice. Unfortunately, response time isn't a distinct quantity that can be separated from other aspects of systems performance. Strictly speaking, a degradation in response time as users join the system is a failure of scaling. As suggested, though, defining an acceptable level of degradation is sensible to achieve something less than infinite scalability. More important, response time in business-to-consumer ecommerce applications is affected by the performance climate out on the public net. From the point of view of the consumer, poor response times represent poor service by the ecommerce site, whatever the true reason for their experience.

As ecommerce applications become increasingly mission-critical—or become the enterprise's mission—organizations need to consider investing in entire replications of their systems. Duplicate systems, running mirrored software and data, and running in alternative locations, provide the most complete assurance of availability, ecommerce's bottom line. Banks and airlines have long accepted that the core significance of information systems to their businesses demands investments of this kind. Ecommerce makes all businesses similarly IT-dependent. Designing for scalability within a system layer, for example, is a sensible, defensive measure, but it requires some brainpower to achieve. Systems replication relies much more on the organization's capability to write checks.

TECHNOLOGICAL ARCHITECTURE

Logical requirements for systems building ultimately map onto technology choices. *Technology* is a broad term, and we tend to use it to refer to coherent sets of tools, rather than single products. The most important toolset in contemporary systems development and integration is the component model, so components form the primary focus of this section. The section also briefly explores the role of databases in ecommerce systems and describes firewalls. It concludes with some examples of typical ecommerce system architectures.

One measure of the success of a technology is its decline into commodity status. Components, of course, advertise their ambitions to be commodities. Databases and firewalls are less obviously commodities, however, they can be thought of as large-grain components in an ecommerce technical strategy.

Components

Layered architectures with application services presuppose some use of specialized, bounded software objects. Software engineering has long treasured the dream of a component-based development process

Objects and Components

Arguments have raged over the difference between the object-oriented approach and the component-based approach to software development. This is perplexing to those of us whose interest in object technology was inspired by hopes of bringing engineering disciplines to the software development activity and, in particular, the concept of objects as composable parts that could be snapped together to form systems.

The confusion may have arisen in comparing the success of object-based development environments, such as Visual Basic, with pre-workbench editions of object-oriented languages. The productivity of environments such as Visual Basic was used as a counter to the purists who complained that it didn't meet the definitions of an object-oriented language. Visual Basic controls formed the largest market of prebuilt components, so it demonstrated reuse on a wide scale. If an object-oriented product, such as Smalltalk, had captured the Wintel development market, then we would now equate components with object technology. Somewhere along the line, the end (assembly of software systems) became confused with the means (competing languages). The arrival of standardized component models clarifies the situation somewhat. Components today are objects with added engineering discipline and commercial credibility. Each of the models described in this section aims to allow creation and interworking of components in different address spaces and (with varying fidelity) across different platforms. Furthermore, the common theme in the development of each model is convergence with the others.

Grady Booch comments that a software component can provide "the physical packaging and distribution of object-oriented abstractions [...] in a manner that is largely language-neutral."[1] In other words, the object technology movement has returned to its original agenda after a period of language wars. The shift in terminology from *object* to *component* signals the arrival in the mainstream of object technology's key notions: the encapsulation and collaboration of software entities. ◼

and the 1990s has brought several efforts to maturity. This section looks at the main competing component technologies, namely Common Object Request Broker Architecture (CORBA), Enterprise Java-Beans, and Microsoft's COM family.

CORBA is the Common Object Request Broker Architecture, defined by the cross-industry Object Management Group (OMG). The OMG has shocked a cynical computing industry by being a committee that delivers marketable standards. Member companies vie to produce standards, which must be backed by demonstrable products, against the OMG's issued requirements. Competing vendors then tend to pool their resources so a single standard is finally presented for OMG adoption. While this gets away from the inertia and design compromise associated with committee productions, it does mean OMG standards tend to be all-embracing. If competing vendors develop separate approaches to a problem, most likely both will be supported in the final standard.

1. Grady Booch, "Components, Continuously Changing Systems, and Urban Spawl," *Object Magazine*, 7(2), April 1997.

CORBA aims to standardize distributed object systems around a common architecture. The heart of the architecture is the Object Request Broker (ORB). An ORB acts as a mediator between interworking objects. An object acting in the client role uses the ORB to invoke methods on a server object. The ORB does the job of conveying the request to the server object. If the server object returns an object as a result of execution, then this is returned to the client again via the ORB. The ORB can be thought of as the software equivalent of a hardware bus, linking up disparate objects, as shown in Figure 5-2.

Operations can be invoked on remote objects in CORBA in two ways: using a static interface and using a dynamic interface. With the static interface, the interface definition written in IDL is compiled into client stub and server skeleton objects. These handle communications for the true client and server objects. When the client calls an operation on the server, the ORB conveys the request to the server, which then executes the operation. The client waits for successful execution on the server.

With the dynamic invocation interface (DII), the client creates a request dynamically, building it one parameter at a time. The client then sends the request via the ORB to the destination object. The requested method in that object executes and the result, if any, is returned. The client that invoked the operation can elect to wait for this

FIGURE 5-2. CORBA objects.

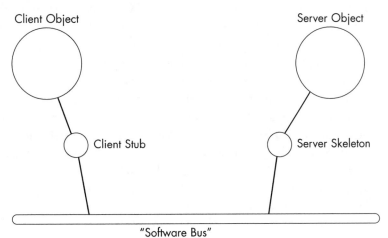

Client Object

Server Object

Client Stub

Server Skeleton

"Software Bus"

result or to continue executing. If the client chooses not to wait, it then usually checks later to see if the operation's result has been returned.

DII enables a client to learn about an entirely new kind of object while the client is executing, and then build requests and invoke operations on that object. CORBA defines an interface repository to support this capability, containing the interface definitions for objects in the ORB environment. When a client encounters a new, unknown class of object, it can query the interface repository for the object's interface. Once it learns that interface, it can then use the DII to build and invoke a request dynamically on the new object. As far as the server object is concerned, no difference exists between the static and dynamic modes.

CORBA predates the rise of the Internet, but the Internet Inter-ORB Protocol (IIOP) was introduced into the CORBA standard to allow interoperability among different vendors' ORBs. Because the problem to be overcome was one of interworking across the broadest possible range of implementations, using the simplest possible means, the OMG looked to the world of Internet standards. Internet standards can even be regarded as a nonreligious, ground-up counterpart to the OMG's activities, where the shared aim is interworking, but the motivation has been pragmatic rather than visionary.

IIOP was predicted to have a profound effect on Web-based architectures, as it would effectively supersede HTTP in many roles. HTTP is oriented around requesting and supplying documents. Because IIOP enables objects to talk to objects, functionality currently embedded within HTML pages can now break out of Web server restraint. This makes the use of Internet/intranet technology for multitier client/server a much more realistic prospect and allows the introduction of thin-client technology with accompanying advantages in terms of administration costs and control and versioning of software.

CORBA is an important tool in implementing functional wrappers for legacy systems. Because ORBs can be found for every conceivable platform, IDL can be written that exposes key behaviors of a legacy system to other application components. A customer lookup, for example, can now look like a method of an object in the community of collaborating objects, regardless of the system supplying the behavior behind the wrapper.

Enterprise JavaBeans (EJB) are another means of encapsulating server-side functionality. Before looking at EJB directly, we need to detour briefly around JavaBeans because the family resemblance of the names can cause confusion.

JavaBeans is Sun's component object model for Java. JavaBeans enable development tool builders to include palettes of Java components within their development environments. For users committed to Java, this enables them to take a component-assembly approach to systems development, similar to what they may be familiar with in Visual Basic. From Sun's point of view, Beans positions Java as a component technology that can happily interwork with other component approaches, notably Microsoft's COM.

From the technical point of view, one of Java's initial limitations was the isolation of objects within applets. Java applets can neither communicate with the page on which they appear nor with other applets. This means the scope of object collaboration is restricted to the applet's packaged classes. JavaBeans moved Java away from this static model to a dynamic model for object interaction.

A Bean has some obvious similarities with visual components such as OCXs. Beans have events, which enables them to communicate and connect together, and they have properties that developers can customize through a tool. In addition, Beans display introspection, which allows tools to analyze how a Bean works. A Bean is, therefore, a kind of self-describing object.

JavaBeans are not restricted to being visual components, but they are oriented toward building visual and, therefore, client, applications. Nonvisual JavaBeans representing database views, for example, are dropped on to GUI panes so their functionality can be accessed, but they do not equate to widgets in the finished screen.

Enterprise JavaBeans, on the other hand, focus on business application logic that sits in the middle tiers of n-tier applications, so they encapsulate common business services such as credit rating and address checking. They run in multiple transaction environments and are highly scalable. So-called session EJBs can be declared as stateless or stateful. Stateless EJBs can be used to provide pools of redundant service objects, while stateful EJBs can be used to create meaningful dialogues with a user.

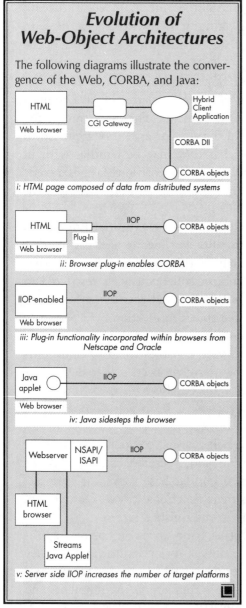

Evolution of Web-Object Architectures

The following diagrams illustrate the convergence of the Web, CORBA, and Java:

i: HTML page composed of data from distributed systems

ii: Browser plug-in enables CORBA

iii: Plug-in functionality incorporated within browsers from Netscape and Oracle

iv: Java sidesteps the browser

v: Server side IIOP increases the number of target platforms

Because CORBA is language-independent, it is possible to mix Java and CORBA development with ease. Using Java-to-IDL bindings, a Java applet can easily act as a CORBA client. The Java applet, therefore, becomes a true part of a distributed object system, with IIOP providing the wire. The Web server's role is reduced to downloading the applet. Thereafter, the applet bypasses the Web server to collaborate with whichever objects it needs.

In addition to CORBA-based communications, Java incorporates an alternative mechanism known as Remote Method Invocation (RMI). This provides similar facilities to CORBA-based ORBs, but only works between Java objects. Assuming the presence of a remote Java Virtual Machine (JVM) allows for a simpler approach than that required for CORBA, where a C++ object on one machine may be communicating with a Pascal object on a second machine and a COBOL object on a third. However, Sun has announced that RMI will support IIOP in the future.

On the Microsoft side of the street, we find COM, DCOM, and COM+. *COM* is the most often used name to describe Microsoft's component model strategy, though other marketing names are used. COM's history is confused by the naming changes along the way, but it is, nevertheless, one of progress.

Early versions of Windows included a data copying mechanism called Dynamic Data Exchange (DDE), which allowed data to be copied between applications. This was followed in 1991 by Object Linking and Embedding (OLE), which allowed the insertion of objects such as charts and spreadsheets into documents. Microsoft's Component Object Model (COM) now provided the common architecture for OLE objects.

In early 1996, OLE 2.0 was reborn as ActiveX, essentially a cut-down set of OCXs (Visual Basic controls). The ActiveX components formed the foundation of the Active Platform, Microsoft's branding for its network ambitions. The Active Platform comprised the Active Desktop, which was essentially the forward development path of Windows, and the Active Server, the forward development path of Windows NT and BackOffice.

Like CORBA, COM separates an object's implementation from its interface using an Interface Definition Language (IDL). COM objects differ from CORBA objects in that a COM object always presents multiple interfaces to its clients, whereas CORBA only presents one. To use a COM object, therefore, a client selects a method of a particular interface. Multiple interfaces are being added to CORBA and interfaces are an accepted feature of Java.

COM uses the notion of class more loosely than CORBA. When a client creates a COM object, it specifies a class identifier, which is essentially a pointer to a file that contains the code for the object. Class identifiers are mapped to file names in a registry so, if a filename is changed, an object's interfaces may also change. In CORBA, objects are directly related to their class.

Distributed COM (DCOM) was released in late 1996 for Windows NT and then for Windows 95. DCOM competes directly with CORBA, but uses RPCs for remote method invocation. Its security services are based on those provided with Windows NT. In 1997, Microsoft Transaction Server (MTS) appeared. This addressed the lack of transaction management and pooling facilities in COM/DCOM. Despite its name, MTS is an ORB as well as a transaction manager. COM+, which appears alongside Windows 2000, should rationalize Microsoft's "Active Platform" offering. Most likely, Microsoft's products will continue to be tied to its operating systems, whereas CORBA is an avowedly open initiative.

Data Staging and Database Choices

The separation of concerns encouraged by layered architectures enables us to treat the data access tier of an ecommerce system as an asset in its own right. But with application servers happily interrogating backend databases and spitting results at Web interfaces, why do we need to maintain any sense of separation? Surely we can promote seamless integration between the user and a backend operational system.

While it is true business systems can be thrown open to new user groups in this way, ecommerce is not solely a matter of unfettered collaboration. The state of your business as represented in its primary operational systems may not be the state you want to expose to your customers or partners.

The chief example of this distinction is the product catalog itself. Internal business systems maintain a view of the company's products and prices. Such systems should naturally be the source of any product or price details that are exposed outside the company's boundaries. A commercial difference relating to the *version* of such exposed information will almost certainly exist, though. Internal systems keep fresh product details and prices, which may even be awaiting effectively. The company's published details and prices are, from the point of view of many internal systems, historical items.

Of course, well-designed product systems maintain a distinction between published and internal data. In this case, an ecommerce application can be directed to the tables that contain the public versions. In many cases, however, the company wishes to add a new distinction between the offers it makes via the ecommerce channel and those it operates through traditional channels. In these cases, it needs to stage that data to declare a version of the product and price data, and to replicate it to an intermediate database.

This has the advantage of creating an artifact with a specific purpose within the systems architecture. Where a legacy system is being used to supply two purposes—its traditional role and its ecommerce function—it is all too easy for subsequent maintenance or modification actions to address the needs of one master while neglecting the other. If a staging database is used to serve the ecommerce channel, then such omissions are less likely to occur.

Of course, it is a business decision as to whether offers should vary according to the channel in which they are delivered. In the early days of ecommerce over the Web, one airline suffered when its online advertised prices were found to differ from those offered through travel agents. Today, we might expect the online price to be cheaper than that offered through a traditional channel. The emphasis in staging databases has shifted from ensuring that ecommerce offerings are restricted in scope and price. Today, the staging database may carry a wider range of goods and services than those represented in a store database. The staging database may contain absolute prices and rules about varying prices according to customer profile.

Another reason for staging data to an ecommerce application is hinted at in the opportunity to provide personalization. Not all customers are equal and many businesses gain their competitive edge through the capability to qualify customers against offers. In this case, exposing the true operational state of the business is the last thing the company wants to do. Consider, for example, a company that sells transportation services. Its operational systems need to know the precise disposition of all its vehicle fleets in real time and their predicted movements against service schedules. The company needs to know the capacity of each transportation unit, its delivery time, and its cost. But this is all information it uses to make decisions about what to offer to whom. Throwing it open to the customer essentially commoditizes the company's resources and removes its opportunity to add value.

In this scenario, a staging database might contain lists of vehicle types and their capabilities, and locations where they might be found. The public ecommerce application could calculate combinations of vehicles and route nodes that would enable a customer's load to be transported from one place to another. The result set would be notional, however. If the customer chooses a particular option, the application could interrogate the backend system to see how practical it would be for the firm to realize that option, given the current disposition of the fleets, other business being transacted, and the payment record of the customer. If the customer is known to pay rapidly and to pay top prices for speed, then the backend system might issue orders to assemble the required vehicle set from a number of outlying nodes and then issue a simple confirmation to the customer. If the customer is unknown, it may mark the orders as provisional, determine a suitable price, and run a credit check on the customer before making a provisional offer to the customer. It could also offer an alternative solution, perhaps suggesting a later, scheduled service for the delivery at a lower price that can be effected by a credit card transaction.

Our ecommerce application is here using a staged database structure to enact some of the enterprise's decision-making intelligence in the ecommerce channel. This is typically a strategy that won't have been deployed before ecommerce arrives on a company's agenda. Although it has always been possible to capture the decision-making expertise of agents within the business, little pressure has usually occurred to do so. Even where rules have been formalized and captured, they have generally been buried in standalone decision support systems, which agents are free to use or not, as they wish. The increase in query volume that ecommerce inspires and its spread around the clock, soon exposes the knowledge that human agents can no longer supply all the individual judgments needed to service them. The happiest outcome is the intelligence built into the ecommerce application is credible enough to make it a primary tool for the inhouse staff as well.

The key issues at the individual database level revolve around standards. The majority of client/server systems built in the past few years have been based on relational databases from companies such as Sybase, Oracle, Informix, and IBM. The interface to such databases is normally in the form of some version of Structured Query Language (SQL). Although a standard definition of SQL (ANSI SQL) exists, the major database vendors have added their own enhancements to support specific features within their own products, such as stored procedures and triggers.

In the early 1990s, object databases began to appear. These were a natural extension of object-oriented programming and represented a transparent method of providing persistent storage of objects. Such databases were extremely efficient for applications involving navigation between objects, that is, applications in which a string of messages were passing between a series of objects, frequently updating the attributes of the objects. They were less well suited to query-based applications, although a common object-querying interface was developed under the auspices of the Object Database Management Group (ODMG). The adoption of object databases was much slower than expected, partly due to the difficulties in supporting queries and partly due to the large and relatively recent investments companies had made in relational database technology.

More recently, hybrid databases have appeared or been announced. Two of the major products in this area are Informix's Universal Server and Oracle 8i. Such products allow relational storage for traditional forms of data and support object storage for multimedia or other data structures with a high semantic content.

Leading Relational Database Management Systems (RDBMSs), such as Oracle and Sybase, have evolved to incorporate a further degree of functionality beyond the structured persistence service described by the relational model. *Stored procedures* are functions that reside with the database, rather than the application partition.

A stored procedure can be an efficient way of exploiting an RDBMS's optimized lookup, traversal, and filtering behavior for complex, data-centric functions. Such functions may be less efficient if coded within a client, particularly where SQL is being used as an enabling layer. Where the data access layer is implemented around SQL, stored procedures can reduce the number of SQL conversations being transacted on the network. In this case, parameters are sent to the stored procedures and the database becomes a *fat server*. Stored procedures introduce a recognizable functional layer to the application and raise the level of abstraction operating at the data interface. This layer is tightly coupled to the database layer, however, and must be co-sited with the database.

Databases are frequently regarded as commodity items within ecommerce applications. The choice of database engine is more likely to be associated with the existing skills base within the organization than any deep analysis of the merits of a particular product. Another important influence tends to be the software development toolset favored by the organization. Developers using the Microsoft platform, for example, will naturally find it easier to work with SQLServer, even though ODBC enables them to work with any major database.

Firewalls

The firewall is arguably the most distinctive ecommerce technology item. In the days when no commercial organization would consider opening its systems to external users, protective barriers were not an issue. For companies embracing the full potential of ecommerce, controlling the gateway between the organization and its environment is a key factor in maintaining operational health.

A *firewall* is neither a product nor a service, but a strategic defensive element of an organization's security policy. In essence a firewall is a system component that sits between the enterprise's network and the external world. The network behind the firewall is hidden from the world at large.

The simplest firewall is a dedicated computer with two network cards. One card connects to the internal network, while the other card connects to the Internet. This machine is often called a *bastion host*. The only bridge between the two networks running at the bastion host is an application called the *proxy server*. The proxy server screens resource requests from internal machines and passes them on to the external network. A proxy server can be set to refuse particular types of request, which allows security administrators to restrict enterprise users' access to the outside world, as well as fending off inbound attacks.

Security control can also be achieved with a packet-filtering firewall. This approach typically uses a network router's configuration options to specify which IP packets are handled and where they are sent. Simple blocking by source or destination address enables the administrator to deny requests from hosts known as disruptive and to discard all packets not addressed to an appropriate host. In the latter case, the firewall can be configured so all HTTP requests are routed to the organization's public-facing Web server.

Another potential layer in a firewall is the use of network address translation. Three ranges of IP address are reserved for use on intranets. Because intranets are by definition closed networks, these special addresses can be used around the world without conflict. Using an internal addressing scheme and controlling the mapping of externally published service addresses to their internal counterparts in the firewall, adds another layer of obscurity to the enterprise's network level.

Some Typical Ecommerce Architectures

As many ecommerce system architectures exist as do development teams, but some common types recur often enough to be outlined as typical of the field. The four architectures discussed here represent distinct stages of maturity in an organization's response to ecommerce. They range from the apparently straightforward task of publishing static sales material to a highly automated transactional environment.

An organization's first brush with ecommerce often involves selecting some product details and publishing them to the web, using an architecture of the type shown in Figure 5-3. This architecture enshrines a separation of responsibility between the enterprise and its ISP, who hosts the site for the company. A report is run against a database that serves an existing business system. This report is converted into HTML, either by hand or using a simple formatting program, and uploaded to the site. Although this may appear crude, it is a safe and relatively low-tech way of putting product data before the customer. The creation of a report effectively declares a publication date on its

FIGURE 5-3. Brochureware.

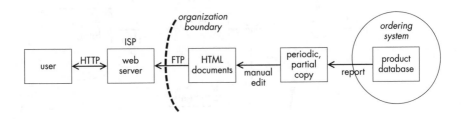

contents, allowing the online version of the company's offering potentially to diverge from the version used by the pre-existing ordering system that "owns" the database.

In the architecture shown in Figure 5-4, CGI is used to generate HTML pages on the fly in response to user requests. The CGI program works against a copy of the company's product information, with the copy refreshed on a scheduled basis. Details are fetched from the staged copy of the product information and merged with HTML document templates. Static information pages, containing less volatile information, are served in the normal manner. This architecture improves the user's ability to find what he is looking for, without threatening the integrity of the existing ordering system.

True ecommerce begins when we enable the functionality of the ordering system to be commanded by the end user. In this example shown in Figure 5-5, we created a wrapper for the ordering system in Java. The *wrapper* provides an interface that exposes the required functionality of the existing system to other Java objects via Java's Remote Method Invocation (RMI) communication mechanism. Java objects can now use the ordering system as if it were a newly made piece of Java functionality.

We have dropped CGI in favor of Java servlets as our means of extending the Web server's capabilities. Linking the Web server directly with the ordering system by creating servlets that co-operate

FIGURE 5-4. Searchable offers.

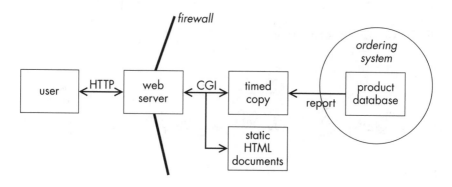

FIGURE 5-5. Ordering.

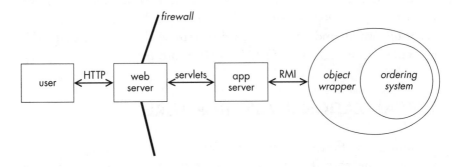

with the object wrapper would be possible. Instead, we created an application server to manage this interaction for us. The application server can, for example, manage parallel accesses to the object wrapper, ensuring performance is maintained when multiple user requests are received.

The architecture shown in Figure 5-6 uses CORBA to create cross-system collaboration among a number of resources. The application

FIGURE 5-6. Transacting.

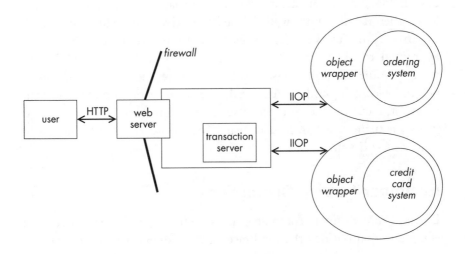

server is now at the heart of the system. Commercial application server products now offer extensive services, of which the Web server and transaction monitor are two key elements. We have wrapped the ordering system and the credit card system so they can participate in object communities using CORBA's IIOP protocol.

ORGANIZATIONAL ARCHITECTURE

Designing an effective organization for any undertaking is a complex task and one that is hard to get right the first time. When novel forms of interaction and challenging new vocabularies are involved, finding familiar models upon which to build can be hard. Add to this that ecommerce typically entails extensive collaboration between different disciplines, and finding an effective team strategy can be a daunting task.

Organizational approaches for ecommerce are currently best defined in terms of negatives and warnings. Highlighting the organizational factors that will inhibit an ecommerce initiative is easier than recommending a sure-fire team structure. In any case, just as ecommerce opportunities vary from enterprise to enterprise, a one-size-fits-all solution is likely to look baggy on everyone.

On a more positive note, if the enterprise has used a generic business model and application-seeking approach as suggested in this book, then it will have a well-defined objective upon which to base its organization. Those executives waking up to find themselves appointed to newly minted titles such as "Vice President of Ecommerce" would be well advised to backtrack to the applications phase before looking for bodies. A crystallized application aim tends to pull a natural focus on the core processes of an ecommerce initiative. This focus, in turn, tends to lead decision makers to the right choices on functions and skills.

Customer Service Distinctions

Business-to-consumer ecommerce has a profound, and often unsettling, effect on organizations that embrace it. A business that has previously prided itself on being customer-facing suddenly becomes customer-driven on a real-time basis. The distinction between sales and nonsales functions begins to blur because an obvious human or physical layer is no longer tasked with enacting the customer interface. At the same time the business discovers that *reach* is a bidirectional phenomenon: the enterprise extends a welcoming hand to its customers, but those customers grasp the hand and start to climb into the organization, operating whatever levers they can find inside.

The most obvious symptom of this effect is traditional forms of customer communication and, especially, telephone calls, do not diminish as online fact-finding, ordering, and status-tracking are rolled out. The nature of the inbound queries changes, with the proportion of nonroutine requests growing as routine transactions migrate to the automated channel. Customers call after absorbing your product information and that of your competitors. They are better informed about their options and about your company's capabilities than they previously were. They may, therefore, see themselves as holding greater negotiating power.

These are, of course, good problems to have. If a company's human communications channels become taken up with discussions only humans can have—while automated channels take care of routine business—then the company is starting to make the best use of its capabilities. Difficulties can arise when responsibility for managing dialogue in the ecommerce channel is mislocated in the organization.

Most commercial Websites grew from marketing department initiatives. Brochures, annual reports, and press releases take comfortably to the Web, and an increasing amount of supplier research is now conducted in this way. The presentational and news values of the Web in its publishing aspect have a natural fit with the competencies and goals of the marketing department. And, for many companies, the establishment of a systems-mediated service that calls for little intervention from the MIS department is a triumph for local autonomy and user power.

As the Web presence develops into an ecommerce channel, the presentational and news values of the site do not diminish, but they are augmented by dialog. The reader bites back and votes with his mouse. The user's comments must be taken seriously and some of his votes translate directly into sales. Where are inbound queries to be directed? Lack of responsiveness to customer requests, whether initiated through email or Web forms, is one of the leading customer complaints in ecommerce.

Two common ways exist in which inbound communications can be successfully fielded. The first approach uses filters to categorize queries and then to prepare automated replies or to route the original email to a selected agent for response. Often a site does both, so an automated acknowledgment is generated. This acknowledgment includes a note about to which email address the original query has been forwarded and, sometimes, a guideline as to how long the reply will take to formulate. Site designers try to train users to channel their queries in a helpful manner, typically setting up email aliases for sales@company.com and info@company.com. These aliases resolve to group lists of agents or cause entries to be added to a queue in a job-management system.

The second approach is to impose further structuring on inbound queries by restricting all dialogue to forms. Customers can be forced to specify a category for their communication from a drop-down list, which is often populated from analysis of inbound emails received prior to the forms strategy. The efficacy of this approach is contested throughout the industry. Some users claim customers do not like filling in lengthy forms and imparting demographic information. They also claim many customers will not contact a company unless there is a prominent email address to use. Others claim most customers find forms helpful and many do not want to compose their own emails.

Wise organizations tend to offer email and forms-based routes together. If the company is going to use human agents to compose replies, it is also worth investing in a relevant support system for the authors. This may include blocks of reusable text, prechecked legal statements, and guidance on greetings. More sophisticated support systems include methods for embedding URLs of relevant offers or information sources, and analysis of the success rates of various message texts, as measured by subsequent responses. That the themes of customer learning and personalization crop up here should be no surprise. Customer-generated dialogue is too valuable to ignore.

Where an organization is successful in building inbound traffic, it may want to consider creating characters to act as correspondents. This can be a way of standardizing the communications approach of a varying team of agents, so they all appear to sing from the same score. Where an organization owns a well-known character, this is a perfect opportunity to add a new dimension to its existence. On the other hand, many organizations find inbound email is the perfect opportunity to exercise a little honest humanity and may outsource response services to trained writers.[2]

The modes of human communication demanded by business-to-consumer ecom-merce are, therefore, somewhat

Seeing Eye-to-Eye

Conversations in the business-to-consumer ecommerce context often share one of these two potential pitfalls, which can waste much time and degrade the customer's opinion of the company:

"You know all about this."

This is an unspoken belief that influences how a customer communicates with an ecommerce company. Most customers have always believed that companies with whom they do business have an instantly accessible full history of the relationship. Any agent dealing with queries in the ecommerce channel needs customer transaction details and account summaries, just as any call center agent does. Where this information is unavailable, whether temporarily or by omission, the agent needs to elicit any required information from the customer and this is best achieved by admission that the information is missing.

"I bought it from you."

Despite a company's best attempt to create a distinctive presence, some customers misremember their buying behavior. The physical and social prompts that remind us where and when we performed some action in the real world are missing in the ecommerce world. It is, of course, hard to prove a negative, but it will be profitable to know what forms of words or graphic styles your competitors are using, so you may second-guess the origin of the enquirer's issue. ■

different from those traditionally used in the marketing department. The audience has fragmented, although it may be found to coalesce into a

---

2. Character strategies can be limiting. I once tried to get some information from the Coca-Cola Company, but the only email address I could find was for Santa Claus. I duly asked Santa to pass my query on to one of his pals at Coca-Cola but he seemed deaf to my plea, insisting merely that I have an exciting holiday.

number of new categories as the volume of inbound communications grows. Where email communications can be economically shifted to the phone, then the call center is the obvious center of expertise for managing the customer dialog. Where the dialog remains text-based, companies need to consider creating "e-centers" (probably virtual ones), where agent-authors take responsibility for the satisfaction of queries and development of the organization's understanding of its customers.

Fulfillment Impact

Just like customer service, fulfillment is an aspect of the organization's responsibilities that is traditionally seen as a discrete and noninte-grated department. Ecommerce bathes fulfillment in a new light. When goods and services can be ordered directly by the customer, no obvious reason exists why there should be a disconnect between intention and satisfaction. Consumers assume all customer-initiated trans-actions are handled automatically and are not interested in matters of system incompatibility. As we shall see, the chief architectural con-cerns on the systems side are to do with systems integration.

From the organizational point of view, companies need to chal-lenge the demarcation of fulfillment as an isolated function. If we are treating ecommerce as an inflected form of retail, then we are likely to see the efficient delivery of goods and services as a means of reducing stock in hand. But if we are to reduce cycle times, we also need to reduce latency in the enterprise's information flow. Confirmed orders should be echoed to production systems, as well as sales and ledger systems. Indeed, any order capture systems developed specifically for the ecommerce channel should be built with onward consumption by production systems as a priority design criterion ahead of manage-ment accounting requirements.

Signs exist that some companies have flipped these priorities, with sales and commissions systems reaching a pitch of sophistication, while delivery requirements are rekeyed to legacy production systems or even printed to paper. Putting management reporting in the foreground can be tempting, especially when expenditure on a new channel must be justified. Failure to meet shipping promises, however, will have a more direct impact on the actual success of the channel.

As well as streaming fulfillment in with order capture and customer service, organizations need to learn from the transaction patterns that inhabit the ecommerce channel and to implement predictive measures. This is a matter of translating behavioral and seasonal knowledge from the physical world to the online world. For example, a favorable review of a site generates new traffic, some of which is converted into sales. Predicting when such an event will happen or what level of impact it will have may be impossible. However, most such events are the result of proactive marketing activities carried out by the company itself. Site reviews tend to follow press releases or to mesh with sector surveys which, in turn, depend on product or service offerings from competitors. Average online demand is readily computed from server logs and companies can measure demand spikes by running test campaigns. In fact, this is the only way to assess the value of different online advertising strategies.

Structurally, fulfillment begins to fade as an isolated concept in favor of a more holistic appreciation of the entire supply chain. This is perhaps the most profound internal result of a move to ecommerce. The shortening of conceptual distance between demand and supply begs a systems response, but it is one of integration rather than a point solution. And, although we have discussed this issue largely in the context of business-to-consumer interactions, the same is true in the business-to-business arena. The most abstract of business-to-business services are now being dispensed on a straight-through fulfillment basis, with customers able to stake out the calendars of their trusted advisors, the relevant personnel being notified after the event. The traditional autonomy of consultants is eroded by their inclusion in an efficient supply chain because they must accept the same kind of ambient workflow long associated with call center staff. So just as customer services staff are becoming better able to act as consultants, consultants are becoming more tightly bound into work practices that optimize their value.

Supply chain integration is a potent topic in the ecommerce market place. As ecommerce erodes the barriers between discrete functions and organizations, so the ability of a player in one part of the chain to own a larger part of the chain grows. Delivery and logistics companies, for examples, are well placed to take more significant roles in the satisfaction of customer requests. Companies that can bind themselves into the chain stand to profit from it.

Ownership

Where does ecommerce "belong"? This is one of the most common questions raised within organizations and, although many people are uncomfortable with raising the question, it is nevertheless an important concern. We have been trained to discard mental constraints relating to organizational structure and to regard local ownership as an inhibitor to innovation and to customer service. Yet, we also all know new initiatives are doomed to failure unless explicit responsibility for their success is identified and publicized.

The key to allocating ownership for ecommerce within the organization lies in recognizing and communicating its constituent facets. Therefore, the branding and corporate voice of a business-to-consumer site should be given solely to the existing corporate communications team, with whatever support they may require from a new media design unit. Customer dialog issues should be located squarely with the existing customer services team. These two teams take the lead in establishing how the company speaks and how it listens.

Ownership of ecommerce systems themselves tends to raise more contentious issues. Most ecommerce systems recruit a range of legacy systems, which are under the control of the organization's IT department. Some ecommerce initiatives require solutions sourced by third parties, sometimes in the form of services rather than software components, for example, a credit checking facility. While the capability in question originates outside the organization, the IT department is the default owner of the relationship. This is even more likely where business-to-business, system-to-system interactions are involved. In this case, the complexity of matching two or more sets of indigenous peculiarities emanating from a set of organizations with their own histories and traditions tends to make the IT team the only player with any hope of understanding the project's critical path, let alone staying on it. It goes without saying that any organization with an established IT department will find its IT team eager to build new functionality or integration bridges, although the alacrity of such teams to collaborate with external suppliers is variable.

IT expertise rests in the IT team and IT departments make good environments for the development of solutions, process expertise, and facility with the firm's data—this is indisputable. Ownership of the associated business processes, however, does not go hand-in-hand with responsibility for the applications that serve them. An IT department may assemble, maintain, and operate a system, but it is a custodian of that capability, not its owner. Ownership remains in the business.

The IT/business divide is an increasingly confusing distinction as ecommerce develops. Clearly, some businesses are electronic and all businesses are tending this way. Business is IT and IT is business; so everyone is on the same side, performing the same dance. Organizationally, however, skills still tend to pool at the extremes of a business-IT scale. More important, loyalties do, too. People with a business orientation tend to see computing folks as obscure and obstructive, while IT people tend to see business people as unimaginative and slap-dash. These are horrific generalizations, of course; but some truth is in the observation that each "side" sees itself as the true keeper of the enterprise's best interests—a role it enacts through the maintenance of certain professional rituals.

No simple answer exists to this conundrum. Smaller and younger organizations tend to have less of an entrenched business/IT divide and the answer to its removal for larger companies may be to spin out new organizations with separate identities, goals, and cultures. This may seem counterproductive because the legacy systems, processes, and other intellectual property of the host organization represent its key value to a future ecommerce-enabled enterprise. Yet all established companies need to go through the process of making themselves appear "strange" to themselves, so they can challenge assumptions about their strengths and weaknesses. Budding off a multidisciplinary team that is tasked with implementing ecommerce capabilities across the company is one way of achieving this perspective. In this way, we can allocate responsibility for the leadership of practical change, without attaching ownership of all its goals and resulting processes.

Support and Development

Ecommerce applications have greater support requirements than most traditional business systems. Business-to-consumer applications need to be operable around the clock and every day throughout the year. Traffic analysis identifies periods when the least impact will be felt from maintenance downtime, though such an analysis may also be used to justify marketing efforts in the relevant time zone. The principal means of ensuring scalability and coverage is to operate mirror sites, with several separate images of the public ecommerce offering. This requires synchronization management, which adds a further level of systems-level functionality to a mix that already contains Internet connectivity maintenance, security monitoring, and component failure monitoring.

The daily impact in the systems department is, therefore, akin to a reformulation of its mission as a real-time business. An established regime with business hours support and overnight batch processing gives way to an environment where transaction streams and background reconciliations and analyses run in parallel.

From the point of view of systems development, most ecommerce applications are developed iteratively. Both business-to-consumer and business-to-business initiatives involve cycles of experimentation and evaluation. A sound practice is to prototype all ecommerce services internally before they are extended to their eventual user community. Inhouse use of online brochures, catalogs, and reservation systems developed in the target technology allow the organization to test its logical and technical architectures in a controlled environment.

Ecommerce systems development is often outsourced, with software components or services supplied by experienced third parties. Much is to be said for using third-party catalog and content management products, and for adopting third-party security frameworks. Where a service cannot be profitably performed inhouse, such as providing real-time currency exchange rates for nonlocal purchasers, third-party providers are the obvious choice.

When it comes to the systems integration task, however, being categorical about sources of expertise is harder. On the one hand, the inhouse team has the best understanding of its legacy systems, their organization, and behavior. On the other hand, they may have little hard experience in making them work together or in yoking them to the technologies of the Internet. Internet experience is growing at a fast rate within organizations, but the need to maintain legacy systems and to develop new point solutions means few internal IT teams can give their whole attention to integration issues. When committed business-to-business ecommerce is at issue, no obvious source of expertise covers all the applications of the partners. In these cases, external help is readily available from the various systems integration houses that specialize in various species of systems glue. Facility with layered architectures and component technologies are important criteria for choosing such partners.

Outsourcing can be extended beyond systems development. Indeed, the use of partners to develop or support aspects of the ecommerce offering is an example of the extended enterprise in action. Small companies may outsource their entire business-to-consumer sales channel to one of the major portals, offering their goods and services for sale to the world without even having a single PC to their own name. Larger concerns may want to host most of the channel's functionality themselves, to enable integration between their Web presence and their backend order and fulfillment systems. But even substantial organizations are likely to partner with external providers for certain specialized services. The two chief services in this category are payment transactions and goods shipment. At the level of the channel's overall format and direction, many organizations choose to buy in design and content origination services from outside. This is often because the organization's original Web presence was built by a new media agency.

Skills Audit

The skills required for ecommerce lie somewhere between the hard, prescriptive assumptions of the general technology follower and the soft, all-purpose requirements often associated with business change. An example of the former assumption is the idea that anyone wishing to get involved with ecommerce needs to learn HTML or Java. It is certainly true that anyone who is seriously interested in business-to-consumer ecommerce needs to devour online experience—buying products online, comparing service levels among competitors, and forming opinions about good interaction design. But it is unnecessary to become a visual designer or an applications programmer.

The other extreme trails a rag-bag of general criteria that it would be churlish to deny to most human activities. Certainly, problem-solving skills and customer orientation are important in ecommerce, but both have been handy since The Stone Age. Team members involved in ecommerce may need to solve problems of systems compatibility, sales message construction, or traffic variability depending on their specific roles and the makeup of the team.

We find the key determinant skills of ecommerce in the middle ground between these extremes. Technology skills include familiarity with distributed systems and object-oriented design. Softer skills include the ability to conceive of the customer as a present force, rather than as an abstract phenomenon, and the accompanying desire to engage with customers when the opportunity presents.

Above all, the most important skill found consistently among ecommerce practitioners at all levels is the ability to perceive and articulate their work as a crucial aspect of business strategy. Where it is successful, ecommerce feels like a crusade. It isn't about fashion or merely incremental benefits, but an element in the reinvention of the business. In the past, we expected business leaders to take responsibility for "the vision thing," while their followers made it stand up. Today, a palpable sense exists that digital connectivity puts its manipulators in control of the vision. The tools of process change, customer connection, and performance evaluation are now immediate and ubiquitous, meaning it's cheaper and faster to test an idea than ever before. Translating idea into action, through the tools of ecommerce, contributes directly to the business's development in a manner denied to earlier generations. The greatest skill lies in recognizing this power and embracing the responsibility to use it.

Can an organization be instilled with this sense of power? It's not as easy as sending everyone away on a course to be sheep-dipped in e-age attitudes. In many ways, it's easier than that. By making the signature technologies of the Internet era freely available to employees, corporates can discover overwhelming sources of ideas, examples, and enthusiasm. Companies that frown on employees using their desktop machines to search for a car or vacation are denying the greatest source of ecommerce learning at their disposal: the experiences of committed individuals engaging in ecommerce behavior. Employees who use today's Web are qualifying to create tomorrow's ecommerce applications. Employees who are encouraged to work away from the office begin to experience a flavor of an extended, virtual world of work. Employees who are encouraged to research via the Internet discover new perspectives on customer desires, competitor offerings, and alternative modes of business. In this environment, a sense of empowerment grows. Wise corporates recognize it is better to be associated with the dawn and development of this new awareness than to let it flourish solely in a nonwork context. As the lifestyle of organizations becomes more information-rich, so the potential of their people grows. Ultimately, the greatest skill required for an organization embracing ecommerce is the capability to foster a climate of learning, experimentation, and confident imagining.

6 | Open Issues

Ecommerce is an issue-driven field. Although its explosion was triggered by the success of an architecture born of the public sector, the growth dynamic of ecommerce is informed by a pioneering spirit that presses restlessly against its frontiers. Ecommerce is a world of trial and error, of rapid introductions and withdrawals.

This book stresses architectural approaches to the challenges of mounting ecommerce initiatives. The fundamental models we have explored continue to create value for managers in the midst of a perpetual tsunami of change. The issues collected in this chapter are neither the superficial ones relating to which companies will continue to be around in five or ten years nor speculations about breakthroughs in technology that will enhance the ecommerce experience. These are interesting matters to be sure, but they aren't of strategic interest in this context.

The issues that concern us here are those with the potential to throw weighty spanners in the works of ecommerce players. They form aspects of a climate that affects all players equally. Open legal, technical, and cultural issues have the power to flex the architectures of the best-prepared ecommerce player. They repay constant monitoring. Hearing about new technologies or new ecommerce products and services isn't hard. Tracking the sense of government policy, the relationship between technology announcements and industry competence, and the developing cultural context of ecommerce use takes a little more effort. Yet, attention to these areas can make the difference between a confident, well-designed ecommerce effort and one that can recover gracefully in the face of tectonic movements in the environment.

We are used to the rhetoric of speed. We believe business and technology change at a bewildering rate. But we often forget the bewilderment is felt on Earth, where we all live. "Internet years" are overlaid on dull old Earth days. The lag between what is becoming possible and what is passing out of practice is an unpredictable area.

LEGAL ISSUES

The law is catching up with the online world. The progressive migration of business to the Web is forcing reappraisal of intellectual property rights and their protection, and clarifying the meaning of intellectual property in a connected world. Responsibility and privacy are issues that touch on the law, though they are perhaps best characterized as aspects of common sense conduct. The political response to ecommerce, particularly its expression in regulatory and taxation policies, is a further source of potential uncertainty for the ecommerce player.

This section provides a taster of the main legal issues, but it is not exhaustive. As new ecommerce applications are developed, so established practices come under pressure.

Intellectual Property

The ease of finding and copying information on the Web leads many users to think that copyright is unsustainable in the wired world, but this is a false impression. Works published to the Web enjoy the same rights as other forms of publication. The World Intellectual Property Organization (WIPO) Copyright Treaty and Performances and Phonograms Treaty of 1996 extended the Berne Convention on copyright to include digital applications. Arguably, copyright is easier to defend online, as it is simple for a company to run a regular search on its own content to see if it appears in any unexpected place.

Intellectual property is a broader topic than just copyright. Types of intellectual property unique to the ecommerce arena include domain names and business process patents.

Most of the initial focus for companies embracing ecommerce was on acquiring a suitable dot com domain name. Some companies found their first choice of name had already been secured by another party and they had to pay to acquire it. Dot com domains were originally free and many Web pioneers speculated in names. Other companies found that although they had managed to buy the domain names they wanted, they had inadvertently allowed external consultants or new media agencies to register in their own right.

Businesses are now aware that memorable, single-syllable dot com names have all been exhausted and are being more creative with portmanteau words and phrases. But many are still unaware that dot com is not a U.S. territorial phenomenon. Dot com domains are assigned worldwide. A business in the U.K., for example, will try to register both as thiscompany.co.uk and thiscompany.com. It does not need to have any geographical or legal connection with the United States or any other country. In fact, the party registering the domain needn't be a legally constituted business in any sense. "Com" designates "commercial" rather than "company," so assuming domain name registration overlaps with trademark registration is wrong. Registering a trademark in one territory may not be sufficient to back your assertion to rightful ownership of the associated dot com.

The domain name regime is being overhauled, with enlargement of the number of agencies empowered to allocate names. The fundamental categorization scheme of Top Level Domains (TLDs) is also being revised to yield more potential names. Dot com has become entrenched as the sign of a commercial site, however, and it is unlikely that ecommerce operators or users will rush to embrace alternative categories. From the marketing point of view, the strings *http://www.* and *.com* are redundant lexical features that efficiently convey the medium rather than the message. To investors, .com in a company name is shorthand for "Internet stock."

That the most treasured intellectual property in online business is the namespace itself is ironic. The RealName service aims to circumvent the problem by maintaining an alternative namespace reality in which commercial concerns can pay for prominence and recognition.

More subtly, the portal movement reduces the need for the user to remember domain names by offering the most relevant links to key commercial sites.

On the firmer ground of patent law, ecommerce has created something of a stir. Patents are being granted for a range of business processes that are, in the opinion of many, generic ecommerce techniques. However, Jay Walker, founder of Priceline.com, who pursues intellectual property breakthroughs through his Walker Digital company, believes the novel modes of commercial practice in ecommerce channels can amount to legitimate innovations:

> "Walker Digital is about reengineering the DNA of the future of business," Walker declares. "What we hope is that a group of thoughtful people can together reinvent whole sectors of the global economy. And not only can we reinvent them, we can own those inventions."[1]

Of course, reengineering is itself the bane of all attempts to protect intellectual property. Ecommerce patents currently remain unchallenged, but the generic nature of many of them may enable competitors to formulate alternatives that achieve similar ends without infringement. In any case, the interest in filing business process patents certainly forces companies to spend on patent lawyers rather than on software and service development. This may help the image of a startup, creating the impression that it has jewels worth protecting. In a dispute, however, the ability to prove early and continuous commercial use of a technology is likely to be important.

Meanwhile, the cost of defending a claim of intellectual property infringement will often be more than the cost of paying royalties to the claimant. Smaller companies have long complained that larger companies restrict their movements with "walls of patents." As always, the cost of litigation is a form of social tax on business.

---

1. Quoted in "An Edison for a new age?" by Dyan Machan, *Forbes Global Business & Finance*, May 17, 1999.

Responsibility and Privacy

The abstract quality of the Web and its apparent autonomous existence as a medium of communication and business often cause uncertainty about personal and corporate ownership of the acts committed through it. Responsibility for content and transactions is not always as clear as in the traditional commercial world, where formal and informal codes of conduct have consolidated over many generations of use. Reliance on electronic communications mediated by networks and machines whose functions are mysterious to the majority of users raises suspicions about privacy and its accidental or malicious betrayal. In one sense, the Internet is the ultimate bureaucracy—a faceless solicitor, aggregator, and router of information. Like any bureaucracy, the Internet can engender distrust.

As we noted when discussing payment mechanisms, responsibility for failed payment transactions can be shifted between merchant and customer depending on the mechanism. Credit card transactions favor the customer in a dispute, while SET favors the merchant.

In other circumstances, allocating responsibility for outcomes is a matter of declaring rights and obligations ahead of a transaction. At this point, the word "transaction" can become treacherous. At least four popular uses of the term exist in ecommerce circles, describing a scale of meaning from "soft" to "hard" (Figure 6-1).

FIGURE 6-1. Four meanings of "transaction".

soft	moment of decision
↑	agreement of terms
↓	exchange of payment objects
hard	completion of data exchanges

At the soft end of the spectrum, a consumer makes a decision to purchase a product or service. From the marketer's point of view, this is the point of closure and the subsequent events are administrative details. The lower half of the scale covers the exercise of a payment mechanism and the completion of record updates in collaborating systems to ensure all participating systems are left in a consistent state.

"Agreement of terms" is the event that can cause problems if it is not addressed explicitly by the vendor. What exactly is the customer signing up for and what does each party undertake to perform as a result of the customer's decision to go ahead? Software vendors deal with this issue by interposing a license agreement in the download procedure for their goods. The user cannot proceed beyond the license text until they have clicked a prominent acceptance button, signaling their agreement to the terms and conditions of the license. This is the online equivalent of tearing the shrink-wrap or breaking the seal of a software product.

Providers of services can learn a lot from examining software vendor practices. First, software vendors sell the rights to use a piece of software, not the actual software itself. In other words, software vendors retain the intellectual property rights in their assets, while customers pay a fee to enjoy the functionality provided by the assets. Providers of other services tend to sell membership rights for similar reasons.

Second, every software license declares the bounds of the vendor's liability. Bug-free software remains a fabled creature, so licenses for full-product releases, as well as beta versions, bear disclaimers to liability. The precise "cocktail effect" of a piece of software running in an unknown target environment demands that vendors cover themselves for unforeseen clashes in functionality and, especially, for loss of data. Providers of ecommerce services need to consider the same issue. For example, how will an enhanced online version of a traditional business process interact with other processes in the target environment? Could a vendor be liable for unforeseen effects in legacy systems or even in the manual processes of the company buying its service? A clickable statement of liability can put bounds on such gray areas. Such a statement also communicates a positive message about the supplier's probity and his insight into the customer's situation.

Third, software licenses declare the legal jurisdiction that will be used in the event of any dispute relating to the agreement. This is usually the home jurisdiction of the supplier, but it needn't be. Every agreement must specify a jurisdiction, as no accepted default court of law exists for online transactions.

Agreements are often regarded as magic spells that ward off the evils of litigation. Of course, writing a poor agreement and leaving oneself open to subsequent challenge is possible. More important, potential customers have the usual right to negotiate a different agreement to the one proffered by a supplier. Mass market consumers rarely do challenge such texts but, in the business-to-business space, the negotiation of online contracts is as significant as it is in the traditional world. A business-to-business agreement may be arrived at after a lengthy exchange of emails involving the principal contacts at each party, their colleagues, and legal advisors. What is important is to capture all this correspondence and to control the proliferation of agreement versions. Digital acceptance of the final text by actors within each organization is almost as important as the final agreement between the contracting business entities. A stray thread of enquiry with a member of one company whose acquiescence does not appear on a final text can leave a leverage point for subsequent disputes.

An agreement text with an acceptance button can be used to implement a set of disclaimers relating to a product or service. Disclaimers play other roles in the determination of responsibility. Email sent from corporate accounts should always contain a statement reflecting the company's association with the text of the message and employees should be encouraged to mail personal messages from personal accounts. Corporate Websites may also choose to deny responsibility for sites to which it links or that link to it. In the case of linking out, no company can ensure the target site always presents the material it expects or that it will maintain similar disclaimers about the sites to which it, in turn, links. No site owner can control who links to it, but it is worth denying any business connection to a referring site that has not obtained permission to so link.

While agreements deal with making a business arrangement explicit, the privacy issue revolves around the fear of exposure. But privacy is a relative quantity, just as security is. The ultimate privacy is nonparticipation. A party that engages in ecommerce can protect its privacy by encrypting the information it exchanges and by taking care not to disclose anything it wishes to be kept secret. When a business suffers invasion of its privacy, this is usually due to a failure of policy, rather than any to ingenuity on the part of an attacking party.

Consider in the first place the huge amount of information companies now make available on their corporate Websites. Companies that in the past jealously guarded details of their employees and their research projects now routinely issue personnel lists, resumes, and research project goals and status via their Web presence. This isn't as a result of changed company policy, but as an effect of devolved responsibility for Web content management. This is also partly a cultural effect, whereby corporate Websites have tended to mimic the early examples set by academic institutions and nonprofit organizations. An astute researcher can often assemble quite precise intelligence about an organization by combing the Web. Information not presented at the corporate Website itself is often gathered from sites belonging to business partners.

Specificity is often the key to intelligence gatherers. This is easily seen by cruising a range of job sites. The same personnel requirements are often transmitted to a collection of employment agencies or online recruitment sites with minor variations. A distinctive pattern of common requirement elements plus location, or some unusual restriction or error, allow the hiring organization to be identified. Then it is trivial to aggregate the various sources to produce a faithful image of the slot being targeted. Analysis across groups of slots quickly produces entire project teams, their goals, and budgets.

Rarely does this level of privacy concern ecommerce players, though. The business value of information rests predominantly in business information. Most users, however, harbor fears about invasion of their personal privacy. We all have something to hide, even if it's only the sad fact that we have nothing worth hiding. A vague fear exists among some consumers that the Internet can somehow peer into their souls and transcribe what it finds there to a global notice board.

Individuals can protect their privacy by taking care of three quantities: Their identity, their utterances, and their hygiene.

Identity is a flexible quantity in the eworld. Free email services enable users to cloak their identities behind any number of aliases.

Membership Websites use usernames rather than real names. A credit card transaction betrays its owner, but passport schemes, such as Qpass, introduce anonymity at the level of the single transaction. Users inevitably leave a connection to their true identity in some system somewhere, though true masters of disguise could create their own network of cross-referring email accounts at any number of free email service providers.

Users intent on privacy can, of course, simply exercise judgment about what they share. Deja.com (formerly DejaNews) effectively preserves for eternity every statement made to a newsgroup or discussion site. Some commentators advise students in particular to avoid making any public statement in such a group that might reflect badly on them a few years down the line when they start looking for a job. Whether employers take the trouble to conduct such searches is a moot point. If one employer becomes known as a newsgroup-trawler, then this is only likely to cause prospective candidates to post self-serving statements to the target group.

On the other hand, Web research is not a precise science. Unless you have a truly distinctive name, it is hard for a researcher to be absolutely certain any statement attributed to you was actually made by you. Information associated with your name at a Website can be disowned. You may even be able to sue for defamation if such information is presented to you. Search engines also vary widely in the representations of the Web they offer. Many of them are concentrating on currency, having formerly silted up with withdrawn resources dating to 1994, the heyday of the early spiders.

In short, assembling a profile of individuals from their utterances in cyberspace is not an automatic matter. If an organization decides to target an individual, then it will benefit from using the Web, but it would be well advised to reserve much of its budget for old-fashioned trashcan sifting. The effort required by a single company to create a lifelike profile of a loyal customer provides some perspective on the ease with which anyone could capture a likeness from a distributed mass of statements.

Finally, comes the matter of hygiene. A user may store something private on a machine, but she cannot be compelled to send it to another party. She could, however, inadvertently reveal private information by installing and executing a virus. Many users consider viruses an affliction of their local environment and associate their actions with corruption of data. But a malicious program that sends data from the infected machine to another host is potentially more harmful. Documents, for example, are easily discovered by their file extensions; user profiles are often handily named "profile." This kind of siphoning can be avoided through normal virus-checking procedures. More simply, no user should ever run a program sent to him by anyone—even a friend—but immediately delete it on receipt. Any reputable piece of software is available for download with a license agreement covering its use.

Regulation and Taxation

The Internet is insensitive to geography, yet geography determines many of our commercial actions in the real world. Restrictions on business practices and taxation regimes vary throughout the world. What happens when we project a global, standardized communications infrastructure on to this background?

The U.S. has established some basic principles that have been echoed by other sovereign entities:

> "Governments do have a role to play in supporting the creation of a predictable legal environment globally for doing business on the Internet, but must exercise this role in a nonbureaucratic fashion [. . .] There should be no discriminatory taxation against Internet commerce. The Internet should function as a seamless global marketplace with no artificial barriers erected by governments."[2]

As well as characterizing the role of government as that of a facilitator, U.S. policy stresses the need for conformity in ecommerce:

> "The legal framework supporting commercial transactions on the Internet should be governed by consistent principles across state, national, and international borders that lead to predictable results

2. *The Emerging Digital Economy {1998}*, page 50-51, US Department of Commerce.

regardless of the jurisdiction in which a particular buyer or seller resides."[3]

In other words, the ecommerce universe should not contain any strange, local physics that makes a mockery of normal practices.

European Union policy has to unify two apparently conflicting viewpoints. The *European Initiative in Electronic Commerce*[4] notes that the Internet is a global phenomenon that has no respect for geographical boundaries. At the same time, the document is concerned to "ensure that a coherent regulatory framework for electronic commerce is created at European level" in accordance with the Single Market project. Ecommerce is, therefore, seen as an evolutionary step in the development of the European market, rather than a challenge to its logic. The European Union is here acting to preserve or enhance the competitiveness of the bloc, just as a single sovereign entity might. Its stated principles for regulation are light in touch and depend on existing models. New taxes for Internet transactions are rejected, but Value Added Tax (VAT) is identified as relevant to electronic trades.

U.S. policy implies that a new global legal framework could emerge to replace the current situation, where contracting parties choose a jurisdiction to govern their agreement. Given the history of global trade development and regulation, this seems likely, but not too soon. On the taxation side, governments will be frustrated from taxing Internet transactions at source because no overarching world tax authority exists. Indeed, such an institution would not have any logical basis for existing without a world government. The history of states cooperating with each other to handle each other's administrative obligations is not sparkling, so we should not expect any concerted effort to enforce or automate taxation on the net.

Regarding the practicalities of the regulatory environment, the OECD notes[5] that many existing retail regulations are inappropriate

---

3. *A Framework for Global Electronic Commerce*, The White House, July 1, 1999.
4. *European Initiative in Electronic Commerce,* Communication to the European Parliament, the Council, the Economic and Social Committee and the Committee of the Regions, 15/04/97, http://www.ispo.cec.be/Ecommerce.
5. *The Economic and Social Impacts of Electronic Commerce*, OECD, February, 1999.

for ecommerce. Restrictions on opening hours, for example, are intended to protect employees and neighborhoods, but become inhibitors on the Web. At the same time, existing regulations governing access to communications facilities become inhibitors to ecommerce because they have the effect of denying entry to some suppliers and customers.

The Internet is often thought of as a wild frontier where order follows some way behind the pioneers. The simple truth is the Internet's disrespect for geography encourages a leveling in business practice. Governments that implement restrictions will see business flow to other territories.

Where policy hits the headlines, it is likely to continue in the area of targeted intervention. Government agencies' right to decrypt encrypted messages is hotly debated and tends to distract attention from the wider issues of electronic—and electronically assisted—crime. With mainstream business migrating to the net, we are hardly surprised illegal businesses are exploiting its advantages as well. The point at which free speech becomes sedition, the responsibility for the caching of obscene images, and the perpetration of fraud are all issues only beginning to dent the public consciousness. Any social response to such issues requires a social mandate that can only emerge through debate and, to date, the level of discussion outside experienced Internet user community groups has been low.

TECHNICAL ISSUES

The pace of change in technology is famously fast. Offering some incantation to slow it down or to send its effects to blow around a competitor's site would be unrealistic. We can still keep some general principles in mind when tackling technical issues, however, and create a sense of perspective to help resolve them.

The technical issues examined in this section are the variability of platforms, the difficulties of communication, and the scarcity of skills.

Platform Risk

Platform risk is a topic that has long plagued technology managers. Making a commitment to an operating system or a hardware family locks the IT department into a set of constraints spanning performance, cost, and skills. These constraints may persist for a management generation or more and they may bar the organization from embracing new technology options as they arise.

Many IT departments have responded gracefully to the introduction of Internet technologies. The support of their existing vendors has been crucial here, with substantial incumbents, such as IBM, leading the introduction of new solutions and services.

Ecommerce raises the issue of platform risk beyond the local concern of the IT department. As ecommerce channels become mainstream elements of a business, they assume bottom-line criticality. Any business system that acquires an undisputed role in the core mission will attract attention from nontechnical management. In the case of ecommerce, we have to factor in the fluidity of a heterogeneous technical environment that is not wholly within the control of the organization.

The historic example of external forces dictating the direction of corporate IT thinking is the introduction of the Web browser. Corporate response to the sudden ability of customers, competitors, and analysts to access information in an intuitive and convenient manner was generally good. IT departments learned quickly about Web servers, HTML, and domain name registration. The rise of the intranet followed organizations' realization that the Web provided an excellent medium for information distribution within the enterprise. The success of the Web is an example of a nonbusiness tool changing the future of business and being absorbed into the armory of business. From the point of view of the IT department, the Web invaded corporate consciousness in much the same way as the PC, an affordable computing solution that began to appear on users' desks in the 1980s, despite the policies or opinions of the IT department.

Ecommerce yearns for ubiquity. It will colonize every connected device and infect every electronic dialog. Ecommerce applications will run in visual spaces as diverse as car windscreens and parking meter windows, clothing, and books. Ecommerce will also exploit audio channels, making broadcast radio an extraordinarily powerful commercial application. Ecommerce is platform-neutral and platform-hungry.

The unpredictability of the technical elements that will convey an ecommerce service is a strong argument for object-oriented design and multitier architectures. There is little sign that connectivity profiles will settle to some equivalent of the standard water supply pressure, so architects of ecommerce applications will have to continue designing service-level versions of their channels. A news application, for example, might negotiate its presentation layer with each accessing device, displaying three-line headlines to a mobile phone while staking a multimedia window on a desktop display.

Platform evolution and obsolescence is unavoidable. Organizations can insulate themselves from the worst effects of technology progress by riding with the changes. Collaborative research and development efforts with other organizations may serve to spread the cost of keeping up-to-date with emerging technologies and may facilitate technology knowledge-sharing across different platform experiences. Even those organizations with a strong motivation toward one platform or platform family—arising perhaps from an investment by a technology provider—will want to hedge with competing platforms.

Established organizations also face another, less subtle, issue relating to their technical platform. This is the freedom of new entrants who are unencumbered by legacy systems. The declining cost of computing has been an important source of new competition in areas such as banking, telecommunications, and travel. A new entrant in one of these sectors can buy or build their core transactional systems to run on low-cost platforms, such as Microsoft NT or Linux, whereas established players would gain no advantage from scrapping their existing investments.

Incumbents should be aware of the growing scalability, stability, and supportability of platforms they may be tempted to disregard as toys. They cannot deny their competitors this advantage, but they are free to reconsider where their principal added value would lie in a more competitive environment. In other words, platform effects can force a company to decide its traditional grunt applications have become commodities and the business's future rests on its interactive applications, customer service standards, brand value, and so on.

Communications Disconnect

Ecommerce is built around networking in two senses. Most obviously, network connectivity is the environmental factor that summons ecommerce into being. Without electronic communications, no electronic commerce exists.

Less obviously, ecommerce creates a new human communications situation within the enterprise. Ecommerce application development spans disciplines. In particular, it exposes business and IT colleagues to each other's values and vocabularies. All business systems development involves such creative combinations across departmental lines. Ecommerce development acts in the same way, but generally across a broader front. Ecommerce thrusts at the heart of an enterprise and impinges on all its organs.

Responsibility for understanding always rests with the initiator of a communication. If a message is misunderstood by a recipient, then the sender needs to construct a different message that better conveys his meaning. Most communications breakdowns arise from differences in the mental models held by each communicating party. The disparity in world view between technologists and business people can be quite profound and is a leading source of frustration in ecommerce channel development.

To generalize somewhat, the default attitude of the technologist to a project is anything is achievable, while the starting point of a business representative tends to be everything is difficult. Both attitudes are defensible and the result of experience. The technologist works in a fluid, abstract world where everything is, indeed, doable, but some solutions have better performance characteristics than others. She seeks to understand the standards and constraints that are operable in any particular project before venturing even a broad solution. The business representative, on the other hand, may begin with well-developed ideas about the look and feel of a system, or its development cost. Both sides struggle to find the characteristics that inform their goal sets. They need to find a common language with which to explore the problem space.

System modeling is the principal vehicle of shared understanding. The section on "Skills" outlines some of the main techniques used for modeling. Whatever techniques are used, it is vital that a neutral, visual means of joint discovery is employed. The team may simply draw blobs and arrows, or make storyboards, and never trespass in the vicinity of a published methodology. They must, however, tackle the project together, treating it as a mystery to be solved, rather than a product of either discipline that must be somehow transposed into an alien environment.

Communications problems during application development are also eased by using rapid prototyping techniques and an incremental development life cycle. *Rapid prototyping* means test versions of a deliverable are built quickly to drive out comment and correction. Many great applications have been kick-started this way. The Web has encouraged prototyping on a large scale, with sites published for feedback and republished with amendments. Incremental development simply means chunks of an application are delivered as they are completed, rather than delaying release until the full functionality is complete. This enables users to experience the system early on and to raise modifications for subsequent releases. Incremental development is particularly important in business-to-consumer ecommerce applications, where inhouse staff typically stand proxy for end customers during development. Inhouse users can create a useful buffer, in turn, releasing increments to the external population in line with business plans.

Returning to the first meaning of communications, enterprises need to absorb the implications of reliance on electronic connectivity for revenue streams. What is the impact of network outage? Loss of the ecommerce channel needs to be covered in some way and certainly addressed by the same order of contingency planning that would underpin, for example, the operation of a physical retail outlet.

Skills

The short supply of IT skills is endemic and is merely magnified by the explosive growth of ecommerce. Policy interventions at school and college education levels take some time to show their effect. Products of the best education systems are free to sell their labor wherever they can, leading to pooling in various "Silicon Wherevers" and drainage from traditional business centers. There will always be a mismatch between skill supply and demand; indeed, one of the most active ecommerce areas is online recruitment.

Structural attempts to solve the skills crisis tend to attract most attention, as they involve tax revenues and local or national pride. Wiring schools or waiving restrictions on startups do have an impact. This approach does much to ignore the wealth of convertible talent already in the work pool, however.

Application development, for example, continues to reach toward a purely visual mode of construction. It would be wrong to suggest that all, or even a majority of, worthwhile business systems can yet be built without reference to procedural logic. Programming is still some distance from being wished away. Yet a great deal of work at the presentation layer can be undertaken by non-IT staff. Page design is an obvious task that is usually best wrested from a programmer. By providing common tools and page features wrapped as plug-and-play objects, IT departments can also encourage a kind of kit development by nonspecialist colleagues.

Systems analysis and design is another area that is traditionally reserved for staff with a programming background, yet its origins are distinct from those of computing. Pure systems analysis disregards the existence of a computer system, making no assumption about how functions are performed in a problem's solution. The conflation of systems analysis with computer systems construction has been one of the factors behind the rise of business process (re)engineering, which is at one level an attempt to reclaim the rights of description and prescription from the IT department. Complex ecommerce systems are best described as collections of collaborating objects and such a characterization may come more easily to a nontechnical person than one steeped in the practicalities of deployment.

For example, a high-level understanding of the uses to which an ecommerce application will be put is essential and must precede any build decisions. In object-oriented methodologies this is likely to be a set of use-cases, together with event models. *Use-cases* are scenarios of system use and can be used to specify system requirements, as well as to test eventual system functionality. Use-cases are associated with Ivar Jacobson's Objectory method and, subsequently, the Unified Modeling Language (UML).[6] Event modeling describes how use-cases break down into individual object interactions. A suitable alternative is a system context diagram, with lower-level flow diagrams. Whatever conventions are used, the team identifies the actors that will use the system and what events they will cause to happen.

Another useful concept from the object technology arena is Responsibility Driven Design (RDD), usually identified with Rebecca Wirfs-Brock.[7] At its simplest, RDD is an analysis and design approach that focuses on the distribution of capability within a system by regarding the system's parts as well-defined, collaborating agents. Responsibilities are allocated much as we would allocate them to specialized professionals or teams in the real world. A Pricing service, for example, might be responsible for determining current prices of all products and releasing them to recognized objects. This enables us to define the Pricing module while deferring consideration of its exact interface, let alone its implementation details.

These analysis and design techniques can be used without any familiarity with computer systems development practice. The outputs of such activities, however, make ideal inputs to systems developers. Recasting the boundary between non-IT and IT skills in this way is a powerful means of defeating assumptions about IT skills. Certainly, not everyone can be a Java programmer, but ecommerce doesn't need everybody to be one.

Another area where skill problems can bite is in project management. The incremental life cycle can be a challenge to project managers used to waterfall approaches, where deliverables are clearly defined, scheduled, and signed off. This typically represents a confused attitude to the incremental life cycle, which is not a label for

---

6. *The unified software development process*, Ivar Jacobson, Grady Booch, and James Rumbaugh, Addison-Wesley, 1999.
7. *Designing object oriented software*, Wirfs-Brock, R., Wilkerson, B., and Wiener, L., Prentice Hall, 1990.

chaotic development. The key to successful management of such projects lies in identifying meaningful increments, which become units of work and of delivery, and distinguishing this from iteration. Iteration is a process of discovery, which is appropriate for architectural activities, but not for component construction. Confusion arises because the generation of increment definitions is driven by the iterative process of analysis. The project manager needs to remember these distinctions and to manage expectations actively both inside and outside the project accordingly. Iterative development is often combined with some project management mentoring and coaching to help managers through their first experience of the technique.

MARKET ISSUES

Ecommerce is progressing from novelty to habituation, but its progress is not steady. Different service types, user populations, and commercial organizations are moving at different speeds. A high-tech worker in Silicon Valley is already used to the Web lifestyle and expects to conduct much of her private and work business from various scattered desktops. Scandinavia, on the other hand, may not have the Bay Area Web culture, but its people are enthusiastic users of the digital messaging services available on their mobile phones and they are embracing ecommerce from a different direction.

The market issues discussed in this section are volatility, locus, and trust. These are as much a product of cultural lag as market structuring. The resettling of expectations, use modes, and customer loyalty will continue for some time as turbulence continues to wash through the ecommerce scene. This section gives some pointers to the likely long-term outcomes in these key issue areas.

Volatility: Free Rides on the Roller-Coaster

The gravity-defying performance of some Internet stocks is matched only by the bizarre business models of many ecommerce players. Free browser and email client software helped to create a mass user community for the net but, in the process, created an expectation that all software can be free. Free email services are widely available and have set a precedent for other Web-based services. The U.K. experienced huge growth in Internet use from the last quarter of 1998 with the launch of Dixons' Freeserve Internet service provider and a host of imitators. British users, who already pay local telephone call charges, fell to the lure of the Web as well-known brands began to offer free access. At the same time, providers of traditional goods on the Web began to follow ruthless price discounting with free products. Business-to-consumer ecommerce is implementing loss-leader tactics with a vengeance; but where is the loss leading?

Companies who do not charge for their products or services are essentially in the business of buying markets. Internet pure-play companies are valued on the basis of their user populations on the assumption that today's users can be transformed into tomorrow's customers. Yet the freebie culture is not one that encourages loyalty. Much of the stock market "bubble" is underpinned by faith in the capability of ecommerce to deliver huge value to companies who have staked out portions of the Internet environment; yet many of the same companies are undermining that very potential through free-ride conditioning.

Where any individual stands on this issue depends on a number of factors, not least his investment horizon. Companies seeking to cash out of an ecommerce position in 12 to 24 months may not need to worry about the sustainability of their business models. Attitudes also depend on how tight a grip we believe ecommerce has on the mass market. This consideration is often brushed aside because little distinction is usually made between the Internet and ecommerce. It is hard to believe that the great effect of the Internet, and particularly the contribution of email to business life, will ever be reversed. But more doubtful is that mass market consumers would pay economic rates for the right to purchase popular items, such as books and airline tickets, over the Web. The alternatives are too well entrenched, so unless the online providers succeed in killing off the physical competition, consumers will always have a low-effort alternative. Those who provide premium services on the other hand, such as Streamline, are already proving customers value their services above traditional alternatives.

A short-term view suggests the conversion of any ecommerce offering into a self-sustaining revenue generator is an academic concern. Success is measured in terms of eyeballs and their growth over time. This metric enables acquisitions and financings as the company snowballs in value. Working revenues may be generated by selling advertising space on the related Web properties or by selling demographic information about the user base. Muscle and speed can lead to rapid dominance of a segment, delivering a category-killer company.

In the long term, mass market ecommerce will tend even more toward entertainment models. This may appear counter-intuitive in a climate that prizes price and convenience above all other factors. However, low prices and guaranteed convenience are attributes that any competent ecommerce player can achieve, given enough investment. Engaging a customer over a long relationship is not so easy. Players in the consumer market need to consider retention as their number-one priority. All eyes are currently on customer acquisition, but retention is a more significant concern for those who are in for the long haul.

Our best model for long-term engagement is the entertainment business—particularly the music industry. Post-war artists have achieved striking longevity by adapting to new styles and movements, and reinventing themselves for new generations while maintaining their core appeal to existing audiences. Arguably, given the diversity of creative and technical talents that go together to make a modern music product, our stars are the persistent brand around which commercial and cultural forces cohere.

As we noted with the pioneer business-to-consumer sites, one key to success is the creation of a sense of community. The nurturing, development, and adaptation of this quality will be a major influencer on the ability of ecommerce players to win through the loss-leader years. Those who are building mindshare, reputation, and above all, personality will be those who remain when the bubble bursts.

In one sense, this market issue is concerned with volatility. User habits are capricious, not yet tamed by long use, and far from loyal. At the same time, the public markets raise novel players to dizzy heights (eBay) and cut them back when they show any slight failure (eBay again[8]). Both consumers and businesses are living in an era where small changes have unpredictable effects.

Locus: Electing into Groups

We have seen how the growing availability of mobile devices and novel connectivity options is delivering a ubiquitous ecommerce environment. A consumer can now engage in ecommerce from anywhere. Ecommerce players need to consider how the current or preferred location of a customer will impact her interaction with the provider. Little wisdom is yet available on how mobile ecommerce differs from deskbound ecommerce but, clearly, communication styles need to vary depending on whether a service is being directed to a fully featured device, such as a PC or TV, or to a restricted environment, such as a car dashboard and audio system.

The locus of users is also relevant to competing or complementary channels. Some observers assume physical retail space will be pressured by the flight to online sales. We believe it is more likely that physical retail space will adapt to act more as a showcase for products and services, rather than a storehouse of goods. People still want to congregate, to see products, to hear explanations and see demonstrations, and crucially to exercise their right to act on impulse. Ordering may be done from devices within the retail space and fulfillment may occur as a separate home delivery event, but many retailers will retain branded physical spaces for the reception, education, and entertainment of their customers. Gateway Computer, for example, has opened several brick-and-mortar stores, but they sell nothing directly from them. All purchases are made through their online storefront and shipped directly to the customer. Gateway Computer also offers educational courses at the store site, optimizing the value of the physical space and enriching the customer relationship.

Stretching the concept of locus a little, we should also note the age and lifestyle groupings that supposedly typify Internet and, supposedly, ecommerce consumption are being challenged in the light of

---

8. Interruptions to service at eBay in June 1999 had immediate impacts on its stock price.

experience. Older people have proved to be some of the most active and adventurous users of the Internet, using email to keep in touch with far-flung family members and exploiting the Web to pursue hobbies and education. At the same time, the assumption that every child connected to the Web collects a bonus in university grades down the road is being questioned by educators and parents.

As ecommerce players become more adept at individuation, gross demographic and access location definitions will become less relevant to marketers. Most current attention is fixed on determining the spending power of the home Web user, as this is the nearest analogue to the traditional family consumer model. Marketers and ecommerce channel designers would be wise to consider that individuals play increasing numbers of roles, depending on their changing responsibilities and location. Their goals and communication preferences will not be fixed in a one-to-one relationship with a single-dimensional profile. The fluidity of work- and lifestyle in the digital era will generate complex buying behaviors in consumers and crude tools will fail to discover the real commercial opportunities amidst the growing noise.

Trust: A Bond with the Customer

Despite the growth in uptake of Internet service in both commercial and private spheres, fear and distrust dominate the average visceral attitude to the development of ecommerce. Many consumers are wary of the breathless excitement generated by technology evangelists and the tension between technology innovation and human values conservation is one of the defining cultural characteristics of our time. The battle between old and new is not without its contradictions with, for example, anarchist groups using the Web to organize and advertise antibusiness protests.

Among people with low affiliation to either extreme a stubborn and reasonable level of distrust relating to ecommerce appears to exist. This is a remarkable phenomenon, in that it seems to apply in the general, rather than in the specific, case. My conversations with customers, managers, and consultants regularly produce generalized doubts about the safety of doing business on the Web, swiftly followed by a list of exceptions they wish to recommend. There is a temptation to ascribe this situation to the novel technologies and terminology of ecommerce. I think, though, it is more likely we are witnessing a simple adaptation of the common approach to commercial activity. Most of us vaguely assume the stores and brands we use are superior to those we don't use and we may even feel slightly sorry for people who patronize other providers. I am loyal to my supermarket, but I suspect it's because I know the way there. Maybe some vestigial part of me believes if I seek out another store, I'll be trapped in a pit lined with sharpened sticks. I can rationalize my loyalty all I like, but habituation and perceived personal security probably play the major part.

Losing sight of the function of brands is easy, living as we do in a world saturated by brands, and where noncommercial activities, such as politics and religion, are accused of using soap-powder sales techniques. Yet the real function of a brand, in a traditional setting or online, is to provide reassurance. Products and services that bear a known brand carry the promise of their producers. They set expectations about quality and redress. They reduce purchasers' distress about making poor decisions: people will sympathize if my brand-name stereo breaks down, but shrug if a store-labeled system does the same.

The real strength of Amazon currently is not its revenues, its losses, its technology, or even its gargantuan virtual inventory. Its true strength lies first in its position as most people's introduction to buying something over the Web. Second, it has a powerful position as the name people will most often recommend to others. Amazon has built an immensely influential brand by giving individual consumers positive experiences, engendering considerable goodwill and word-of-mouth advertising as a result. Interestingly, many Amazon users have difficulty in describing the company's logo when asked. The word alone has become a potent brand.

Trust is encapsulated, maintained, and delivered through brands. It seems established brands stretch to ecommerce with particular ease when they are themselves concerned with conveying trust concepts. The success of credit card transactions on the Web, for example, derives partly from convenience, but partly from the credit card companies' reputation for efficient and reliable purchase handling. Brands such as the *Wall Street Journal* or the BBC bring their reputations for truthful coverage to their Web properties. Consumer associations are starting to offer consumer protection services for ecommerce sites. Consumers tell researchers the backing of a major financial institution would increase the likelihood of their making an online purchase.

Most of this chapter has concentrated on the business-to-consumer space, but all these issues apply equally in the developing business-to-business market. On the issue of trust, the successional entry of Microsoft, IBM, and Hewlett-Packard as big e-players provided definite boosts to the development of ecommerce applications and strategies on each occasion. Hewlett-Packard's public conversion to ecommerce and ebusiness came as late as 1999 when it launched its "e-services" campaign, yet the declaration of one of the industry's oldest and most respected names was mostly greeted with relief rather than cynicism.

Brand building and brand migration form one angle of attack on the trust issue. The other main management option for building trust is relationship management. Ecommerce efforts are often fixated on transactions, but relationships are the human channels for transactions.

Physical retailers have discovered, often to their pain, that much of a customer-supplier relationship is rooted in the physical. Retail banks, for example, found customer relationships melted away as the bank dematerialized into a mass of convenient encounters. Supplier and customer both benefited from economies and efficiencies of automated services, yet counter service is hard to beat as an opportunity for establishing real emotional identification. Ecommerce players need to work hard to maintain visibility with customers and to continue dialogs with them. They are currently constrained on the outbound channel by plain-text email, which is difficult to differentiate and enliven. The failure of "push" technologies to establish richer channels to the user has left players to rely on the utility and interest of their Website as the primary means of communication. Although many email clients now accept HTML email, few commercial operators dare to use it because it isn't universally available and because many users will not tolerate incoming mail with large embedded images.

Maintaining the relationship at a basic level by stoking dialog is crucial to long-term viability for any ecommerce offer that cannot command a monopoly on some species of transaction. Managing that relationship effectively allows trust and tolerance to grow, and can create the most valuable tool an ecommerce player can own: a champion who will promote the brand to friends, family, and associates.

# Recommended Resources

No shortage of material relating to ecommerce exists, especially online. This section lists only those resources we have found consistently informative, accurate, and readable.

ONLINE

One of the best sources of general industry news and background is Cnet News.com (www.news.com), which also maintains a comprehensive ecommerce news section.

The Industry Standard (www.thestandard.com) is an invaluable source of news, analysis, and opinion on the developing ecommerce landscape and much else.

Iconocast (www.iconocast.com) is particularly useful for research results and for first recordings of new trends and terms.

PRINT

Most newspaper business sections carry stories on ecommerce, particularly on the fortunes of publicly quoted Internet stocks and predictions for the growth of different ecommerce application types. Among the general business magazines, *Forbes* and *Fortune* provide clear and lively coverage of ecommerce topics.

Red Herring magazine is a reliable, attractive, and alert commentator on the developing technology business, and it is particularly strong on emerging technologies and companies.

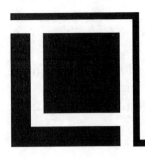

Glossary

aggregation   The compilation of collections of data items or content of similar type; also applied to the creation of markets from disparate customers and to the concentration and matching of supply and demand in a market.

agora   An assembly place and market; a venue for online transactions.

applet   A set of Java classes that can only be run within some larger, more complex environment such as a Java-enabled Web browser.

applet runner   An environment that runs applets.

authentication   The validation of a party's identity.

availability   A measure of a system's effective user uptime.

b2b   *See* business-to-business.

b2c   *See* business-to-consumer.

bastion host   A machine that acts as part of a firewall.

brand inflection   Adaptation of a brand for the online environment.

business-to-business   A term denoting ecommerce applications oriented to users acting in employee roles or to collaborating systems operated by business partners.

business-to-consumer   A term denoting ecommerce applications oriented to individuals acting in a personal or family capacity.

category standard   *See* retail category standard.

Common Gateway Interface (CGI)   A protocol for taking data from Web forms and processing it, thus extending the functionality of a Web server.

channel   A branded carrier of entertainment or information; a permanent route to a group of customers.

channel partner   A company that handles product distribution on behalf of a manufacturer or packager with which it is allied.

churn   The propensity of a service provider's customers to terminate their contracts.

client/server   A type of systems architecture that distributes computing tasks among two or more machines.

Common Object Model (COM)   Microsoft's component model strategy.

community guidelines   Rules of behavior provided for users of electronic marketplaces.

connectivity   Participation in an electronic network.

content   Text and images displayed at a Web site; usually refers to noninteractive parts of a site.

content negotiation   A tactic whereby a Web server sends different content to a client depending on the HTTP headers it receives; used more loosely to refer to strategies for displaying content relevant to a particular user or group of users, as initiated by more explicit means.

cookie   Data written to a client machine by a server for subsequent reference by the server.

corporate data modeling   The identification and description of commonly occurring entities about which the enterprise stores information, such as Customers and Products.

cryptography   The science of rendering communications meaningless to all but their senders and receivers.

customer self-administration   *See* downstreaming.

datagram   A collection of data accompanied by addressing data.

dematerialization   The replacement of a physical good or document by the information required to assemble it.

digest   A value computed from a data set and used to check that the data set has not been subsequently altered.

disintermediation   The removal of established intermediaries from commercial relationships and their replacement by direct connections between the parties formerly serviced by the intermediaries.

downstreaming   The shifting of clerical tasks to a customer or business partner by giving her access to business system functionality.

Digital Subscriber Line (DSL)   A means of increasing the bandwidth of existing copper cables by using a greater range of frequencies than in traditional telephony.

ebusiness   A term introduced and popularized by IBM to express the use of Internet technologies throughout an enterprise's activities.

Electronic Data Interchange (EDI)   A means whereby computer systems can exchange standardized documents relating to transactions across dedicated communications networks.

Electronic Funds Transfer at the point of sale (EFTPOS)   A means of taking payment instantly from a customer.

expert system   A system that processes a collection of rules to suggest possible courses of action.

extended enterprise   A view of an organization that takes into account its partner relationships at the moment of examination.

extranet   An extension to an intranet allowing third parties to access some corporate resources.

e-zine, zine   An online magazine publication.

fat client   A type of system architecture that places processing responsibility predominantly on the client device.

firewall   A system component (hardware and/or software) that sits between the enterprise's network and the external world.

File Transfer Protocol (FTP)   The standard means of moving files between machines connected by Internet standards.

fulfillment   the satisfaction of a customer order.

globalization   The erosion of trade and communications barriers, accentuated by the reach and functionality of the Internet.

host   A computer attached to a network.

HyperText Markup Language (HTML)   A scheme for embedding instructions about how text should be rendered within the text itself.

HyperText Transmission Protocol HTTP   The means whereby HTML resources are fetched across network connections.

hypertext   Digital content containing executable links to other digital resources.

Internet Inter-ORB Protocol (IIOP)   A protocol added to the CORBA standard to allow interoperability among different vendors' ORBs.

incremental development   A software development strategy whereby usable pieces of an application are delivered to the user community as each piece is completed.

individuation   The identification, profiling, and targeting of individual customer relationships in an ecommerce channel.

inflection   *See* brand inflection.

intellectualization   The trend toward knowledge- and dialogue-based products and services.

intermediation   The activity of a third party that acts as an introducer and facilitator of commercial relationships and transactions on behalf of pairs of parties.

interoperability   The capability to make dissimilar systems work with each other.

intranet   A network running inside an organization, using Internet protocols.

Internet service provider (ISP)   An organization that supplies email and Web services to end customers.

Java   An object-oriented programming language developed by Sun Microsystems, intended to allow platform-neutral software development.

Java bytecode   The intermediate language interpreted and executed by a Java virtual machine (JVM).

JavaScript   A general purpose scripting language.

JVM   Java virtual machine: a notional machine that runs Java bytecode.

Jini   A federated operating system architecture developed by Sun Microsystems.

legacy systems   An organization's installed computer systems, so called for their continuing value in subsequent development or the difficulty of removing them.

logical architecture   A type of generic systems model.

markup   Instructions embedded in a document that control its rendering.

memex   A Web-style information network envisioned by Vannevar Bush in 1945.

mobile commerce   Electronic commerce using mobile devices such as cel phones as clients.

near end crosstalk (NEXT) A form of interference that can cause data degradation in some DSL architectures.

nonrepudiation The assurance that a completed transaction cannot legally be denied by either party to the transaction.

n-tier architecture A layered system model, where distinct but communicating software layers each manage a specific class of tasks.

object A package of data and function that does some coherent job.

Open Buying on the Internet (OBI) An architecture for business-to-business procurement systems.

offer A combination of product and service elements; also used by Open Market to designate an object representing a purchasable item.

one-to-one marketing The practice of addressing commercial offers to individuals as individuals rather than as members of groups; *see also* relationship marketing.

operational data Data collected as a result of an enterprise's core transactional systems, such as sales in a retail organization or calls in a telecommunications network.

Object Request Broker (ORB) A piece of software that acts as a mediator between interworking objects.

partner inclusion System-to-system collaboration between business partners.

Personal Digital Assistant (PDA) A handheld electronic device normally combining notebook, address book, and calendar functions.

Public Key Infrastructure (PKI) A security architecture that combines specialist authorities, digital certificate management systems, and directory facilities to create secure networks on top of unsecured networks, such as the Internet.

plug-in A piece of software that extends the functionality of another program, typically a Web browser.

portal A branded gateway to resources and services; increasingly the home page of an ISP.

presence A basic commercial Website.

procurement The business process of acquiring products and services.

proxy server An application (or application and machine) that screens resource requests from internal machines and passes them on to the external network; used as part of a firewall.

public and private keys   The pair of keys used in a leading crypto-graphic solution; the keys are mathematically related, but one cannot be derived from the other.

rapid prototyping   The practice of building and releasing test versions of a software system in order to provoke comment and correction.

Responsibility Driven Design (RDD)   A systems analysis and design approach that focuses on the distribution of capability within a system by regarding the system's parts as well-defined, collaborating entities.

reach   The extent of potential interaction between connected parties.

relationship marketing   The practice of creating a personalized dia-logue with a customer to discover and propose attractive offers; *see also* one-to-one marketing.

refill   A product attribute designed to ensure repeated consumer/supplier interactions.

retail category standard   The set of design elements that suggest, in any one era, a particular type of store.

scalability   The capability of a system to grow in size to service an increasing number of clients.

screen-scraping   A technique for creating a new interface to an existing system by emulating user inputs and redirecting system outputs.

servlet   A Java object that runs on a server.

Secure Electronic Transaction (SET)   A payment mechanism that performs authentication of both parties to a transaction.

Standard Generalized Markup Language (SGML)   A way of describing the treatment of any kind of document in a processing system.

slot   A bounded, atomic, and historical value opportunity that may be sold or traded.

smart card   A plastic card with an embedded chip, typically used to store customer account data in automated payment applications, such as payphones and turnstiles.

staging database   A replica of a corporate data source, used by a Web-based application.

state   The data present in a system at any one time.

stored procedure A function that is executed by a database management system.

tag A symbol denoting an embedded instruction in a document.

teletext Information pages encoded within spare lines of a broadcast TV program.

thin client A type of system architecture that places processing responsibility predominantly on the server.

thread A named sequence of processing tasks.

Transaction Processing monitor (TP monitor) A software tool that ensures transactions are either completed or abandoned and, therefore, never left in an inconsistent state.

transaction In the commercial sense, the agreement of contractual terms or the exchange of goods or services for value; in the technological sense, the completion of complementary data updates in two or more entities.

transformation agent An intermediary that gathers data, collates, and processes it, and then sells it to other users.

trickle-down royalty The extension of previously exclusive products and services to the general population.

Unified Modeling Language (UML) The leading object-oriented systems analysis and design methodology.

use-cases Scenarios of system usage used to specify system requirements; part of the Objectory analysis and design methodology and subsequently part of UML.

value chain The group of organizations implicated in the production of a final product or service.

Value Added Network (VAN) A data communications network predating the rise of the Internet, used for transmitting EDI messages.

viewdata An early online information service type.

virtual organization An enterprise created around contributed skills and knowledge resources, rather than physical plant.

virtualization The process of redefining the boundaries and structure of an enterprise to include partner organizations and free agents.

vortal A vertical portal; a portal targeted at a specific industry, market, or interest group.

Wireless Application Protocol (WAP) A scheme for conveying data between wireless devices.

Webcam A still or video camera that feeds images to a Website.

Web server A piece of software that returns resources to a client in response to HTTP requests.

Wintel Slang for the Microsoft Windows/Intel software/hardware platform.

Wireless Markup Language (WML) A stripped-down version of HTML used with WAP, optimized for rendering on small displays with limited graphics capabilities.

workflow The automated routing of work items between nodes in a business process.

wrapper A programming interface that provides access to a legacy system.

eXtensible Markup Language (XML) A means of defining documents with associated structure and semantics.

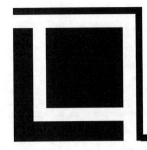

Index